TOKENS OF AFFECTION

Postpartum depression is hard on a marriage.

In their private practices, authors Karen Kleiman and Amy Wenzel often find themselves face-to-face with marriages that are suffocating, as if the depression has sucked the life out of a relationship that was only prepared for the anticipated joy of pending childbirth. What happens to marriage? Why do couples become angry, isolated, and disconnected? *Tokens of Affection* looks closely at marriages that have withstood the passing storm of depression and are now seeking, or in need of, direction back to their previous levels of functioning and connectedness. The reader is introduced to a model of collaboration that refers to eight specific features, which guide postpartum couples back from depression. These features, framed as "Tokens," are based on marital therapy literature and serve as a reminder that these are not just communication skill-building techniques; they are gift-giving gestures on behalf of a couple's relationship. A reparative resource, *Tokens of Affection* helps couples find renewed harmony, a solid relational ground, and reconnection.

Karen Kleiman, MSW, LCSW, is a well-known international expert on postpartum depression. She is founder of The Postpartum Stress Center, a premier treatment and professional training center for prenatal and postpartum depression and anxiety.

Amy Wenzel, PhD, ABPP, lectures internationally on issues relevant to mental health and psychotherapy, and provides ongoing supervision to clinical psychologists, social workers, and psychiatric nurses.

TOKENS OF AFFECTION

Reclaiming Your Marriage After Postpartum Depression

Karen Kleiman
with
Amy Wenzel

NEW YORK AND LONDON

First published 2014
by Routledge
711 Third Avenue, New York, NY 10017

and by Routledge
27 Church Road, Hove, East Sussex BN3 2FA

Routledge is an imprint of the Taylor & Francis Group, an informa business

© 2014 Taylor & Francis

The right of Karen Kleiman and Amy Wenzel to be identified as the authors of this work has been asserted by them in accordance with sections 77 and 78 of the Copyright, Designs and Patents Act 1988.

All rights reserved. No part of this book may be reprinted or reproduced or utilised in any form or by any electronic, mechanical, or other means, now known or hereafter invented, including photocopying and recording, or in any information storage or retrieval system, without permission in writing from the publishers.

Trademark notice: Product or corporate names may be trademarks or registered trademarks, and are used only for identification and explanation without intent to infringe.

Library of Congress Cataloging in Publication Data
A catalog record for this book has been requested

ISBN: 978-0-415-81044-9 (hbk)
ISBN: 978-0-415-81045-6 (pbk)
ISBN: 978-0-203-07097-0 (ebk)

Typeset in Minion
by EvS Communication Networx, Inc.

TO BRUCE,
I am grateful every single day.

CONTENTS

About the Authors		ix
Foreword		xi
	Introduction	1
1	Your Current Married State	7
2	When Depression Descends	24
3	The Connection	41
4	Secrets of a Successful Marriage? The Tokens	57
5	Connection Strategies	65
	Part I: Communication 101	65
	Part II: CBT 101	72
6	Token of Esteem	78
7	Token of Collaboration	92
8	Token of Compromise	102
9	Token of Selflessness	113
10	Token of Sanctuary	127
11	Token of Expression	138
12	Token of Tolerance	156

CONTENTS

13	Token of Loyalty	175
14	Bumps in the Road	188
15	What's Next?	201
	References	211
	Index	220

ABOUT THE AUTHORS

Karen Kleiman is a well-known international expert on postpartum depression. Her work has been featured on the Internet and within the mental health community for decades. In 1988, Ms. Kleiman founded The Postpartum Stress Center, a treatment and training facility where she treats individuals and couples experiencing prenatal and postpartum mood and anxiety disorders. More recently, she founded The Postpartum Stress & Family Wellness Center in New Jersey.

Ms. Kleiman has been featured in many television and radio shows, magazines, and health websites. Her national television appearances include *Inside Edition*, *The Oprah Winfrey Show*, and *NBC Nightly News with Tom Brokaw*. Currently Ms. Kleiman is affiliated with a number of websites where she writes articles, facilitates support chats, and addresses the concerns of pregnant and postpartum women and their families. She also serves as a parenting expert panel member for BabyCenter.com and Storknet.com and an expert blogger for Psychologytoday.com.

In 1980, Ms. Kleiman received her master's degree in clinical social work from the University of Illinois in Chicago. In addition to her clinical practice at The Postpartum Stress Center, she instructs a postgraduate training course in the treatment of postpartum depression and mentors advanced clinicians specializing in this unique field of practice.

Ms. Kleiman is the author of several books on postpartum depression. Her first book, *This Isn't What I Expected: Overcoming Postpartum Depression* (Bantam), co-authored with Valerie Davis Raskin, forged new territory in the self-help book market on postpartum depression. She is coauthor of *Dropping the Baby and Other Scary Thoughts: Breaking the Cycle of Unwanted Thoughts in Motherhood* (Routledge). *The Postpartum Husband* and *What Am I Thinking?* (xlibris) are self-help books that offer practical advice for couples struggling with depression. Her book, *Therapy and the Postpartum Woman: Notes on Healing Postpartum Depression for Clinicians and the Women Who Seek Their Help* (Routledge) is a groundbreaking resource for clinicians who treat women with postpartum mood and anxiety disorders.

ABOUT THE AUTHORS

Amy Wenzel received her PhD, ABPP, in clinical psychology from the University of Iowa, followed by her clinical psychology internship at the University of Wisconsin Medical School. She has served on the faculties of the University of Pennsylvania School of Medicine, the American College of Norway, and the University of North Dakota. Her research has been funded by the National Institute of Mental Health, the American Foundation for Suicide Prevention, and the National Alliance for Research on Schizophrenia and Depression (Brain and Behavior Foundation). She is author of *Anxiety Disorders in Childbearing Women: Diagnosis and Treatment* (APA Books) and editor of the *Handbook of Perinatal Psychology* (Oxford University Press), as well as author or editor of books on topics such as cognitive therapy, cognitive research methods, and close relationships. She co-authored *Dropping the Baby and Other Scary Thoughts* with Karen Kleiman. Her areas of research and clinical expertise are in perinatal anxiety disorders, interpersonal functioning in anxiety disorders, suicide prevention, and cognitive therapy, and she has published more than 100 articles and chapters on these topics. She lectures internationally on issues relevant to mental health and psychotherapy, and provides ongoing supervision to clinical psychologists, social workers, and psychiatric nurses. She currently divides her time between scholarly research, training and consultation, and clinical practice.

FOREWORD

Karen Kleiman and I are as different as two kindred spirits can be.

She is the only person I know who submits her books to the publisher *before* the contracted deadline. I sometimes push the envelope and am writing up until the book goes into production (as is the case with this Foreword!). I like fancy statistical models. She says they make her head hurt. We bicker (playfully) about the need to develop an outline before beginning to write a book. We sometimes end our conversations with a simultaneous "ugh!" and burst out in laughter before we hang up the phone.

But we both share a passion for working with postpartum women and men, as well as a passion for writing and sharing our knowledge with clinicians and consumers, alike.

Clinically, we come from very different theoretical orientations. Karen is a strong believer in supportive psychotherapy and has developed exquisite metaphors for communicating hope, understanding, support, and nurturance to her postpartum clients. Her approach is described beautifully in her 2009 book, *Therapy and the Postpartum Woman: Notes on Healing Postpartum Depression for Clinicians and the Women Who Seek Their Help*. My background is distinctly cognitive behavioral, and I have published many treatment manuals for clinicians to consult as they deliver cognitive behavioral therapy (CBT) for a host of different clinical presentations. When I first met Karen, she expressed doubt about whether CBT is a good match for postpartum women—is it too rigid? Too much for postpartum women in acute distress? And I wondered about the evidence base for her supportive approach. Both of our concerns would be proven incorrect.

Over the years, we have influenced one another clinically and professionally, and we're finding more and more of the other's wisdom incorporated into our own work. Almost every day, I use Karen's metaphors with postpartum and non-postpartum clients alike. And Karen has asked for copies of some CBT worksheets that I regularly use with my clients. I remember once that she had an "a-ha moment" and said to me, "I think I do CBT with many of my clients and didn't even realize it." In fact, our next collaboration is a treatment manual on CBT for perinatal distress (also to be published by Routledge), which will demonstrate the delivery of standard CBT in the context of a supportive therapeutic relationship and appreciation for the subtleties in perinatal clients' clinical presentations. It will represent a hybrid of both of our greatest clinical strengths.

The *Tokens of Affection* described in this book emerged from Karen's vast clinical experience with clients who recovered from postpartum depression but whose relationships were still damaged from the fallout. This premise is an important one that is often overlooked—most people just want depression to be over and expect that their lives will fall back into place as they had been before the depression. This book normalizes the experience of relationship distress following postpartum depression, provides a heuristic for understanding how to repair the relationship (i.e., the Tokens), and describes tangible tools that we use in our clinical practices and that have been incorporated into countless treatments for couples. She even allowed me to work in some of the foundational principles of CBT to help readers facilitate effective communication and accurate interpretations of their partner's behavior. The main message that resonates throughout the book is one originally articulated by relationships expert John Gottman—that couples need to "turn toward" one another rather than "turn away." The means that couples need to refrain from "keeping score" and instead devote themselves to implementing the Tokens because the relationship is worth it. It is valued. Even if it feels as if one person is doing more work than the other person.

Just last week, I described the concept of "turning toward" with a couple on the verge of divorce. Their arguments regularly devolve into insults, name calling, and blows below the belt. In other words, not good, and not anywhere close to John Gottman's 5:1 ratio of positive to negative interactions that Karen references later in the book. The husband said, "I can stop using that word she hates so much, but what about her smirks? That attitude?" "Let it go," was my reply, "in the spirit of not getting derailed away from the main issue you're addressing in your interaction. In the spirit of repairing the marriage that you so very much want to remain intact. In the spirit of turning toward your marriage, rather than turning away." There was a big pause. "I can do that," he said with surprising resolve. This man just gave his wife the Token of Expression by refraining from name calling and the Token of Tolerance by letting go of any perceived slights by his wife. Karen's Tokens have given me a much richer framework than I had before I read her manuscript to teach simple but powerful communication skills to this and many other couples.

Karen and I both recognize a need to be authentic in our clinical work with our clients and in our writing as a vehicle to form a relationship with our readers. Part of this involves being a little bit self-deprecating and even goofy when appropriate, and, believe me, Karen and I are both self-deprecating and goofy. When I educate my clients about exposure therapy for anxiety disorders, I disclose that I am a diehard spider phobic and give a vivid example of how my avoidance of spiders has only made my phobia worse and highly irritates my husband, on whom I call to get rid of even the tiniest of spiders. Sometimes I even imitate my shrieks, which makes my clients roll with laughter. Karen has peppered humorous examples from her own marriage throughout the book to show that even therapists have communication differences with their husbands. My favorite is Karen's example on pp. 16–18 of this book, in which she describes becoming more and more angry as she sat out on the curb waiting for her husband to come after her after a disagreement, only to find that her husband was intentionally leaving her alone because, from his perspective, he thought she wanted space. I often use this example with my own clients to illustrate what I call the "Men are from Mars, women are from Venus" phenomenon first described by John Gray. Our examples from our own lives illustrate key take-home points for our clients and readers and show that it is only human for problems and misunderstandings to occur in our relationships and lives in general. My hope is that readers will resonate with these examples and rely on them in their own lives to make decisions that help them to turn toward their relationships.

I stated at the beginning of this Foreword that Karen and I are as different as two kindred spirits can be. As I've written about the way we work with our clients and communicate to our readers, I'm realizing that maybe we aren't so different after all. And we seem to be converging to a greater degree as time goes on. It is a pleasure to collaborate with and learn from you, my friend, and be a small part of this gift (perhaps we can call your gift a Token?) that you are giving to your readers.

Amy Wenzel

INTRODUCTION

I love being married.

In our marriage, I am the self-proclaimed master of all things relationship oriented, while my husband, well, he does everything else. We each surrender to the other's area of expertise. Like everything else in life, our marriage has its good days and cranky days, and days when the relationship simply must take a back seat to everything else. Now that our children have grown and moved out of the house, we have the luxury of looking back at the early days through the forgiving filter of long-gone precious moments and hindsight.

While I admit I am quite comfortable with my role as our relationship healer, and agree that it is something I do fairly well, for the most part, I am equally aware of the countless things I do wrong, or not-so-well, or not at all like other people might do them. In fact, those closest to me are often taken aback by my willingness to reveal my flaws and expose my vulnerabilities to the outside world. Friends and family, often stunned by my frankness, weigh in that I should, perhaps, be more discreet and less impulsive when it comes to disclosing my vulnerabilities. They may be right, to an extent, but it is a reflex of mine. I know no other way to be. When circumstances dictate, I can restrain myself to keep up appearances, but it's not a natural state for me and I believe with great confidence that this inclination to be forthright is one of my greatest assets—one that accompanies me into every session with every client. I am quite certain it's part of what disarms a new client who is often paralyzed by unspeakable anxiety and hopelessness.

Though I suspect my affinity for directness has been a lifelong proclivity, the longer I work with postpartum men and women, the more value I see in balancing my professional expertise with my perceived "weaknesses." As a therapist, bringing one's entire self into a session is risky, to say the least, and an act that should only be carried out with the wisdom of what it will mean to the client. I believe it's critical to my work, that my clients see me as real. While initially it may seem counterintuitive, ultimately, it's more human. Our genuineness as a therapist is our supreme tool. It holds infinite healing power.

INTRODUCTION

What do my personal vulnerabilities have to do with the message of this book? I believe we all must work hard to put our best selves out there, in our work, in our marriage, in our lives. At any given moment, each of us may be challenged by the discrepancy that exists between what we expect and what we experience. Nowhere is this discrepancy more prominent than in a relationship recovering from the wrath of depression.

You see, there are powerful paradoxes within each of us, all the time. For example, a person can be competent and emotionally accessible at the same time. Someone can be proficient in one area and less skilled in another. A person can be successful and symptomatic, simultaneously. This last example is hard for postpartum couples to come to grips with. Depression has a way of darkening everything in its path. Perceptions become skewed. Clarity is clouded by the force of the illness. This is true for the one who experiences the depression as well as the partner who lives with the sufferer. The couple, unwittingly, takes on these misperceptions and, all too often, misinterprets symptoms as a reflection of who they or their partners are. If someone feels bad, everything is bad. If someone is feeling hopeless, there is no hope. If someone is scared, everything feels scary. That's because things appear very black and white for postpartum couples who are struggling to resume control over their lives after depression and reconciling these apparent contradictions can feel impossible.

Additional examples of paradoxical thought patterns that can emerge during postpartum depression are:

If I'm anxious all the time, I can't be a good parent.
If I want to go back to work so badly, I must not love my baby.
If my partner isn't acting lovingly toward me, I must be unworthy.
How can I attach to my baby if I feel so unlovable?
What if pain from my troubled past means I cannot be a good parent?
How can I possibly take care of my marriage if I can barely take care of myself?

These dichotomies are difficult to resolve, especially for new parents who are trying so diligently to do everything right. People forget that life consists of opposing forces much of the time. And after a baby comes into the picture? These contrasting desires and urges can squeeze the joy right out of the high expectations of this time in a couple's life.

That is why it is essential that you begin to understand that paradoxes do exist right now. Yes, you can be worried about the way you are feeling and still take care of your marriage. Yes, you can be a good mother while you are experiencing excruciatingly scary thoughts. Yes, you can be a good father even if you are ashamed that you feel so bad. And yes, your marriage can sustain high levels of painful resentment and misunderstanding and still be a safe place for both of you to rest comfortably.

Depression sets the stage for many such paradoxes for any postpartum couple. It is precisely these paradoxes, fueled by depressive thinking, which can drive a wedge into the connection between the two of you. Self-doubt permeates the marital system after symptoms take hold. Unexpectedly, the relationship can be seriously jeopardized by ties that have shattered and replaced by an unfamiliar landscape of misunderstandings and ineffective communication.

Things that used to make sense, now feel unsteady and vulnerable.

Vulnerability can be an uncomfortable state, but it can also serve as a catalyst toward a better sense of self and a deeper relationship. In order for that to happen, you need to be willing to take the risk of letting yourself sound stupid, be wrong, be seen, be heard, be messy, make a mistake, or feel pain, in order to achieve authenticity and ultimately, greater intimacy between you and your partner. Brené Brown, a research professor, refers to this as "the courage to be imperfect" (2012, p. 218) and believes this is the root of earnest parenting and partnering. Being comfortable with your own vulnerability is not easy but it is something you can learn. It begins with trusting yourself and believing that you have your own best interest at heart.

This is the only prerequisite for your work here. Open your mind. Believe in yourself enough for you to expect the best from your relationship. Find the courage and give yourself permission to lean into your marriage and see where that takes you.

The Driving Force Behind this Book

I am grateful to the postpartum couples who have been brave enough to share their stories, expressing what they needed most from me and from each other. Some express this with their words. Some convey it with the silence of what they cannot say. At present, almost 30 years into my clinical practice and 30 years of marriage, I am in position to merge these parallel life experiences into this book, on behalf of postpartum couples who have struggled with depression.

Sometimes it seems that couples put too much effort in the wrong direction and are unable to see what is often right there in front of them. Couples with new babies are tremendously preoccupied and busy worrying. They are too tired to understand what their partner is saying. They are overwhelmed by the demands of their schedule and too depleted to give anything back. So they often bark back and forth or decide to take care of things themselves, because it's just easier that way.

When depression has been part of this picture, one or both partners may continue to feel angry, resentful, or unworthy. These negative emotions can remain hidden by daily distractions, or they may blast into every single interaction. Either way, they are apt to fester. Even when the welcomed relief of recovery from depression brings renewed hope and anticipation of good things to follow, the fallout from the illness can confuse intentions and lead the marriage both astray.

Postpartum couples crave and deserve relief. The birth of a baby is associated with some of life's most poignant contradictions: joy and despair, pleasure and grief, elation and exhaustion, euphoria and anxiety. The impact of these incongruent states of emotions can wear heavily on the spirit of a marriage. This book is a response to working with couples who have become disheartened by the weight of this unremitting pressure, in an effort to help revitalize their connection.

About the Book

No one will argue the point that postpartum couples need to take better care of themselves. For a period of time, postpartum couples understandably feel obliged to focus solely on the baby or how the baby is impacting their lives. It's hard not to. This book, however, will not focus on the baby. In fact, the baby is barely mentioned. Nor will this book center on the transition to parenthood or how a baby drastically transforms a relationship. Also, this is not a book about a troubled marriage. Nor is it about couples who need marriage counseling or who need guidance on how to navigate through the transition to parenthood.

It's time to focus on you as a couple. This book provides a roadmap leading back to your baseline functioning, an effort to rebuild what depression has taken away from you. This book offers a couple-based intervention aimed at increasing your awareness and overall satisfaction in your marriage. For now, it's about you. Although we are extremely sensitive to the myriad changes and challenges that babies bring to a marriage, the primary goal here is to take the spotlight off of the baby for a brief time and redirect your attention to each other.

The book will begin by helping you assess where the two of you are right now in terms of your connection and help you understand how the depression contributed to this current state. After examining your marriage, you will be introduced to the concept of the Tokens and basic strategies to keep in mind throughout the chapters. Subsequent chapters will describe in detail each of the Tokens: (1) Esteem, (2) Collaboration, (3) Compromise, (4) Selflessness, (5) Sanctuary, (6) Expression, (7) Tolerance, and (8) Loyalty. Though these terms may not be new, they will be applied to your marriage in specific ways that will focus on reciprocal desires and your growth as a couple. All of the Tokens are interrelated, and you will find that many overlap. This is because although the specific skills may be different, all of the Tokens rely on the fundamental notion that you both believe your marriage deserves this attention and that commitment resonates within the description of each Token. Every time you work on one Token, you will be strengthening another one. Note that each chapter ends with a list of Token Tools, which are relationship-enhancing strategies based on the material in that chapter. Pay particular attention to the skill-building nature of these tools so you can begin to apply them in your daily exchanges. Keep in mind that you may learn things about yourself that surprise you. Or irritate you. You may also find some of the suggestions infuriating, particularly if you feel you are doing most of this work yourself. You may be living with a partner who is unenthusiastic about this or simply appalled by the notion of working on or improving your marriage. All perspectives will lead you to the same conclusion. You are trying. You are putting forth effort to enhance your relationship. You get lots of points for that and, in the end, if you continue to follow these guidelines, both of you should expect to feel better.

A word on the frame of reference for this book: Amy Wenzel and I collaborated while writing *Dropping the Baby and Other Scary Thoughts* and found the combination of our two very different theoretical perspectives extremely gratifying. Amy is a researcher, teacher, consultant, practicing psychologist, and a prolific writer. Her expertise in the field of cognitive behavioral therapy and other evidence-based treatments is extensive and an asset to every project I undertake. My strengths, on the other hand, lie in my good instincts where the evidence is based solely in my office and in the hearts of the women I treat.

One could easily say that our writing partnership incorporates the very essence of the Tokens we refer to in this book. Our teamwork is successful because of our mutual regard (esteem), our desire to join forces with a common goal (collaborate), our ability to surrender to the other's area of expertise (compromise), and our willingness to assess and honor each other's different perspectives (selflessness) and writing styles (expression), accept each other's literary idiosyncrasies (tolerance), respect the other's imposed and sacred schedule (sanctuary) and lastly, our passionate and mutual dedication to educating and supporting the needs of postpartum couples (loyalty). With that said, Amy's work is behind each written word, although the voice of the book is mine. You may notice that there a few "we's" sprinkled throughout the chapters when referencing our shared clinical experiences or viewpoints.

Finally, any reference to my own marriage is not intended to sound self-congratulatory in any way. I refer to my personal experiences with the insight and appreciation of all the mind-boggling mistakes I have made along the way. It is my hope that the telling of these stories is not perceived as arrogant or self-righteous. My intent is to acknowledge that we are all human and perhaps you can learn from the emotional openness and from my mistakes, as I did.

INTRODUCTION

If you* have recovered from postpartum depression or anxiety and feel that your marriage could benefit from some thoughtful attention, you are poised to do this work. The book is specifically written for couples who have experienced depression following the birth of a baby and have recovered with or without professional treatment. Although the book makes many references to marriages and sometimes, specifically to men and women, this book will be useful to any partnership, including same-sex relationships. Regardless of who experienced the depression, this book was written for both of you, or either of you. Your desire, motivation, and readiness to address your marriage are great predictors of how things will go from here. The two of you have endured the worst of it and now face the challenge of fortifying the foundation of your marriage. That foundation is based on the core relatedness between the two of you—a relationship that, perhaps, has been shaken, or set off course from the upheaval of depression and recovery. My hope is that with the help of this book, you will take a closer look at where you are together and embrace this opportunity for growth on the most fundamental level, from a place of compassion and desire for a renewed connection.

The Tokens of Affection will help you reconnect.

---

* Statistically, as well as, in our clinical practices, more women struggle with postpartum depression then men, but attention to male depression is rising, which will benefit the postpartum couple. Additionally, we are aware that the readership of self-help books leans heavily toward women. For those reasons, some of our references the individual with postpartum depression may sound as if we are speaking directly to women. We are not. However, in an effort to avoid the overuse of disclaimers and qualifiers, our words may reflect a bias toward mothers as the sufferer of the postpartum depression in the family. We apologize, in advance, if it sounds as if we are excluding any father who has experienced depression after the birth of his child. Our intent is to make sure both partners will benefit from this book.

1

YOUR CURRENT MARRIED STATE

What has happened to my marriage? I thought things would be better now. Instead, we are both irritable and more distant than ever.

—Support group participant

Just when you think things are finally starting to feel normal again, symptoms have resolved, everything seems to be getting back on track, everyone should be moving forward ... suddenly both of you are stymied once again by an unforeseen obstacle.

If everyone is now feeling better, why does your marriage feel so difficult some of the time?

You've recently had a baby and you are both exhausted. Maybe it's your first, maybe it's your second or third. Maybe it's your last, maybe not. Regardless, if the two of you have recently withstood the ravages of depression, you are in a far different place than you expected to be in at this time. Perhaps one or both of you are feeling relieved and hopeful. On the other hand, you might be angry and bitter. Or exhausted and unmotivated. Or anxious and uneasy. Or grateful and appreciative. Or perhaps you are feeling many or all of these feelings simultaneously.

One client said she noticed something wasn't right soon after she told her husband she was starting to feel better. Before long, she was hesitant to tell him she was feeling better because she was afraid he had forgotten how bad she recently felt. She was afraid his expectations might change and she would fail to live up to them. For months, she has visited a therapist weekly, taken her medication as instructed, and learned how to cope with her ever-present intrusive thoughts that challenged her on a regular basis. At last, Nicole felt invigorated as she emerged out her period of "dark and daily devastation." It was light again. The sun was shining again. She could breathe once more. She describes how her hard-earned desire to share this relief was short-lived as her husband impatiently and mistakenly concluded that everything would automatically return to normal, "We would now proceed as if nothing had happened; as if we should fall right back into line. You do your job, I'll do my job, let's have sex and oh, did I tell you I'm playing golf all day Saturday?"

It's understandable that one or both partners yearn to return to previous behaviors and levels of functioning, partly fueled by denial but mostly because non-depressed spouses are eager to bring joy back into the household. However, recovery from depression does not happen overnight, thus, creating a lag between the crisis and a renewed sense of well-being. Anne Sheffield, author of several books on depression, calls this phenomenon and one of her books, *Depression Fallout*, describing overlapping stages of confusion, self-blame, demoralization, resentment, anger and the "desire to escape the source of so much unhappiness" (Sheffield, 2003, p. xv).

Pause for a moment and consider how you feel about your partner right now. Where are you both in terms of your relationship? How close do you feel? Do you feel loved? Do you feel listened to and understood? Next, think about how you felt about your partner before the baby. Before the depression. Before your life changed so dramatically. How did you envision your life together at this point? How did you think you'd be act and feel as a couple? It's quite possible things feel good, but if you are reading this book it is likely that you feel something is missing. There may or may not be high degrees of conflict in your marriage. Good, solid marriages can experience periods of time when one or both partners feel discontented. Undoubtedly, life has become enormously hectic and it may seem as though the two of you are rarely in the same space at the same time. The experience of having a baby and depression is a volatile combination. Although statistics vary, the worldwide estimate for the prevalence of postpartum depression (PPD) ranges from 5% to 25% (Gaynes et al., 2005) and about 10% of men (Paulson & Bazemore, 2010). Unfortunately, these numbers are likely to be on the low side because postpartum depression is generally under-recognized and under-treated in both men and women. The prevalence rates (up to 26%) have been noted to be higher in some urban women with low incomes (Hobfoll, Ritter, Lavin, Hulszier, & Cameron, 1995). (Note that this book refers to *postpartum depression* and *depression* to include all postpartum mood and anxiety disorders, including anxiety, panic, obsessive-compulsive disorder [OCD], and post-traumatic stress disorder [PTSD].)

It would be a mistake to presume that the volatility of depression would not take a toll on the marriage. If the impact of the depression is ignored, the couple might conceal true feelings of resentment, disguised by bickering, criticism, irritability, and generally unpleasant dispositions. Although these are normal reactions to such a series of shockwaves to the marriage they are nonetheless certain to make things worse instead of better. A marriage in gridlock can result in a downward spiral of anger, blame, and isolation.

Postpartum Depression Is Hard on a Marriage

No one expects to be blindsided by depression after the birth of their baby. Although it's true that increased awareness is enabling more couples to better prepare for the possibility and thereby reduce its impact, still, when it happens, it doesn't matter how well you've prepared. You feel cheated. You *are* cheated. Even later, after symptoms have improved and healthy coping skills begin to emerge, remnants of the earlier ambush can, and will, create various degrees of turmoil in your marriage.

The early postpartum weeks and months divert couples away from themselves and invariably diminish the time they have for each other. More specifically, it diminishes the time a woman has for her partner, which can reduce his marital satisfaction (Barnes, 2006). Studies show that depression has been linked with "marital problems" (Whiffen & Gotlib, 1993) and poor "marital adjustment" (Whiffen, 1988). Do poor marital relationships *cause* postpartum depression or does postpartum depression *cause* poor marital relationships? Both are true, depending on the circumstances, but there is no clear causal association that would hold true across the board. Without a distinct definition of poor marital relationships, it's difficult to generalize, but it's interesting that despite the research which supports this, many couples exhibit a consistent, though frustrated, effort to settle what has been disrupted during the crisis. In fact, many women report after the fact, that their relationships were strong and their partners were particularly supportive. I have been witness to countless numbers of women and men who fight tirelessly to regain the love temporarily lost in the shuffle of emotions.

In 2011, The Postpartum Stress Center distributed an informal questionnaire in preparation for this book, exploring the impact of depression on the marital relationship. Ninety-five percent of the 55 respondents were women. Of these women, 93% identified themselves as the depression sufferer in the relationship. By far, the majority of participants reported that their marital relationship suffered but continued to be loving and strong. While only 7% responded "No," they were not in the slightest worried about their relationship, 62% said they were "not really worried, but postpartum depression did take its toll on the marriage," and some were "a bit worried" but trusted in the strength of the relationship to help them navigate the rough waters. Consequently, more women than not, were hopeful that their relationship could withstand the tumult caused by the depression. It seems that many of the couples continue to put forth great energy and effort toward the marriage, and may do so despite, or because of, the extraordinary strain. This apparent incongruity speaks volumes in favor of the incentive to repair the connection during depression's aftermath.

Taking a look inside your relationship is probably the last thing you feel like doing right now. It may even feel like a waste of time. Digging into your marriage just when you have recovered from the tumult of postpartum depression, may present a hardship for which you simply cannot muster the energy.

But you should.

Here's why: As far back in 1957, LeMasters reported that 83% of new parents experience moderate to severe levels of crisis during the transition into parenthood. Although initially disputed, other researchers have validated this high degree of distress during the transition to parenthood (Stamp, 1994). In fact, one study shows that marital quality decreases sharply for 40% to 67% of couples during the first postpartum year (Shapiro, Gottman, & Carrère, 2000). When we factor in postpartum depression, the picture is even bleaker. Research shows that husbands of women with postpartum depression report less satisfaction in their marriage and feel less capable as parents compared to husbands of postpartum women who are not depressed (Zelkowitz & Milet, 1997). Additionally, there is evidence that women with postpartum depression report inadequate communication with their partners (Paykel, Emms, Fletcher, & Rassaby, 1980) and, specifically, that they feel less able to talk openly about problems with their partners than postpartum women who are not depressed (O'Hara, 1986). In summary, there is (a) a high degree of distress during transition to parenthood (without depression), (b) a decrease in marital quality during first postpartum year, (c) less satisfaction reported by husbands of women with PPD, and (d) inadequate communication with spouses reported by women with PPD. Additionally, lesbian couples, who conceived a child through artificial insemination, showed an increase in relationship conflict after the birth of their baby (Sayer & Goldberg, 2006).

Another reason why you should rally around this effort is that research shows that couples therapy reduces depression, especially in women. This is partly based on the finding that women tend to use emotion-focused coping, and blame themselves for marital problems, which puts them at greater risk for depression. It follows, then, that if couples learn to attend to the relationship with effective tools, this could conceivably relieve depression or likely protect from relapse (Beach, Fincham, & Katz, 1998).

Thus, we see that the impact of postpartum depression on the marriage has striking implications and can potentially damage the relationship. This is true whether it is the mother who has suffered from depression or whether depression affects the father. Do not make the mistake of minimizing the impact, regardless of who suffered from depression. As one woman told me, "Postpartum depression changed my marriage. It actually made it better in some ways, I think. We learned things about each other we never knew. But it crushed our spirit and it hasn't been a smooth road home. It rocked our foundation."

If you are the depression sufferer, right about now, you might be feeling guilty about how the depression affected your marriage. Not only will that not help, it will keep you locked into some of the old distorted thinking patterns that emerged during or, perhaps, triggered your depression. I know, first you felt guilty about the depression and now you feel guilty about the state of your marriage. Right now, it's important that you exercise the ability to ignore your temptation to feel guilty about this. Do not blame yourself. Save your energy for this work you have ahead of you. If you are the non-depressed partner, it will be helpful if you can remind your partner that they are not to blame and that the two of you are on the same team here, working on making things feel strong again. Note that if your marriage feels either too fragile or too volatile, self-help measures will not be sufficient. In those instances, you should seek professional assistance for further support.

In my clinical practice, I find myself face-to-face with recovering couples who appear to be suffocating by each other's fumes, as if the depression had sucked the life out of a relationship that was best prepared for the anticipated joy of pending childbirth. Couple after couple report an agonizing new married state; one that emerges after the acute depression has resolved; at a time when joy is expected to permeate the demands of this life transition. Even without depression, the postpartum period challenge each and any marriage with stressors of unprecedented proportion. You already know how sleep deprivation, unpredictability, idealistic expectations, and a new baby can combine in combustible fashion! When we factor postpartum depression into the mix of two individuals trying to make sense out meeting each other's needs, it can get pretty messy, pretty fast. All systems are interrupted and abruptly forced to recalibrate.

Whether or not depression has interfered with the family dynamics, partners do not always understand what the other one wants. This happens, from time to time, in every marriage. Sometimes it is due to poor communication. Other times it may be the result of a misperception. Still other times, it is because one or the other may be unclear about what it is he or she really wants. When we are talking about *your* marriage, believe it or not, what matters most is how you feel about the way your behavior, words, body language, and actions make your partner feel. Let's repeat that, what really matters, what is most fundamental to the well-being of your marriage, *is how much you care about what your partner is feeling.*

Sounds a bit outdated, doesn't it? It may also feel completely out of sync with your tired soul and, quite frankly, not enough about *you* at this moment. Nevertheless, the aim of this book is to set forth my personal, professional, and evidence-based assertion that partners in a relationship will feel better if they pay attention to how the other partner is feeling. If you were the depressed partner, no matter how bad you feel or how depressed you were, or currently are, it still holds true. While it is a prospect that may wound your weary heart, it remains a cornerstone of this theory of intervention. Taking care of yourself and each other will revitalize your marriage. For this to work, all you need to do is suspend your disillusionment and trust the process.

This is not just a good idea; it is also supported by research which points to a concept called *relationship awareness* (Acitelli, 2002). Relationship awareness is defined as focusing your attention on interaction patterns thereby viewing the relationship as a unit. The focus of attention (thinking patterns and talking patterns) by the individual (you) is relational (your marriage), rather than just focusing on your partner. There is even evidence that couples in conflict are less likely to remain in conflict if they are able to shift the focus of their conversations from an individual partner (which is usually blame-oriented) to the relationship (Acitelli, 1988, 1993; Bernal & Baker, 1979). Relationship awareness can be implicit or explicit (Acitelli, 2002) and generally includes the understanding and referencing the relationship as an entity. Partners are in this together. Research indicates that implicit relationship awareness, such as talking or thinking about the other as part of a unit, is associated with positive relationship results and ultimately predicts an increase in marital happiness (Acitelli, 2002). However, it probably will not surprise anyone to discover that explicit awareness, or, addressing the relationship in direct conversation, although certainly good practice if done right, does not guarantee a positive outcome.

Setting Yourself Up for Success or Failure

Your expectations and fantasies of how your life would look once you got back on track after the depression hit may have more influence on the way you feel right now than you might think. We are all disappointed in our relationships from time to time. If you are disappointed now, as you are both trying to navigate a smooth recovery, your displeasure may carry more weight moving forward than you would like. All marriages learn to negotiate a multitude of negative emotions, pretty much on a regular basis. During a crisis, expectations are often put on hold in support of more pressing lifesaving gestures. In other words, if I'm choking, I don't care if you are nice about it or not, I just want you to help me breathe.

We don't always know what is going to be revealed about our partner or ourselves after an unexpected disturbance in the relationship. Your knight in shining armor can become ornery and short-tempered right before your eyes. Your gentlewoman can morph into a demanding, argumentative source of ongoing angst.

Let's take a look at how things are right now, relative to how you thought or hoped they would be. See if any of these unfavorable statements reflect any part of how you feel *now* with regard to your marriage and your most recent experience with depression:

- *I am surprised by how empty I feel.*
- *I did not expect to feel abandoned by my partner.*
- *I thought these persistent feelings of anger and/or sadness would have lessened by now.*
- *I know my partner loves me, but sometimes I just don't feel it.*
- *I wish I weren't so bitter.*
- *I miss the way things used to be.*

- *I worry that things will never feel good between us again.*
- *I blame myself for the distance in our marriage.*
- *I blame my partner for the distance in our marriage.*
- *I wonder if our marriage is worth the effort it will take to fix things.*
- *I am surprised by my partner's lack of awareness regarding my feelings.*
- *I am disappointed by how we responded to each other when we needed each other the most.*
- *I thought my partner would have been more understanding.*

If you related to even one of these responses, you already know there are issues that need to be addressed that are important and timely. The good news about feeling so badly is that these are common responses to depression and they will lead you to a deeper understanding of yourself and your marriage. When either one of the partners is sick or weakened by symptoms, it makes sense that he or she would be soothed by an extra dose of compassion and special consideration from the non-depressed spouse. During the postpartum period, however, regardless of good intentions, there are too many other people, tasks, and obligations literally crying out for attention. Sometimes, the best we can hope for is that no one is screaming, bleeding, weeping, or hurt. If things feel stable, we are likely to postpone getting our emotional needs met on behalf of keeping the peace and secretly hoping things will just get better in time. When this happens, it can end up that no one's needs are being met sufficiently.

I'm waiting for you to meet mine. You're waiting for me to meet yours.
I'm tired. You're tired.
I'm waiting. You're waiting.
Here we sit.

Family Rules

It has been shown that the most gratifying relationships are those in which both partners rally around collectively established expectations and rules. Rules are often based on preconceived notions from your early childhood experiences, from your peer groups, from society which combine to form your expectations of how life should be. Most of the time, your rules probably work well for both of you. Some family rules are expressed, many are unspoken.

Here are some examples of random rules:

- Wash the dishes after each meal.
- Pick something up off the floor if you walk by it.
- Don't swear in front of the children.
- No cell phones at the dinner table.
- Pizza on Friday night.

Here are some additional examples of rules that are more aligned with our purpose here:

- Don't go to bed angry unless you talk about it together in the morning.
- A kiss in the morning and a kiss at night.
- Don't bring up past mistakes or weaknesses.
- Do not criticize each other's parents.
- Do not post, boast, or otherwise advertise your personal issues.

The problem with unspoken rules is that unless you are on the same page and unless you express what the expectations are, someone may be disappointed by making assumptions or misinterpreting the expectations. Therefore, rules and expectations must be expressed and, ideally, agreed upon. What are some of your family rules?

Household rules and responsibilities may seem easy to divide, but they are often the cause of conflict. *Who's doing what and how much* can lead to areas of dispute. In some situations, it can seem easy enough: *You do this part. I'll do that part.* This leads to clear expectations, for example: *You cook dinner. I'll clean up.* Be clear. Express gratitude. Of course, these task-oriented rules are always flexible, and many couples find that sharing responsibilities or switching it up sometimes is a nice way to share the burden.

Rules can also refer to more complicated opportunities, such as: never go to sleep angry, or don't bring up past mistakes or weaknesses. In these circumstances, rules are important because they establish agreed upon expectations and when things occur the way we expect them to, we tend to feel grounded. We feel safe with predetermined boundaries that regulate the marriage. However, if you don't act the way I expect you to, or if I don't do something the way you anticipated I would, confusion sets in. This is one of the ways depression makes its enduring mark on a marriage. Roles shift, rules are broken, expectations are crushed and agreements are shaky. It is no wonder everyone feels unsettled.

The focus here is to learn how to regroup and focus on the two of you. How to realign the expectations so that disappointments are minimized and shared goals are reestablished. This will work whether you are reading this book out of concern about problems in your relationship or whether you are reading it in the hopes of revitalizing your lost love.

A Balancing Act

At the heart of this book is the concept of connectedness, a concept we will explore in detail in Chapter 3. For our purposes, connection refers to a couple's dedication to the marriage demonstrated by mutual respect, caring and a core belief in the interrelatedness of these three constructs: *you, me* and *us*. It's a straightforward equation.

YOUR CURRENT MARRIED STATE

(You + me) = us

How simple is that? It's amazing how many couples forget this basic concept. There's you. There's me. And there's us. If you find yourselves blaming, or keeping score, or wanting credit, or taking the other for granted—you offset the equilibrium and are not acting as if you believe in your marriage. Even if you do. There is compromise in every good marriage. Sometimes it's more about *me*, sometimes it's more about *you*. That's the way it works. The key to maintaining connection is balance and cooperation.

Hallie and Andrew were in their mid-thirties negotiating life with a baby and toddler. Hallie was thrilled to start looking for a new house now that she was feeling better. They were running out of space after their second baby was born and things were temporarily until they all felt healthy enough to think about moving. "Andrew doesn't even want to move. What's wrong with him? He says this house is fine. Are you freakin' kidding me?! I mean, I have no backyard for the kids, they are sharing one bedroom. I have a toddler in with my baby, for Christ's sake! My kitchen is from the 1950s, and he thinks if we upgrade it everything will be fine. I'm moving. He can either come with me or stay here, but I'm moving."

I thought she was kidding. She wasn't.

Eventually, her husband conceded. They moved. They were both unhappy. He hated the house. She hated the neighborhood. He cursed, she screamed back. He isolated himself, she ignored him. He blamed her. She blamed him.

They weren't sure at what point they both stopped listening. Or caring. But they were both convinced they were in this alone. And they continued to conduct themselves exactly that way.

I asked Hallie why she was so angry; why was she willing to pick up and move with or without him, and if that was just an idle threat, why would she say something so hurtful?

Her flush face radiated with pain, she rolled her eyes and cracked her voice:

"I have no clue. He's just never fucking there for me. Never fucking there. Never."

"Never?"

"Well he certainly wasn't there for me when I was sick. WERE YOU?!!" She glared at Andrew, her sad eyes masked by anger.

Hallie was hurt by her perceived abandonment by her husband. Not too long ago, she felt she was drowning in symptoms yet still expected to maintain "life as usual." She describes herself as someone who is in touch with her feelings but not able to express them in ways that helps her get her needs met. Often, she resorts to anger, which is typically aimed directly as Andrew. They are fighters. Sometimes, couples are so used to fighting that it is the only way they know how to express themselves—even when the underlying feelings are sadness, loneliness, or fear. Not that these feelings aren't worth fighting for.

They are. Even so, Hallie and Andrew will learn that there are more effective ways of doing that, if they are willing to let go of old patterns and learn.

As depression deposits bitterness on either side, the effort to navigate around the unpleasantness can feel insurmountable. When emotions run high, and couples are distracted by life and chores and babies and sleeplessness and the trauma of depression, sometimes, the path of least resistance is the most tempting. Often, that pathway has room for only one and when stress is high, solitude can be quite appealing at first. However, respite quickly turns to isolation and soon, no one's needs are being met. When couples advance along parallel paths, without speaking the same language, it is easy to see how polarized a twosome can become. As the spirit of cooperation shuts down, connections shatter.

The message is clear: it is not only about finding the right words or avoiding conflict. Instead, it is about respecting and honoring your commitment to each other and your marriage by changing unproductive patterns and realizing the power you both have to work together. Even when there is conflict; *especially* when there is conflict. This notion of focusing on *how* (process) to resolve conflict as opposed to *what* (content) you are arguing about has been shown to be directly related to divorce potential (Stanley, Markman, & Whitton, 2002). Couples frequently get tied up in the content, such as details of who said what, and lose sight of the larger process. Again, it is, at this beginning stage, all about restoring the connection. You will see in subsequent chapters that this theme of connectedness is the concept that unifies all of the Tokens.

Are You Ready to Use the Tokens?

Most of us married folk think we are right, much of the time, and we believe we know what is best for us and our marriage. This is especially the case for women, who typically take the plunge when it comes to initiating marital repair tactics. However, what is true all of the time, without fail, is that each and every interaction between two people is just that, an interaction between two people. While it might feel like one event (we went to the park) and may be perceived by both as the sharing of one experience (we had a wonderful time), it is actually the convergence of two people and two experiences. Neither of which is more right than the other. Still, we each think we are right.

I learned this early in my marriage. Back when my husband and I were just discovering the fine points of how to arbitrate terms of a young marriage, something caused me to storm out the front door with a harrumph and a half. Off I went, propelled by self-righteous fury, and plunked myself on the street curb. Like a 4-year-old tantruming in protest while simultaneously checking back to make sure Mommy is there, I repeatedly glanced behind me, expecting to see my husband, dutifully chasing after me. *Surely, he knows how upset I am, I know he will come get me and apologize or at least make sure I'm okay!* But the trail from the house to the curb was silent with only the exasperated sigh of my unmet needs. *I can't believe I have to sit here and feel bad by myself.*

This is not okay. I sat and sulked a bit more, all the while peering back at the doorway in disbelief. *He was not coming out to look for me. Unbelievable. Who had I married? Was he really this selfish? Was he heartless? Did he not care? Did he not even know?*

Grudgingly, I sucked back the tears, took a deep breath, and went back to the house. There, I found my husband sitting on the couch watching TV, as if nothing had happened. "Hi Babe," he quipped, "Where were you?"

Really? Wow. Is this A.D.D.? Is this Men-Are-from-Mars stuff? Is he kidding?

"I was outside. Crying. By myself. Waiting for you."

"You were? Why were you crying? Why were you waiting for me?" He looked at me as if he had no idea what I was talking about—his eyes and mouth wide open like a toddler being punished for doing something he didn't know was wrong. Almost immediately it was obvious that he, really, honestly, and most assuredly, had no idea what I was talking about.

"Did you know I was upset?" I asked incredulously.

"Yes." He replied proudly, positive that he had the right answer for me.

Silence.

"Well if you knew I was upset, why didn't you come out after me? I mean, hellllooooooo?? I went out, upset. WHY DIDN"T YOU COME AFTER ME??!!"

"Because ... I ... I thought you went out because ... you wanted to be alone?"

Now, it was my turn to look at him as if I had no idea what he was saying.

"Why would you think I wanted to be alone?"

"Because you went outside, and I was inside?"

Omg, I thought, *do I have to teach him, coach him, tell him every single thing I need?* I would find out later that yes, of course I would.

"Okay, so let's be clear about this," I began slowly, "When I'm upset, and you know I'm upset, and I bail out, leaving a dust trail behind me, I do not. want.to.be.alone."

"Okay." He responded gently. Probably thinking something like, *that doesn't make sense to me at all, but I'll buy it.*

"So," he calculated, "when you crash out the front door in disgust and say something like, *I can't stand this,* and you slam the door behind you, that means you *want* me to come after you, is that what you're saying?"

"Yeah, something like that."

"Well, for the record," he continued, "I thought that meant you wanted to be alone. Because when I'm upset and I walk out to be alone, I actually want to be alone. I assumed that what you wanted, too."

Wrong.

"Okay, so when you're upset," I tried to make sense out of this, "You do NOT want me to follow you and talk to you about how you are feeling?"

Um. Right.

"Really? I thought the best thing for me to do, if you are upset, is to help you express it so we can talk about it together."

"Nope. The best thing for you to do is let me be alone. At least for a while. Then we can talk about it later."

Hmmmm.

I concluded, "So when I walk out by myself, I want you to come be with me. But since you want to be alone, you presume (mistakenly) that that is what *I* want. Therefore, by leaving me alone, you think you were doing what I want, but I feel abandoned and unloved. On the other hand, if *you* walk out and want to be alone, I presume (mistakenly) that you need to me to come help you express yourself (major misperception) so by following you, chasing you, stalking you, I am making things worse, instead of better?

Oh, yeah. Definitely.

This is an example of the good sense that two people can actually make, when they are not quite making sense to each other. Couples often take two divergent paths to reach a common goal. This is true for couples in conflict and couples in harmony. Thus, while the common goal may be marital satisfaction, each partner may maneuver the pathway with opposing tactics and without understanding of what is happening, feelings can get hurt and resentments can mount. The revelation that opened my eyes that day was as simple as this:

I will feel better if I better understand what he needs.

Overshadowed by our tender marriage of cluelessness, prior to that instant of divine enlightenment, we had strolled along with naïve confidence. Until that moment, I wasn't ready to think in terms of how he was thinking. I really believed much of that would just take care of itself when two people love each other. Isn't that how it works in the movies? Truthfully, as an insanely sensitive person who is empathetic by nature, it didn't always dawn on me that I would have to do more than that sometimes! I just presumed my husband would have the same instincts I did. Rule number one that I learned early on: Never presume.

That's the moment I realized I was ready. Ready to dig in and figure out what I needed to know to help him help me and, by doing so, enable me to be a better partner to him. When we think about that seemingly simple statement, I will feel better if I better understand what he needs, we elucidate the underlying motivation for the use of Tokens and the paradox it presents. It is a paradox all parents are familiar with. Take good care of yourself and then you can take good care of your children. If you aren't healthy, you won't have the resources to care for your children or each other. It's the oxygen mask in the airplane theory. Oxygen mask on Mommy before baby. If you can't breathe, you will not be able to help. With this in mind, your task now is to (a) become aware of what you need to feel better in your marriage, (b) take the steps necessary to help make that happen, then (3) share it with your partner so you can both feel better.

Do you feel ready to give? Are you ready to breathe in the air that comes from taking care of yourself and spend some energy understanding what your partner needs or wants? Ask yourself these questions:

Do you feel you understand how your partner's needs and desires differ from your own?

Do you feel ready to examine this and take the steps required to ease some of the current discomfort?

Are you willing to risk stepping out of your comfort zone in order to increase the probability that you will both benefit in the long run?

It's easy to know that your baby needs oxygen on the airplane. It's not so easy to know that your partner needs air in your marriage. You, without a doubt, are the one in the best position to provide that sustenance. As Patricia Love and Steven Stosny say, "Developing the ability to experience the world through your partner's eyes, while holding on to your own perspective, may be the single most important skill in intimate relationships" (2007, p. 141). You will know when you are ready to use the Tokens, because it won't feel like work, it will just feel like the right thing to do.

Rationale for Tokens

The Tokens we refer to in this book are principles that have shown to be associated with an increase in marital happiness; they are gift-giving gestures that you will learn to share on behalf of your commitment to each other. By definition, a token represents an object of value. Each Token of Affection, which will be explored in detail in subsequent chapters, is designed to help the two of you restore connections that have unraveled due to ongoing stress and depression. If you thought your partner would be more loving and responsive to you if you understood him/her better, would you go to all this trouble?

The decision to move forward with the Tokens is best positioned if it comes from a feeling of strength, rather than weakness. In other words, putting effort out on behalf of your marriage will be more productive if you are motivated by the desire to reconnect, rather than out of a feeling of frustration. If you find that feelings of anger or guilt or resentment are getting in the way, try to give yourself permission to suspend some of these negative feelings for the time being. Although that might sound counterproductive, you may actually find that you feel *less* angry, guilty, or resentful as you engage in this process. For now, try to move these feelings aside temporarily and open yourself up to the possibility that these feelings, while valid, may get in the way.

How did these Tokens come to be? In my work, I have seen many couples struggle and survive the emotional turmoil imposed upon their marriage by postpartum depression. It is always an uphill climb. I have witnessed the emotional apathy, couples who are too tired to climb, so they stay stuck, stumbling through their unhappiness. I have also seen couples who claim the depression brought them closer as they cautiously scaled the mountain together. Still other couples continue to hang onto the cliffs, losing traction, dangling, and smashing their bodies against the mountain in their arduous effort to reach the peak of comfort.

The Tokens are your foothold. They will give you something to hold on to while the two of you find your way back to each other. These eight Tokens have been demonstrated in my clinical practice and in my observation of life, to hold great promise for recovery from pain as well as increasing long term mutual fulfillment. The Tokens are the gateway back to the connection that the two of you already have.

Let's start by taking a brief look at each Token.

1 **Token of Esteem**
   This first Token refers to how much and how well you value yourself and your relationship. It is common for self-esteem to be thwarted by depression. It's hard to feel good about yourself when everything feels so dark and impossible. That's why your first step is to work on regaining this sense of self. This will then move you in the direction of esteem for your relationship. What it means to you, how much you value it, what significance it holds for you and how much you are willing to invest in it.

2 **Token of Collaboration**
   The second Token is the first bridge between you and your partner. It provides the foundation for teamwork. Again, this is hard to do if remnants of depression or unfulfilled expectations flood the scene, but early on, it's important to start viewing your partnership as just that, a partnership.

3 **Token of Compromise**
   The third Token can be a greater challenge for some couples more than others. Highly competitive couples, Type A personalities, for example, might find compromising a bore. Or, irrelevant. You will learn that the art of give and take is one of the cornerstones of long lasting happiness. When I give up on behalf of you and you give up on behalf of me, and it is fair, balanced, and in the spirit of affection; we are each giving to the relationship.

4 **Token of Selflessness**
   The fourth Token refers to the ability to view this giving (or giving up) as gaining something, rather than losing something. We all know the old adage that it is better to give than to receive. Unfortunately, most postpartum couples emerging from depression report to me that they just aren't in the mood to give. They are tired and tired of being tired. The relationship simply does not look or feel like a place to go for nourishment or fulfillment. Nevertheless, this is exactly the point of the book. The relationship is the place to go to find the goodies you are seeking. It's all there.

5 **Token of Sanctuary**
   This fifth Token is how you mark your territory for well-deserved comfort. It is the most tangible Token, the one that refers to a physical space

that you each have and another one that you both share. A space where everything feels warm and cozy, thoughts are whispered, and problems are solved.

6 **Token of Expression**
The sixth Token refers to how you communicate, both verbally and nonverbally. In Chapter 5, you will review the basic elements of fair fighting techniques and see how to intervene if some of your thoughts or feelings are actually misperception. Here, you will learn how you might be getting in your own way and how to maximize the art of conversation between the two of you. Moreover, you will see how many ways you might be sending messages when you may or may not intend to do so.

7 **Token of Tolerance**
The seventh Token is hard for a lot of people. Couples tell me they thought it would get easier as years pass, but instead, they find they are less tolerant of each other. Perhaps because there are so many distractions; perhaps it's because everyone is tired and overworked; perhaps it's because it's just plain easier to be cranky than it is to be tolerant. Still, the inability to accept things on a small scale, can lead to larger disappointments, which can then lead to resentments that are forever engraved.

8 **Token of Loyalty**
The last Token refers to a commitment to the relationship and learning skills to transform your good intentions to meaningful and lasting connections.

Now let's see if we can establish a preliminary sense of which areas you feel most vulnerable in, which translates into which Tokens you need to work hardest on. Take a look at the list of eight Tokens in Table 1.1. Indicate how much of a problem area you think each might present for you, from 0 to 5 (0 = no problem, 5 = very problematic). Mark an "x" in the column that reflects how much of a problem you think *you* have in each area. As you complete this, consider what each Token word means in terms of the marriage as well as yourself in the context of your marriage:

> Esteem = value for self or other
> Collaboration = teamwork
> Compromise = give and take
> Selflessness = thinking of others
> Sanctuary = feeling safe
> Expression = ways to communicate
> Tolerance = ability to accept
> Loyalty = trust and commitment

Table 1.1 Token Assessment

	0	1	2	3	4	5
Esteem						
Collaboration						
Compromise						
Selflessness						
Sanctuary						
Expression						
Tolerance						
Loyalty						

Now, think about what this means to you and your marriage. What conclusions can you draw from this?

- Are you where you want to be?
- Do any of your responses surprise you?
- Are you particularly worried about your ability to tackle any, or many, or all of these?
- Are you skeptical about your partner's interest or ability to participate in this process?
- Do you feel ready at this early stage to engage your partner and review the Tokens together?
- Do you worry that your efforts here may be dismissed or not taken seriously?

This initial exercise is the first step in training your heart and your brain to feel and think in terms of a team. While each Token is oriented toward connectedness, the inherent paradox is that the successful use of the Tokens depends on individuality and self-determination. In other words, the presumption is that *healthy coupling depends on the union of two healthy individuals.* Keep this in mind as we explore the Tokens and the interrelatedness that underscores this work: *The better you feel about yourself, the more clarity you will have with respect to your partner.* The more clarity you have, the more positive influence you will have on your marriage. Again, the core principles that highlight your success potential are: (a) Your independent strength and well-being and (b) Your desire and ability to identify your partner's needs. If it sounds like you will be doing all the work, you are right. You will be doing all of your own work. The payoff will be that your partner will feel better and, with belief in this process and mutual hard work, will return the favor by reciprocating the effort.

There are all kinds of reasons for you to be optimistic right now. First of all, the depression is behind you so you and your partner are on the precipice between the past difficult months and all the good things that will soon unfold. Second, you are being mindful enough to pay close attention to the nitty-gritty nuances that make your marriage unique. This is not a casual journey. Rather, it is one that is embarked upon with love and great hopefulness. It is evidence of your deliberate regard and consideration for the promise the two of you made some time ago. Third, those vows you shared will underscore each Token in this book and remind you both of what attracted you to each other in the first place. And finally, you might be wondering if the principles in this book will hold true if only one of the two of you is motivated to strengthen the marriage. The answer is yes.

2

WHEN DEPRESSION DESCENDS

Character cannot be developed in ease and quiet. Only through experience of trial and suffering can the soul be strengthened, ambition inspired, and success achieved.

—Helen Keller

Andrew said he noticed a change in Hallie even before she was depressed. They were married for 3 years before having children. During that time he described both of them as carefree and more relaxed. "Ever since we had kids, she's turned into a crazy woman, always checkin' and doin' and running around," he elaborated. She became hyperfocused on the baby and seemed to worry about everything. He recalled that nothing felt fun anymore and pleasure was replaced by details, organization, schedules and anxiety. When things didn't go the way she expected them to, Hallie would melt into a frenzy that would temporarily paralyze her. Andrew admitted that her heightened vigilance made him feel uptight, almost as if her anxiety was contagious, he would say. Sometimes, he would just have to leave the room so he could regain his composure. This made Hallie feel deserted. "He was a total jerk." She proclaimed. "I had to do everything. And when I couldn't do it all and freaked, he just checked out."

Here we see how abruptly things can seem to change and how easy it can be to misinterpret the intentions of our partners. While Hallie believed she was being abandoned, Andrew was stifling his overwhelming feelings of anxiety. There appears to be little awareness of what the other person was experiencing and needing. The continuing isolation of separateness and excessive worry that permeates a home under stress can squeeze the life out of a family under attack during a postpartum crisis. The result can be a marriage starving from lack of attention and affection.

What is Postpartum Depression?

Postpartum depression (PPD) is complex and multi-faceted, but most experts agree it is the result of the interaction of biological, genetic, psychological, environmental, and social factors. There is no one single cause. Depending on individual vulnerabilities, for some women, the illness is more biological in nature, for others it has more psychological or environmental influences.

Postpartum depression and postpartum anxiety disorders are getting more attention now than ever. There is more information, greater clarification, and improved screening protocols. Regrettably, however, misunderstandings and misdiagnoses continue to be widespread and the social stigma of mental illness persists. This is true even within the families that are struggling. Postpartum depression is very real and its impact on the family can be devastating.

As previously mentioned and worth repeating, anywhere from 5% to 25% of all postpartum women and about 10% of men experience major depression during the postpartum period (Gaynes et al., 2005; Paulson & Bazemore, 2010). The numbers vary when we take into consideration (a) women who are misdiagnosed, (b) women who experience perinatal losses that trigger a depression, (c) women who experience minor depressions (less severe than major depression) or anxiety symptoms such as panic or obsessive-compulsive disorder (OCD), (d) women who do not seek medical attention for their symptoms, (e) the timing and types of screening mechanisms. A recent study led by one of PPD's foremost researchers, Katherine Wisner, confirmed that 14% of the women studied screened positive for depression. This is significant because it is the largest scale depression screening of postpartum women to date (10,000 women) and the first time a full psychiatric assessment has been carried out for the postpartum women who screened positive for depression. Since the postpartum time frame presents the highest risk period for mental health issues in a woman's life, this current research underscores the necessity for prenatal and postpartum screening and assessments (Wisner et al., 2013).

In women with previous episodes of postpartum depression, the risk of recurrence is 1 in 4 (Wisner, Parry, & Piontek, 2002). Although awareness of male depression following the birth of a baby is increasing, the preponderance of help-seeking behaviors for depression and for marital support is facilitated by women. Because we presume that, by and large, women will be the primary readers of this book, much of our language will be directed toward them. We are hopeful that men reading this book understand this decision. One endearing man I was treating for depression after the birth of his child told me the impenetrable blackness and extraordinary pain was completely overwhelming. He said being depressed was the worst pain he ever experienced, "Suddenly, everything went dark." He didn't feel weak or disempowered by the pain, nor did he succumb to the standard withdrawal response. He quickly identified the seriousness of his state and reached out for help. He didn't care who thought what, or who labeled him, or whether the books were written for men or for women. When I expressed regret that my own books had been written specifically for women suffering from depression, he said, "Hey, the books helped me feel better, I read right past that stuff. Besides, I have you here with me to help me get through this, all is good."

What remains unequivocal, regardless of who seeks treatment, is that the birth of a baby alone, and certainly in combination with of depression, creates a jolt to the entire family system.

Symptoms

As a matter of review, postpartum depression is the presence of a clinical depression during the postpartum period. The postpartum period is loosely defined as the first year following the birth of a baby. A clinical depression refers to a serious depression that meets diagnostic criteria for a major depressive disorder according to the *Diagnostic Statistical Manual of Mental Disorders* (American Psychiatric Association [*DSM-IV-TR*], 2000). Depression can be mild, moderate, or severe. Some of the symptoms of a major depressive episode can overlap with what is considered normal postpartum changes, such as fatigue, loss of libido, and anxiety, as a result, the diagnostic picture can be obscured. Thus, it is not just the symptom or emotion itself, it is the *frequency, severity,* and *intensity* of the symptoms that define depression during the postpartum period (Kleiman, 2009). For example, while it might be common for new mothers to feel weepy from time to time, if the crying is persistent, doesn't seem to let up, or interferes with the way she typically functions, then it is not okay.

Some of the more common symptoms of depression include:

- Extreme sadness
- Depressed mood most of the day
- Fatigue/insomnia
- Inability to enjoy pleasurable activities
- Irritability
- Difficulty sleeping
- Feelings of worthlessness or guilt
- Change in appetite
- Obsessions
- Loss of interest in sex
- Thoughts of suicide
- Perception of inadequacy
- Impaired concentration
- Agitation

Anxiety can manifest as physical or non-physical. Some general common symptoms of anxiety are:

- Fear of pending doom
- Pressure in the chest area
- Stomach queasiness
- Shortness of breath
- Trembling
- Numbness
- Heart palpitations or "skipping beats"
- Restlessness
- Irritability
- Fatigue
- Trouble falling asleep

Symptoms of anxiety are almost always present in some form, but if the anxiety is pervasive and predominant, a diagnosis of generalized anxiety disorder (GAD), panic disorder, OCD, or post-traumatic stress disorder (PTSD) may be given, depending on the particular set of symptoms. The term *postpartum* depression can be misleading, because so many suffers present with high levels of agitation and obsessive thinking. By and large, the medical, academic, and lay communities sanction the use of the term *postpartum depression* to include all postpartum mood and anxiety disorders.

The symptoms of postpartum depression must not be confused with the *baby blues*, a common phenomenon affecting the majority postpartum women. Symptoms such as sadness, weepiness, irritability, and anxiety can emerge shortly after birth and typically resolve within the first 2 to 3 postpartum weeks (when hormones settle down). This time-limited syndrome resolves spontaneously and requires no treatment. When moms feel particularly blues-y it is recommended that they increase their self-help measures, such as rest, nutrition, exercise, sleep, and social support. Unfortunately, many healthcare providers continue to misinterpret this 2–3 week cut off and may misinterpret or discount a postpartum woman's lingering presentation of symptoms. Therefore, let me repeat this so it is clear. If feelings of distress persist beyond 2–3 weeks postpartum, they should not be dismissed as the blues. Screening for prenatal and postpartum depression and a referral for potential treatment is indicated.

It has been shown that depression or anxiety during pregnancy, poor social support, stressful life events, previous history of depression, and a family history of depressive disorders are strong predictors of major depression in postpartum women (O'Hara & Swain, 1996; Swendsen & Mazure, 2000; Wisner & Stowe, 1997). On the other hand, the following do not appear to be linked to a higher incidence of postpartum depression: The woman's educational level, the sex of the baby, whether she breastfeeds or bottle feeds, whether the pregnancy was planned or the type of delivery she had (Wisner et al., 2002).

Most Significant Predictors of PPD	Not Predictive of PPD
Previous history of depression	Educational level
Family history of depression	Baby's gender
Depression or anxiety during pregnancy	Breastfeeding or bottle feeding
Stressful recent life events	Planned or unplanned pregnancy
Poor social support	Mode of delivery

Treatment for postpartum depression usually consists of either psychotherapy, antidepressant medication, or both therapy and medication. Because depression so often causes the sufferer to misconstrue what is being said or done, much of the focus of early treatment is to address these misrepresentations in order to reduce the anxiety associated with them. Treatment modalities include *interpersonal psychotherapy* (IPT), *supportive psychotherapy,* and *cognitive behavioral therapy* (CBT). Briefly, the idea underlying IPT is that depression occurs in an interpersonal context, and that improving close relationships can lead to symptom reduction. Supportive psychotherapy is a psychodynamic approach that is largely based on the relationship between the therapist and the client and aims to reinforce the client's healthy adaptive patterns in order to reduce symptoms. CBT is another psychotherapeutic approach that helps the client understand how their thoughts and feelings can directly influence how they are feeling. During the short-term course of treatment, individuals learn how to identify and change destructive or distressing thought patterns that have a negative impact on how they feel and their behavior.

Who Was Depressed? Mom? Dad?

In the United States, the ratio of women to men suffering from depression is 2 to 1 (Keita, 2007). Regardless of who experienced the depression after the birth of their baby, both partners invariably suffer. Mothers and fathers who are depressed feel enormous responsibility for their symptoms and generally understand how hard they can be to live with at times, but feel powerless to do anything about it. Guilt takes center stage. The non-depressed spouse typically picks up the slack and though may be initially supportive and sympathetic, in time, often becomes weary and resentful. Typically, men and women both state they feel embarrassed about the way the depression makes them feel and wish it would just go away. Despite the improvement in awareness initiatives, depression is often perceived as a weakness (*If only I were strong enough, I wouldn't feel this way!*) by the sufferer and by the larger society. Moms and dads, both describe feeling cheated from the joy of experiencing the precious moments with their baby as well as with their partner. Mostly, they feel robbed of the life they expected, fantasized about, and to which they felt entitled.

Men and women respond to depression and marital distress, differently. The basis for some of these gender-related differences is not clear, raising the question of whether the numbers reflect biological differences in how men and women respond to stress or something else, such as their willingness to seek treatment, as one example. Because women are nearly twice as likely as men to experience depression (Nolen-Hoeksema, 1987), it's important to consider gender specific responses in the discussion of depression and marital distress.

The conclusions in this area of research are equivocal, but, by and large, studies show that women who are distressed in their marriage have a higher risk for depression than husbands who are distressed. However, depressed husbands and wives are at equal risk for marital distress (Gotlib & Beach, 1995). Subsequent research went on to show that for men, depression predicted marital distress, while for women, it was the other way around—marital distress predicted current and future depressive symptoms (Choi & Marks, 2008; Fincham, Beach, Harold, & Osborne, 1997). Researchers are careful to point out that causal associations between depression and gender are not consistent but most agree there is a bidirectional relation. In other words, most of the studies show that low marital satisfaction is linked with depressive symptoms, in one direction or the other. Clearly, this reciprocal association can tie couples up in an endless cycle of depressive symptoms and marital distress.

According to Terrance Real, author of a number of books on male depression, women tend to internalize their distress, often blaming themselves or feeling responsible and are more likely to ask for help. Men tend to externalize their distress and may blame outer circumstances and are more resistant to treatment. His research also shows that men have less tolerance for the high levels of distress and are more at risk to escape their pain with the excessive use of alcohol or drugs, or overworking, or seeking relief through an extramarital affair (Real, 1997). It's interesting to note that in his work, Real also discovered that an underlying root of depression in men was a feeling of disconnect from their own needs and from the significant people in their lives. He notes that the key is reconnection. One might wonder if this vulnerability is the fault line that the postpartum period disturbs so abruptly, leaving some men feeling isolated and neglected. If this is so, then our premise in this book which highlights reconnection may help ease the discomfort that some men may not even have identified.

Did my depression cause my marriage problems or did my marriage problems cause my depression?

As previously mentioned, depression is linked with lower marital satisfaction. According to one study, there are three possible ways in which marital satisfaction and spousal depression are entwined. Here are the likely scenarios:

1 **Marital dissatisfaction and disappointment exist before the depression.** It has been shown that dissatisfaction with the relationship predicts maternal depression (Beach, Sandeen, & O'Leary, 1990). It makes sense that when either partner is unhappy in the relationship it could lead to emotional deprivation, either real or perceived, which could then lead to withdrawal and depression.
2 **One partner's depression may precede marital problems.** In this situation, depression may cause dysfunction that triggers marital conflict. Additionally, I have seen that women under stress may perceive their partners as less supportive. They also tend to evaluate their partner's behavior in negative ways (Notarius, Benson, Sloane, Vanzetti, & Hornyak, 1989). It is possible that depression plays an important role in uncovering or generating issues that are pivotal to the couple's ultimate well-being. On the positive end of the spectrum, some clients have reported to us that their depression served to help them better understand each other, thereby increasing their continuing satisfaction. On the down side, some couples report that the depression surfaced issues that ultimately were insurmountable.
3 **Any stressful life experience, such as childbirth itself, can be solely responsible for the link between marital satisfaction and depressive symptoms.** There is evidence that women may be particularly sensitive to their partner's negative attitude when they become parents (Buehlman, Gottman, & Katz, 1992) which may or may not be the result of depressive thinking. Regardless of which partner experiences depression after the birth of their baby, it is a well-documented trigger for both marital stress and depression (Salmela-Aro, Aunola, Saisto, Halmesmäki, & Nurmi, 2006).

Emotional Residue

The effect postpartum depression has on a marriage can manifest in myriad ways. Whether your marriage was steady and strong prior to depression or not, the force of symptoms can break down the best of ties. Not long-term. Not irrevocably. But when the pitch-black landscape engulfs one half of a partnership, it's hard for either one to breathe. Think about it. Any time one of the couple is in anguish, it promptly becomes a family issue. We easily recognize it in simple terms: When dad is sick, no one is happy. When mom doesn't feel good, dad gets cranky. When dad is tired, mommy has to pick up the slack. There is a great deal of sharing and division of labor intrinsic to a postpartum setting. You do this, I'll do that. In an ideal world, the sharing and partnering and exchanging of roles and tasks is part of the dance that moms and dads negotiate during the first months and years of adjustment. This life transition is a constant challenge with constant accommodations. Sometimes, it works well. Sometimes, it doesn't.

Depression makes all that harder.

Once the acute symptoms of depression have been treated and both parties salvage their composure, lasting emotions continue to permeate the air. Even though the dust has cleared, and everyone has reclaimed their rightful position in the family domain, remnants of the postpartum upheaval pollute the breathing space. It feels okay for the most part. Maybe even better than it did before in many ways. But still, something's amiss. Too much awareness, perhaps? Or not enough? Not enough attention? Or too much of the wrong kind? Too much distance? Or not enough? Too much anger? Whose? Too much guilt? Definitely. This residue can become part of the problem, or part of the solution. The solution involves applying the lessons learned, as painful as they may be, to the advantage of the marriage. If part of the problem, the emotional residue can lead to (a) communication collapse, (b) ambivalence, or (c) disengagement.

Depression affects the way you think and how you think can affect your depression. When someone is depressed, their perception of the world around them, changes. If you are reading this as the non-depressed spouse, especially if you have never experienced depression, you might take notice of some of the TV commercials that depict the world from the viewpoint of the depressed person. Everything is portrayed as dark, and slow, and sad, and stuck. Everything within reach feels far away. Everything that could bring comfort feels heavy and improbable. Everything that is good, feels bad.

That's not the worst part.

The worst part about all of these complicated emotions is that after a while, they don't feel like symptoms.

They feel like *who you are*.

If being with my baby makes me so nervous, I must be a bad mother.

Since my husband is getting on my nerves all the time, we probably shouldn't stay together.

I cannot stand the way I feel. I'm certain my husband will leave me.

If I tell my wife how I'm really feeling she will think I am weak and useless.

And the worst of all:

My baby would be better off with a different mother (or father).

Regardless of who is depressed, mom or dad, by far, the prevailing emotional burden consists of some elements of guilt and anger. For example, when a woman becomes depressed after the birth of her baby, she suffers from more than deep sorrow and feelings of hopelessness that accompany a depressed mood disorder. The emergence of depression at this time of her life often forces her to misinterpret the symptoms and view the depression as her experience of motherhood. She does not know how or does not feel able to separate it and thus, believes she is inadequate and unprepared for this role of mother. She is angry at the depression. She is angry at herself. She is angry at her partner. This is often accompanied by overwhelming guilt because she is believes she is failing to meet her own expectations and those of her family and society. Many mothers describe feeling guilty because they are not feeling what they think they should be feeling.

Once these feelings set in, it's difficult to extract them from one's current sense of self, as distorted as they may be. Treatment will help. Unfortunately, not all women with postpartum depression seek treatment. Either way, the ripple effect of scary thoughts or misdirected emotions runs deep. It is quite possible that even after successful treatment, one or both of you may still hold intermittent feelings of regret or deep disappointment, or any number of other potent emotions. Without treatment, it is highly probable.

It's not hard to imagine that such strong emotions would continue to lurk, even after you thought everything was better. Emotions are complicated. In addition to the circumstance (for example, an internal thought or external event) that may give rise to a certain emotion, they are also understood in terms of your experiences, your judgment of the event, your bodily state, your DNA, and all kinds of complicated neuroanatomical and neurochemical systems. The intricate synergy between these forces is something scientists continue to study. Each of us has been a victim of our own uncontrolled emotions, at times, regardless of our ongoing dedication to control ourselves! We may believe we have a certain feeling under control, then, bam! Suddenly it overcomes us without warning!

Since we tend to act in ways that correspond directly to our emotional state, let's begin with understanding which emotions are driving you and your behavior at this time. Derived from our clinical practice, the list below represents some of the emotions that are common for couples adjusting to life *after* postpartum depression. See how many of these feelings resonate for you right now, regarding your marriage. This will provide a prelude to the focus of your work ahead:

Rate each emotion from 1-5 according to how strongly you feel that emotion, with 5 being the strongest.

blank = none
1 = weak
2 = slightly strong

3 = moderately strong
4 = very strong
5 = extremely strong

In Table 2.1. place "x" in column under the number that best reflects your level of emotion toward your partner right now. Leave blank if you are not experiencing that emotion. You will notice that the majority of the emotions are negative. This is so we can cut to the heart of some of the pain in order to move the process along. We included positive feelings in order to balance out your experience and facilitate a broader picture of the current emotional state. In the "other" space at the end, write in any strong emotion you are feeling that was not listed. Next, repeat this with the second set of numbers as it relates to how you believe your partner is feeling toward you.

Any negative emotion that you checked with a 3 or above is likely to be causing interference in your relationship. The primary goal of this exercise is to identify what feelings you have, determine how bad the negative feelings feel and how good the positive feelings feel, and begin to discover whether or not they are hindering your recovery or your relationship. It would be helpful at this early stage to engage your partner in this exercise in order to determine whether your perceptions are aligned with those of your partner, or not. And vice versa.

Although we have listed slightly more negative feelings than positive, here's some interesting information about the positive feelings in your relationship. John Gottman, a leading relationship researcher and author of several excellent books on marriage, talks about a *magic ratio* of 5:1 (Gottman, 1993). This ratio refers to the relationship between positive and negative interactions between couples during conflict resolution. He says that in happy marriages that are working well, there are five times as many positive things going on, than negative. He defines positive things as interest in each other, empathy, kindness, affection, humor, asking questions, and generally being nice. And this is during conflicts, too!

Conversely, in the couples that he studied that ended up divorced, the ratio was 0.8:1, a tiny bit more negativity than positivity, but approximately 1 to 1. He explains that if you behave in a way that hurts your partner's feelings, you have to make up for it with five positive things! His research shows that happy couples tend to express more positive feelings and actions than negative ones whether or not they are in conflict and regardless of their particular styles of communicating. Statistically speaking, partners who demonstrate constant criticism, negative feedback, lack of appreciation, or act disinterested in their partner are setting themselves up for potential demise (Gottman & Silver, 1999).

While this next section will examine the effect of emotional residue and subsequent areas of vulnerability, keep this magic ratio in the back of your mind. The reason you should remember this message of five positive things for every one negative one, is because the Tokens will be your tool for upholding

Table 2.1 Your Emotional Experience

Emotional Experience	Self 1	2	3	4	5	Partner 1	2	3	4	5
Frustrated										
Sad										
Unloved										
Resentful										
Hurt										
Disappointed										
Guilty										
Explosive										
Insecure										
Contempt										
Anxious										
Disillusioned										
Angry										
Distant										
Irritable										
Disapproving										
Shameful										
Rageful										
Disgusted										
Judgemental										
Indifferent										
Bored										
Grief										
Criticism										
Hostility										
Depressed										
Afraid										
Loss of control										
Appreciative										
Happy										
Admiration										
Intimate										
Devotion										
Loving										
Grateful										
Optimistic										
Grateful										
Curious										
Gentleness										
Respect										
Humor										
Other										

that ratio. Despite your previous behaviors and response patterns, you are now in a better position to make a difference and increase your ratio!

Communication Collapse: On Shaky Ground

Communicating when someone is depressed is difficult. Whether you are the one who suffered, or the partner of the sufferer, the depression will affect you both and make understanding each other more challenging. Any time feelings become raw from chronic pain, effective communication is in jeopardy. It's hard to dialogue with someone when you're holding a grudge or privately furious, or heartbroken. Gottman states that couples tend to turn *toward* each other, or *away* from each other, simply by how they respond, both verbally and nonverbally.

For example, he points out, how does it make you feel when your partner calls your name from another room, when you are in the middle of doing something? Do you respond "yes?" with a voice that implies you are listening and open to what may be asked of you? Or do you say, "WHAT?!" with a voice that implies you are busy, or annoyed, and not interested? The YES, is turning inward toward the relationship and the WHAT is turning away. Gottman further describes how every "bid for attention" (2007, p. 99) is a bid for emotional connection. When we feel rejected (which is so often present of depressive thinking), we tend to retreat, or ask less often. All of the little moments, of turning toward one another, or away, add up, as an investment in the relationship, one way or the other. In this way, Gottman shed lights on the main thrust of this book when he writes "turning toward leads to more turning toward" (2007, p. 153).

Communication patterns associated with depression are often marked by:

- Avoidance of conflict and avoidance of attempts to reconcile.
- Perceived feelings of failure may lead to self-blame.
- Lack of motivation and energy to change or focus on positive.
- An inability to accept positive feedback due to persistent misinterpretations of unlovability.

Unfortunately, these behaviors can actually reinforce the disconnect and deepen the isolation. Even after the depression has been treated, some people tend to prefer the familiarity of their rigid preferences and may not have the clarity to see how this may negatively affect their ability to communicate.

During and after postpartum depression, both partners often feel alone in their anguish and misunderstood. They have become partners in agony. Once treatment begins to take hold and there is less focus on the illness and symptoms, both work fervently to get back to the business at hand. Back to being a family, focus on the baby, back to making up for lost time, as women often tell me. This spontaneous desire to return to normal is common and can play out in a couple of ways. Some couples may inadvertently put their relationship on the back burner so they can focus on the baby and other aspects of their life demanding immediate attention. Somewhat ironically, it is often the stronger relationships that get abandoned temporarily, in support of the rest of the family obligations. This may be because *if I trust that you aren't going anywhere, it is easier for me to let you be, while I go and take care of all these other things that require my immediate attention.* Make sense?

On the other hand, relationships that are more unstable or unpredictable may resume a familiar posture of constant bickering or other unproductive tactics. It may not feel good, but it's what they know and are comfortable with and easiest to take up as they reenter their lives together. Regardless of which path they take, couples can quickly forget how to take care of each other when they are so busy and tired.

Warning signs that communication could be breaking down:

- *I struggle to think of things to say to my partner.*
- *I am rarely interested in what my partner has to say.*
- *Every time we talk, we fight.*
- *I try not to criticize but I feel so negative much of the time.*
- *I'm too tired to argue so I just don't say anything.*
- *When my partner talks to me I notice I am easily distracted.*

Do you feel as though your communication has started to break down?

Ambivalence: The Great Divide

We've seen how communication pathways are thwarted by depression. Paradoxically, as emotional needs become heightened, relationship numbness can ensue. Numbness in this case does not refer to a complete lack of feeling. Rather, it refers to a defensive position, a shutdown of sorts, usually because of the extreme emotional complexities we reviewed earlier in this chapter. Too much anger, resentment, or guilt can make anyone tired and weary. This kind of emotional fatigue, if not attended to lovingly or professionally, can create the numbing response. Remember Hallie from earlier in this chapter? Her anger has driven many of her conversations into fiery balls of circular and unproductive dialogue. When she came to see me she felt smothered by the emotional residue. She described this way, "I just don't care anymore. I'm so sick and tired of him not listening to me, not being there for me. It's like what I say doesn't matter. If what I want isn't what he wants, well, then, so what. We'll do it his way. I don't care, really. It's fine. It's not worth it. Really."

It's as if someone says, "I don't care" out of protest or despair.

Hallie rolled her eyes as she tried to explain how she just "didn't care" anymore, during a session that Andrew was not able to attend. "It's really not worth it."

"It's not?" I asked, responding to the pain I had seen in her eyes and heard in her words for weeks.

"The more I try, the less he has to give me. Or at least that's how it feels. We do better when we do our own thing, you know, he plays golf all weekend and I spend the days with the kids. Woohoo! Fun for me, right?"

Hallie and Andrew are experiencing a communication breakdown that has led to ambivalence. She protests and pretends not to care because the ambivalence feels better than the pain of rejection. Her attempts at humor also serve to protect her somewhat, but in reality, she is not as good at defending herself as she would claim she was.

Sometimes, when ambivalence drops in on a marriage struggling to recover from postpartum depression, it can result from sheer exhaustion. It is no secret the sleep deprivation can be the greatest enemy of all. Working on the marriage can just feel like too much to do, with so much going on and so little energy to draw upon. Moreover, depression is an extremely self-absorbing illness, forcing the sufferer to worry and hyperfocus on how she or he is feeling most or all of the time. This distorted perspective can lead to uncertainty and doubt in the relationship, because, quite frankly, nothing feels good. When this happens, a recovering couple can find themselves completely polarized, where there is not necessarily contention or hostility, but there is now a division between the twosome. And that never feels good.

Keep in mind that ambivalence can be a real phenomenon; such is the case when someone is transitioning from communication breakdown to total disengagement, on the road to a marital crisis. Or, it can be defensive. It can take the form of apathy but in actuality it is concealing the hurt and vulnerability. It's crucial that you know the difference. If it's defensive, it is a cop-out, relied on by people who choose not to be accountable or responsible. Even with a silly example like, do you want to go see a movie tonight? "I don't care" is a weak response. Of course, you care. Take a stand. Have an opinion. Share it with your partner.

Warning signs that ambivalence has set in:

- *I don't care anymore.*
- *I feel stuck.*
- *No matter what I say, it doesn't make a difference.*
- *Whatever ...*
- *My partner doesn't seem to be invested anymore.*
- *Some days things feel great. Other days, I can't believe we are still together.*
- *I'm honestly not sure how I feel.*
- *Every time I offer a solution, my partner backs down and avoids any effort to make something feel better.*

Do you feel you are experiencing the early stages of ambivalence?

Disengagement: The Mortal Wound

This is the most painful scenario, but not the most common. Most couples do *not* completely disengage as a result of their experience with postpartum depression. It may feel like that at times, but that is not what is happening in the majority of families. In rare instances when the marriage really is at stake during this time, it is likely that the severity of the depression reinforced troubles or vulnerabilities that existed before the baby and before the depression. The added stress of having a baby along with a depression that shocks the family system will cause a couple to drift toward areas of weakness. That's what we do when we are tired and overwhelmed and irritable. We revert to more primitive states of functioning. We all do it. When our defenses are down, it is easier to complain, whine, and nitpick. None of which are good for a marriage, but they are not indicative of enduring problems, unless, of course, there are enduring problems.

Long-standing difficulties in a marriage are not the focus of this book. Still, as noted in the first chapter, up to 67% of couples report declining marital happiness after having a baby (Shapiro, Gottman, & Carrère, 2000). This is without factoring in the fury of postpartum depression! This number of discontented couples is striking and obliges us to take a closer look at how we can intervene and help couples manage better, considering the magnitude of distractions and disruptions. The truth is that without paying attention to this, some couples will gravitate in an outer direction, away from each other and settle in a quiet corner. Sometimes this is done out of anger. Sometimes this is done out of despair. Whatever the motivating force, once one or both of the partners sink into a private space leaving no room, no energy, no interest in the other partner, the impasse can prove fatal for the marriage. This is when we might see the emergence of unhealthy responses and choices which can range from neglecting to take care of oneself, to risky behaviors such as the misuse of drugs or alcohol, infidelity, or domestic abuse.

Some of the warning signs of severe disengagement that signal trouble and the need for intervention are:

- *I prefer to be alone all of the time.*
- *It's a relief to not be with my partner.*
- *I never enjoy his/her company.*
- *I do not want to be touched.*
- *We never talk, and when we do, we fight.*
- *Nothing I do is ever right.*
- *We have nothing in common.*
- *I don't care how she/he feels.*
- *There has been no progress for months and every time I bring up how serious this is, I am dismissed.*

Keep in mind that some of these statements may be uttered from time to time with little consequence. If, on the other hand, these statements reveal feelings that are more constant, reflecting a more chronic state of mind, then both partners would cope and feel better with supportive counseling.

Could your marriage be suffering from the early stages of disengagement?

The Approach Track: Back to Each Other

We've seen how the emotional residue of postpartum depression can find its way into the tiniest crack in your relationship during this extended recovery period. Negative feelings and actions have more ability to damage the relationship than positive feelings have to heal and make things better. Remember Gottman's magic ratio? For every negative interaction, there needs to be five positive interactions to balance it out. Without the positives, relationships simmer in negativity which eventually infects even your best efforts. Right now is the time to turn this around, if need be, and stay on track toward a healthy connection.

In summary, the sequence of steps are shown in Figure 2.1.

As mentioned, the emotional residue which can remain even after successful treatment for postpartum depression is normal. One factor that shapes the health of your marital relationship is which track you take as you journey

Birth of Baby
↓
Postpartum Depression
↓
Successful Resolution
↓
Emotional Residue
↙   ↘
Approach (Token) Track   Dismissive Track
↓   ↓
Collaborative Efforts   Thwarted Efforts
↓   ↓
Connection   **Disconnection**

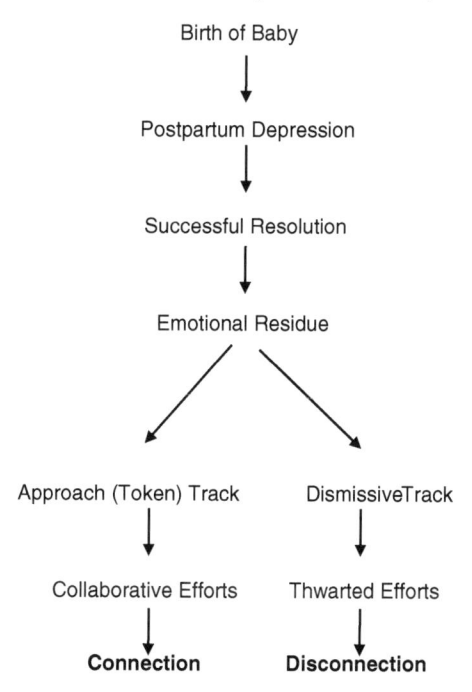

Figure 2.1 The Track to Connection

beyond the treatment phase. You can see that dismissive track (hoping it will go away or get better on its own), which is characterized by mutual disregard, is likely to sabotage or thwart efforts to improve things and can worsen the emotional distress. It is characterized by avoidance and very little, if any, energy is put forth. Ultimately, this contributes to various degrees of disconnection in the relationship.

On the other hand, the approach track, which is just another way to view the Tokens, encourages a collaborative effort and is likely to promote a stronger connection. On this track, energy is put forth toward paying attention to the emotional signals.

You are now on the approach track. You are in position to respond to the emotional residue with attention to lingering symptoms and the emotional aftermath. Being mindful of these areas of vulnerability will increase the resolution potential while decreasing the chance that things will fall off track and get worse.

3

THE CONNECTION

The greatest degree of inner tranquility comes from the development of love and compassion. The more we care for the happiness of others, the greater is our own sense of well-being.

—Tenzin Gyatso, the 14th Dalai Lama

When depression unexpectedly inhabits a postpartum household, it does not discriminate. It often takes on a life of its own, affecting healthy marriages, marriages in trouble, new marriages, or long-term marriages. When the disturbance is severe, it can affect the way the couple views each other and themselves as a unit. Remember that depression changes the way you feel about yourself and your perceptions of the world around you, including your marriage. What ends up happening is that the depressed partner may misinterpret an event (words, thoughts, actions, looks) and then, if this version of the event is not checked out, it is internalized as "real." Perceptions that sift through the filter of depression are frequently biased against the depressed spouse. That's because it all feels bad. Everything feels bad. Even in good, strong marriages.

What do I mean by a good, strong marriage? One that is based on deep friendship and mutual regard. At the core of every good relationship is the connection. The connection is what protects and inspires you as a couple. The connection defines the companionship, it's what helps you share responsibility whether you are laughing or arguing. It's what holds you together when needs are not being met, when frustrations are high and when disappointments arise. The connection between you and your partner gives purpose and meaning to your life together and provides the core strength for a successful marriage. In this context, connection refers to your mutual sense of awareness, empathy, intimacy,* and the capacity for understanding and growth. When two people are dedicated to each other, it can manifest in many ways.

Commitment is what you know to be true. Connection is what you feel.

At the center of this book is the notion that we are hard wired for connectedness and feel lost and isolated without it. When depression unravels connections, it can expose a vulnerability that transforms previously confident people into those who feel unworthy of such connectedness. The paradox here is that this belief of unworthiness, which is largely shame-driven, is incompatible with the need to connect. That is, if the shame of depression takes over, the desire for connection may increase but the ability to connect becomes more difficult.

Fear, Shame, and the Connection

In Chapter 2, we looked at some of the research-based gender differences that play into this discussion of depression and connection. Typically, men tend to solve problems through action and reason. Words and feelings do not feel useful during problem-solving. When feeling unsafe or threatened, taking action helps many men feel in control of a dangerous or vulnerable situation. If they are unable to do that, men often experience shame or a sense of failure. Women, on the other hand, tend to feel safer when connected to others. Expressing their feelings is a way of relating, which ultimately decreases stress. Love and Stosny (2007) describe this as a *fear-shame dynamic* (more on this in Chapter 12) and say that without insight into this dynamic, men and women unknowingly intensify each other's area of vulnerability. Think about it. A wife wants to talk because she is feeling anxious. Her husband responds by taking action. She doesn't want action, she wants closeness, so she points that out. He feels criticized and ashamed, on some level, that he cannot understand or meet her needs. He responds with defensiveness. She feels abandoned.

Depression adds fuel to the fire.

Regardless of who is depressed, the woman may try to seek comfort through words and emotions, which may irritate her husband to some degree. He may seek comfort by instinctively trying to fix things, perhaps without asking for or receiving help from others. When things don't go as planned, he views himself as a failure and she views herself as alone. Whether it is right or wrong,

---

* For clarification purposes, we will be highlighting the exchange of affectionate gestures as a measurement of your emotional involvement within your relationship. We will not be focusing on your sexual relationship. While undeniably a critical component, it is beyond the scope of this book. A majority of postpartum couples report that sex takes a back seat when factoring a new baby and depression. For some couples, this is not the case, and sex continues to hold a significant place in their relationship. If, however, your sex life feels like it also needs some attention, you may find that working with the Tokens to secure a stronger emotional foundation will simultaneously strengthen your sexual expressiveness. That would be a secondary bonus from doing this work!

true or not, many men and women struggle with how to support each other because of this dynamic. Recall the example when my husband so dutifully left me alone because he presumed that's what I would want, because that's what he would want (see Chapter 1). Sometimes, what the support giver thinks will be helpful to the other is, in fact, not what the partner (support receiver) wants, it's what the support giver would want! Martha Manning, psychologist and author, pursues this disconnect in a poignant exchange between her and her therapist-husband in her book, *Undercurrents*: "'I don't want you to help me. I want you to be with me.' He looks at me as if he has no comprehension of the difference of those two things" (1994, p. 77). That line resonates with many couples. Many men tell me, *I'm doing all the right things, I'm doing everything she asks for and needs. I'm doing my best to take care of everything. What am I doing wrong?*

This is where we see depression tumbling into the marriage.

Manning elucidates what she needs during her own depression, "Just hold me, sit with me. Put your arm around me. Listen as I struggle to tell you what it feels like" (1994, p. 78). But it's hard for a man to sit with his wife in so much pain without being tempted to fix it and take the pain away. Likewise, when the man is depressed, it's hard for a woman to not to nurture and respond to his isolation by pulling him in closer to her, which may, in fact, make him feel worse (shame). In *Therapy and the Postpartum Woman*, this issue was explored in detail:

> Communication between the couple may deteriorate as symptoms shuffle through their relationship. Women often say they feel pressured by the demand on them to express what they need during a time when they feel least equipped to do so. Women do indeed have to tell their husbands what they need. Yet, when they do, they may be met with frustration or apprehension. Husbands are tired, too. They are working hard and trying to understand something that may be threatening their sense of security. It's a hard time for both of them, often polarizing them and making it less likely for either to be there for the other during this time of stress.
>
> (Kleiman, 2009, p. 208)

Shelby was a 31-year-old mom who loved her job as a social worker in a private practice and planned to return as soon as possible. She was excited about having her second baby and agreed with her husband Matt that this was the perfect time to have a baby. Their 4-year old would be in pre-school by the time the baby was born, and Shelby thought carefully about how she would work up until the last moment. When she went in for a routine ultrasound 20 weeks into her pregnancy, Shelby was diagnosed with a short cervix and sent home on bed rest. In an instant, her life turned upside down. She left the doctor's office stunned and saddened by the news. No lifting, no cooking, no housework, no going up and down the stairs, no working, no playing. That's all she heard, no, no, no. Her anxiety soared while loved ones around her tried to reassure her that everything will be fine. But still, her thoughts whirled inside her head: *What if there's something wrong with the baby? What if I deliver prematurely? What will I do all day? How will I lie around all day doing nothing? Who will take care of my daughter? Will it even help? What if I endure this nightmare and there is still something wrong with the baby? What will they do at work without me?*

Over the next few weeks, she struggled with a perception of uselessness and intense feelings of despair. She perceived that she was isolated and irrelevant, despite encouragement from her husband and close friends. Her longing to take care of others and to be in control of her life, stifled by circumstances, remained a restless ache in her heart. As the weeks passed, she increasingly perceived herself as incompetent as a mother and wife. Matt noticed her withdrawal and tried to offer his support, but Shelby was sinking and Matt's fear and frustration led him to rely on the help of family and friends while he buried himself at work.

Their son was born at 38 weeks and all went well. What a relief after such an agonizing wait; he was strong and healthy. Soon, Shelby started experiencing a cluster of symptoms that scared both her and Matt. She was dizzy, constantly. She complained of feeling disoriented, as if she were out of her own body. She didn't feel at all like herself and most troublesome, she didn't feel at all like being with her baby. After self-help gestures proved futile and her vague symptoms of feeling shaky and confused persisted, Matt and Shelby went from doctor to doctor. First, her obstetrician. Then, a neurologist. Next, an endocrinologist. Then, an ENT. They ran tests, took tons of blood, and asked scores of questions. In the end, all concluded she was "fine." Her pediatrician suggested she see a therapist in light of her pregnancy-related stress and her family history of depression and anxiety.

That's when I met Shelby and Matt for the first time. She sat curled up in the corner of the couch, telling me how worthless she was. Not how worthless she felt, how worthless she *was*. She was no good to her daughter, no good to her new son. She cringed every time he cried and screamed at her husband to comfort him because she would only make things worse. She sobbed in between telling me this is not at all what she expected, that she used to be so capable, caring and in control and now she just wished someone would take her baby away. She used words like, embarrassed, ashamed, humiliated. Matt sat close beside her, alternately looking intently at her, and back to me, hoping for answers, for help, for immediate relief. He, too, sat helpless, as he filled in the blanks to her story. He appeared loving and present, though frightened by the intensity of her regressed state. The three of us talked about the combination of her history of previous depression, her mother's history of severe depressive episodes, the enormous stress of prolonged bed rest, and the anxieties attached to pregnancy complications. We talked about the numerous losses Shelby experienced and the crushing impact on her sense of self and purpose. We talked about how undeserving of Matt's love, she felt she was, and that kept her from reaching out. We talked about how frustrated Matt was after weeks and weeks of taking care of things in the house, only to sit by as she spiraled down deeper. They were both exhausted. Then we turned the discussion to our step-by-step plan to help Shelby get relief, and by doing this, help them both feel better.

Recognizing the Signs

As weeks passed, it was gratifying to see Shelby progress through her treatment and rediscover the pleasure in her children. She was a wonderful mother, with precise instincts and creative energy that flowed from her, through her children, and back to her again. Her heartwarming smile was the perfect mirror of her renewed connection with herself and her life. Except for one piece.

"I miss Matt." She started our session after a few weeks of focusing on how good she was feeling.

I waited for the story. Her tears preceded her words.

"I don't know, exactly. I don't know where he is or what's going on. It's just not the same."

Of course it's not, I thought to myself. *How could it be?*

"Tell me how it's different."

"He's more distant. I mean, I know he works hard, so he comes home tired. And of course, I'm tired from being with the baby all day and taking care of Cara after school, but it's hard to put into words, I guess, it's like that shit show we went through back then really wiped us out. It's like something burned a hole in the heart of our perfect family. Everyone is going through the motions as if everything is fine, but it's not right. Something's not right."

"What is he doing or not doing that feels off to you?"

"Um, he's not there, like he used to be. When he's home, he's distracted, or he's watching T.V., or he's playing on his phone, or texting someone. He's always busy with something. He checks out. He seems to spend more time at work and exercising, it's like he's looking for reasons not to be home. Not really, I know, but sometimes it feels that way."

"Have you talked about this with Matt?"

"Not really. You know how it is, we try to talk but between the two kids and work and stuff, it's not easy to get to the point before something distracts us. He knows I'm upset because I cry all the time. Every time I need something or ask something, it's a big deal all of a sudden and I'm like, what the hell, what happened to us? Then he gets all weird and says I'm overreacting. I think he's afraid I'm going to spiral out of control again or something. When I cry, he completely flips out and says he can't do this anymore. I know that's not what he means, I know he's just scared, he's not used to seeing me like this, I know. But it feels terrible and it makes me feel so guilty. I'm sad."

Shelby and Matt were in an unfamiliar state of separateness. They were used to doing everything together, topped off with hand holding and giggles. What scared them most was the feeling that they could no longer rely on the other one the way they were used to doing. They had to kick into crisis mode, which left them both feeling alienated from each other. They felt able to take care of things, for the most part, but no longer able reach out to each other. Though they both felt the loss, each experienced and expressed it differently.

He is scared and irritated, so he withdraws in shame.

She is sad and lonely, so she cries and feels unloved.

Generally speaking, I trust a woman's instinct if she tells me she thinks something is wrong. However, it's important that we balance a postpartum woman's good instinct with her current state of heightened sensitivity. After having a baby and after having postpartum depression, all systems remain on high alert for a considerable period of time. With anxiety at an all-time high, and depression commanding the spotlight, many worries become internalized and reflect a loss of confidence in self. However, with regard to the marriage specifically, anxieties tend to zero in on what has been lost and whether or not the marriage can return to a previous level of mutual satisfaction.

For example, when mom is depressed, she might think like this:

I feel so guilty that I wasn't there for him.
How can he love me when I'm so messed up?
How can he trust me after I said all those awful things about him and the baby?
Does he see me differently?
What if I relax my focus and I slip and feel bad again?
What does he mean when he says he hopes I never get sick again?
What if I do get sick again, will he leave me next time?
Was he just pretending to care when things were so bad?
Why does he act like it never happened sometimes?
Can our marriage survive if I get sick again?

When dad is depressed, he might think like this:

What if this happens again?
I cannot stand that I cannot get my act together.
What if she thinks I'm too weak to take care of her?
What does she really think of me taking medication?
What if she tells people that I totally lost it?
What if she prefers someone stronger and healthier?
I'm so ashamed and embarrassed and I'm sure she is judging me even if she says she is not.

When Shelby expressed these anxieties to Matt, he was able to quickly reassure her. He wasn't going anywhere. He would be there always. He could handle her symptoms. She would get better. Still, his behavior indicated otherwise.

He did spend more time in front of the TV. He did snap back at her when she obsessively asked the same question several times for ongoing reassurance. He did express discontent on his face when she would weep uncontrollably out of the blue.

As a result, despite his best intentions and kind words, their connection was weakening.

Why Connections Matter

We know that the postpartum period is a busy, unpredictable, constantly changing stage of life. This is an understatement. Therefore, the last thing people often think about during this time is what their social life and relationships look and feel like. Still, consider the research behind this: Numerous studies have shown isolation to be detrimental to postpartum adjustment. It has been shown that women tend to function best in relation to others (Surrey, 1984) and benefit from support. In fact, the loss of connection with significant others has been associated with feelings of sadness, anger, loneliness, and depression. Furthermore, it has been suggested that during the postpartum period, some women experience a feeling of distance from their primary source of support (usually partner) as a result of the intense connection they have with their baby (Paris & Dubus, 2005). Some women describe feeling uniquely attached to their baby and simultaneously less able to view themselves as intimate partners. One woman I was treating said she was "reserving her body for her baby" and being touched by her husband in any intimate manner did not feel consistent with that. This was not, however, how her husband viewed things.

As we've seen, postpartum partners are often forced to spend much time apart. Parallel activities and zigzagging schedules are typical. Comments such as *we're like two ships passing in the night* and *we never see each other because one of us is always sleeping* are common. For some couples, this transitional withdrawal is experienced as par for the course and not reason for concern. For other couples, this disconnection can indicate an emotional distancing that has become a significant and painful reality. Despite the increased awareness of postpartum depression and the availability of information that might prepare couples, women and men both tell me they are stunned by the toll it takes on their marriage. Many say, after the fact, that had they known, they would have prepared better with appropriate support.

A marriage out of balance can tilt in one of three directions:

- The relationship can rely on its own resources and move forward toward healing.
- The relationship can become polarized when one or both partners disengage and co-exist on parallel paths.

- The relationship can remain in a state of perpetual discontent for a very, very long time.

Our goal is to help your marriage move forward by tapping into your personal resources, and helping you and your partner tap into the wealth of tools that have been temporarily shelved.

Sue Johnson, author of *Hold me Tight* (2008) and clinician who contributed to our understanding of Emotionally Focused Therapy (EFT), teaches us that isolation for a couple is traumatizing; that they have a primal need to seek and maintain contact and a secure connection. Her theory is based on the attachment system which is believed to be paramount to the success of a marriage. Attachment in general, refers to the emotional bond to another person. Psychologist John Bowlby was the first attachment theorist, describing attachment as a "lasting psychological connectedness between human beings" (Bowlby, 1969, p. 194). While this theory originated in terms of infant attachments to caregivers, the central theme of attachment theory—basic security—has tremendous implications throughout a person's life.

Johnson explores the attachment theory and translates it into marriages, "Attachment theory teaches us that our loved one is our shelter for life" (2008, p. 30) and describes a state of panic where couples react to a perceived fear of abandonment and loss of connection. She also tells us that the longer couples remain disconnected, the more negative their interactions become. Johnson believes, as we state here in this book, that there is a pre-eminent need to remain attached and secure. The fundamental questions that underlie almost every fight and every fear are questions of connection:

Do you care about me?
Do I matter?
Am I safe here with you?

Relationship Interrupted

One of the best reasons to reflect on your marriage is because it feels good to do so. Perhaps not the process itself, but the results of your hard work will be worth it. Babies interrupt marriages. Postpartum depression interrupts marriages. The trajectory of love gets sidetracked by life events.

So what do we do about this? It is generally agreed upon that men tend to think talking about their feelings is less useful than women do. Authors Love and Stosny maintain that just talking about your relationship will not improve things. They say couples should place less emphasis on communication and more emphasis on connection. Specifically, they suggest men prefer to connect through activity and women prefer talking, listening and interacting with their partner (Love & Stosny, 2007). Men yearn to feel connected; they just don't always want to do it by talking. Still, within this unique context of postpartum depression and your marriage, unless the two of you find a common ground with which you can address and resolve any underlying emotional residue, the connection will languish.

All of this focus on expressing yourself and deepening the connection may sound good on paper, but when depression has flattened the very brightest of expectations, it's much easier to stay put and hope that things to get better on their own. Sometimes, working on a relationship simply feels like too much work: *Intimacy? Now? I don't think so. Empathy? Really? What about ME? Awareness? Are you kidding? I'm already too aware! Understanding and growth? Gag. Right now I'd rather sit home alone, order a pizza and call it a night. Relationship? It's there. Connection? I'm exhausted.*

When life gets in the way, and all systems are stalled, someone needs to shift into high gear.

Perceptions or Misperceptions?

We've seen that depressive thinking distorts feelings and perceptions. These distortions can then lead to exaggerated states of misinformation which linger long after the crisis has begun to resolve. It's interesting to note that in terms of your mental health, your perception of your partner's support is as important as actually receiving the support (Dennis & Ross, 2006). That is, even if your partner makes himself available and provides positive feedback and emotional support, if you are not feeling well and do not perceive this as helpful, you may focus on the conflicts in the marriage. It makes sense that women with depressive symptoms tend to perceive lower levels of their partner's investment and their relationship quality. The association between partner support and postpartum depression suggests a reciprocal link. That is, a poor relationship with a partner can contribute to postpartum depression and untreated postpartum depression can contribute to chronic marital conflict (Patel, Rodrigues, & DeSouza, 2002).

Depressed partners are not always the most reliable informants. Loss of pleasure is one of the hallmarks of depression. If the depressed partner had negatively evaluated aspects of the marriage, references of incompatibility or discontent would now need to be understood within the context of depressive thinking. If the non-depressed partner is not professionally trained, it is easy to see how these perceptions would be vastly misunderstood, and perhaps, taken very personally. It's hard not to take it personally if your depressed partner tells you that you aren't helping enough when you think you are, or you're not supportive enough when you feel you are rising to the occasion and putting forth tremendous effort.

We saw this played out with Hallie's misdirected anger at Andrew. Although her feelings were valid, she disguised her hurt and expressed it as anger. Subsequently, she pushed her partner further away and had no idea how to pull him back. His response was to lash back.

Here are some steps to improve your perception sensitivity:

1. If you are experiencing a strong negative emotion, label that feeling. When you label your feeling, it helps you become more aware and more objective. You are less likely to get sucked up by the negative emotion if you name it and allow yourself to step back a bit.
2. Check out your perception. For example, you might feel inadequate, but inadequacy isn't really a feeling, it's a perception. I *believe* I'm inadequate. Or, you might feel unloved, but your partner may love you very much and you may even know that in your head but not feel it in your heart because your perceptions are distorted, due to emotional residue.

    Ask for verification from your partner. Express how you feel and ask if this is how your partner views it.
3. Be open to the possibility that your perception is misguided. Just because you believe something to be true, does not mean it is.
4. If you are feel angry much of the time, with no precipitating event, chances are good that this anger is shielding you from a different painful emotion you do not want to feel, such as hurt, loss, loneliness, sadness, abandonment, or fear. Take a serious, but gentle look inside your heart and try to determine what other feelings may be contributing to your anger.
5. If misconceptions are present, try to replace your thought with a corrective one. *I'm not inadequate all the time. I'm very good at putting my toddler to bed and reading to him throughout the day. I should spend more time focusing on things I feel good about right now.*

Remember, when left unattended to, misperceptions can lead to assumptions about yourself, your partner, and your marriage that may or may not be true. Your feelings are valid, always. Still, your perceptions need to be confirmed by your partner to insure accuracy. Otherwise, it inserts doubt into the connection.

Are Your Roles Reversing?

In our first book, *This isn't What I Expected*, Valerie Davis Raskin and I described the occurrence of a role reversal that may emerge. If you had a baby and suffered from depression, you may find:

> As you continue to recover and resume normal activities, an interesting phenomenon may occur. You may find that your partner begins to decompensate. As you get stronger, the equilibrium of the relationship often shifts, and your partner may relax his hold on whatever psychological resources helped get him through this crisis. Though he, too, was overwhelmed, he may have suppressed these feelings. It is as if when you needed oxygen, he held his breath, but now he needs

extra air. As you get stronger, he may begin to let some of these feelings surface and may become disillusioned, exhausted, irritable, or depressed. When this occurs, women often respond with confusion and anger, *I'm finally feeling better, and now you fall apart?"*
(Kleiman & Raskin, 1994, p. 252)

This switch in roles shakes the connection up a bit. In the above scenario, with mom being depressed, just when she is eager to return to her previous level of functioning within the family, she may be blindsided by her partner's decline in participation or worse, the emergence of depressive symptoms. Unfortunately, mom's depression puts her partner at risk for depression. Spouses living with a depressed partner reported more depressed mood than the general population (Benazon & Coyne, 2000). In fact, one small study showed that 12 out of 24 partners of women admitted to a psychiatric unit were depressed themselves (Lovestone & Kumar, 1993). And finally, depression in fathers during the postpartum period has been shown to be associated with both a previous history of depression themselves and the presence of depression in their wives during pregnancy and the postpartum period (Areias, Kumar, Barros, & Figueiredo, 1996).

When these dynamics are explained to couples, it can offer great relief. Psychoeducation regarding the impact of the depression on both partners can diffuse the tension and open the possibilities for better coping and understanding. Returning to Shelby, she was not surprised and immediately relieved when she heard this explanation. It made sense to her that Matt would be retreating after so much pressure on him to be attentive and dutiful in all aspects. It also made sense to her that any hint of trouble or crack in the recovery process could instantly elicit alarm or an *uh-oh* response, as in, *Uh-oh, here we go again...*

When we see this phenomenon arise and potentially threaten the core connection, the best repair is early recognition. When partners become aware of and better understand *why* disruptive behaviors are taking place, compassion emerges. Shelby realized that although she wasn't "done" recovering completely, she needed to reconnect with Matt strictly on a post-depression healing level. She began to understand this was not about her or the marriage; rather, it was merely a posture her husband eased into by default. Awareness of this dynamic will enable the couple to talk about it and better meet each other's needs.

The reason this is so relevant to your work here is that you want to make sure that both of you are in position to contribute to this process as much as possible. Therefore, even though the one who was depressed is feeling better, if the non-depressed spouse begins to need extra support, you both need to pay attention to that. If either one of you is experiencing symptoms that require professional support, take the time to follow up with this before going further here. Symptoms that compete for attention should surpass any other agenda.

Any depressive symptom in full swing will sidetrack the two of you, so make sure you are both feeling ready to step out of your selves for the time being, to take care of each other. Repeat that phrase if your roles reverse, it should become your mantra: *Take care of each other. Take care of each other. We need to take care of each other.*

Old Issues?

Another phenomenon that disrupts the connection is ongoing marital issues that are put on hold during the depression and then rise to the surface all at once at some point during recovery or after. In our book, Valerie and I point out that "couples who are aware that this [previous marital stress] latent pressure on their marriage is a natural part of this process are much more likely to be prepared for this transition" (Kleiman & Raskin, 1994, p. 253). Preparing for it may mean attending therapy together at some point, even far into recovery, so both partners have equal opportunity to explore the issues and identify ways to begin problem solving.

It makes sense that couples automatically prioritize issues on behalf of the crisis at hand. Certainly, they are not going to quarrel over old issues when one of them is bleeding, figuratively speaking. Typically, enduring family disputes find a way to slip into the background while both parties rise to the urgency of the moment. As things settle, previous areas of discontent and old baggage can creep into conversations that have nothing to do with them! Finally, you are beginning to feel like yourself again, and you turn around and all the old grievances are still there!

Ironically, this creates the gap between needing to speak about issues and needing not to. A fascinating exploration of the roots of female depression can be found in the work of Dana Crowly Jack who frames the concept of depression as a response to social and relational pressures and feelings of anger, pleasing, dependence, goodness, low self-esteem (Jack, 1991). In essence, she describes the way women actively seek to silence themselves in order to maintain intimate relationship. Perhaps to avoid conflict? Perhaps to respect their partner's aversion to the discussion? Regardless, it has been proposed that "Silencing the Self" puts women at risk for depression when they hide their true thoughts. Results of a research study indicated that both men and women who perceived their marriages to be conflictual tended to suppress their anger while pretending to go along with their partner's wishes (Thompson, Whiffen, & Aube, 2001). The silencing model appears to lead to the development of depression in *both* men and women in conflicted relationships. Learning to differentiate old issues that need to be gently placed aside for the time being from current issues that need to be addressed, requires careful skill and compassion.

As you continue through this process, it will be normal to expect intermittent moments of defeat. Try to stick with the issue at hand without referring to past grudges or resentments. One issue at a time. Complaints and disappointments in a marriage do not go away. They are a normal part of life together. There are nice ways to let your partner know you are unhappy about something and there are ways to do it that attack your partner's character. You will learn how to express some of these nuances as you proceed through the Tokens. For now, be alert to the fact that old issues that have been problematic for a while do not miraculously vanish when the marriage is distracted by a crisis. Return to these issues with care and good timing.

Partner Support?

It may be difficult to support a spouse that has worn down all available resources, but one cannot ignore the fact that continuing to provide support will increase the chances of a positive outcome. Partners can help reinforce positive interpretations of events, which will help to neutralize the impact of persistent negative thinking. In fact, it has been shown that social support actually helps alleviate symptoms of depression and accelerates recovery (O'Hara & Swain, 1996). The very good news is that there is evidence that supportive partners play a significant role in protecting women from relapse. In fact, it has been shown that women with psychiatric histories who did not relapse in the six months following delivery had partners who were more positive about them than women who did relapse (Marks, Wieck, Checkly, & Kumar, 1996).

The increased burden of living with a depressed person cannot be overlooked and obliges us to encourage mutual support, particularly in the early recovery stages. During this transition into the role of parent, partners are often taken aback when depression descends after childbirth. Despite all efforts to have a smooth postpartum period, the non-depressed partner is now faced with their own transition issues as well as the stressors and repercussions of postpartum depression.

Although the depression has subsided in your household, the value of direct spousal support, both emotional and practical, cannot be overstated. As roles shift and continue to readjust to this challenging time, partner support is, perhaps, the most powerful weapon against the return of intermittent depressive symptoms.

Here's how we link partner support and your connection:

If *you* were depressed:
- Do you feel your partner was supportive during that time?
- How do you wish things could have been different?
- What specific things could your partner have done that might have helped you feel more supported?
- What specific things could your partner *not* have done that might have helped you feel more supported?

- Were you surprised by the amount of support you received while you were depressed?
- Have you had conversations about any support concerns in the past?
- Do you think some of your strong feelings now are related to the degree to which you felt supported or unsupported?
- Do you think that's important information to share with your partner? Why or why not?

If you were depressed, the answers to these questions can be the starting point for a deeper discussion about how your needs were or were not met during your depression.

What Put Your Connection at Risk?

We have seen that even solid marital connections will be challenged from time to time by unforeseen obstacles. Stop for a moment and ask yourself how some of the risk factors below have affected your marriage. Below is a partial list of some of the barriers, in addition to the depression itself, that can come between the two of you and make your marriage more susceptible to instability and an impaired connection. While it is important to identify these potential disruptions and understand their influence, it is equally important to distinguish them from current issues and keep them as separate as possible.

1 **Expectations.** The extent to which your expectations of marriage were confirmed or not confirmed can influence your degree of contentment. Everyone has fantasies of how things will be, after the baby, even after the depression. It sounds like a downer, but couples who are prepared for the worst, usually do better. In other words, we have found that couples at risk for depression who receive therapy during pregnancy as a preventive measure to ward off postpartum depression are generally more resilient during the postpartum period than if they had not prepared in that way. Likewise, couples who receive therapy during or after the treatment of postpartum depression, usually do a better job protecting their marriage from the fallout.

   Are you surprised by how things feel right now? If you are, then, why? Think about the specific things that are disappointing you about the way your partner is or is not meeting your needs right now. Does this align with what you had in mind?

2 **Prior discontent.** Anything that made you question the commitment to your marriage, or any unresolved point of contention prior to your baby and postpartum depression will soon take center stage again. Be alert to any huge, looming problem that is sure to overshadow the topic of the moment. Make sure and keep things separate.

3 **History of previous abuse in the marriage.** Any evidence of any level of emotional, mental, verbal, sexual, or physical abuse is a serious game changer. Dysfunction to this extent is immensely destructive to the marital core and needs to be addressed before self-help strategies can be applied.
4 **Family of origin issues.** Any lingering issues that stem from your family history will slink through, around, and in between the obstacles that exist at this stage of the game. This happens all the time, of course, but when you are trying to reconcile the recent pressure (depression) with current expectation (marriage that feels good), identifying and separating those issues which continue to haunt us from our past from those that are pertinent to the present work is vital.
5 **Family legacies.** Sometimes we inherit a proclivity toward certain behaviors or tendencies. For example, if no one ever discussed their feelings aloud when you were growing up, it would be easy to see how that would make you inclined to repeat this behavior, believing that it was best for you because that is what you were "taught." Sometimes we are aware of these legacies and try hard to preserve something of value to the family, and sometimes they evolve into behaviors that we often subscribe to involuntarily, almost by instinct. If family legacies interfere with an adult partnership, it's important to balance the merit of the expectation against the possibility that it may be getting in the way.
6 **Predispositions/Genetics.** As we've seen, we cannot escape our past. Or our DNA. Tune in. Identify what's what and focus on today. Be here, now. Your history is a part of your marriage, to be sure, but it will not help you move forward if you lean backwards or fixate too heavily on those aspects you cannot control.
7 **Pregnancy-related pressures or losses.** Any complication during pregnancy has the potential to cause strain on a marriage. This includes any unforeseen medical condition or emergency that forces the couple to recalculate steps along the way. Emotions are high and unpredictable. If something unthinkable occurs, such as a pregnancy, newborn, or infant loss, the pain it brings is indescribable. One study established that parental relationships have a higher risk of dissolving after miscarriage or stillbirth, compared with live births (Gold, Sen, & Hayward, 2010). Couples with unstable relationships prior to the traumatic loss are especially impacted.
8 **Infertility.** The stress of infertility is associated with increased marital conflict and decreased sexual self-esteem. The impact appears to be stronger for women than for men, but both report a negative effect on quality of life issues regarding marriage, intimacy, and health (Andrews, Abbey, & Halman, 1992). Many couples seen at The Postpartum Stress Center during or after infertility treatment, share similar accounts, describing the constant tension brought on by nonstop procedures, extreme guilt

or blame, financial strain, hormone treatments and side effects, waiting and waiting for results. Of course, men and women differ greatly in their responses to infertility treatment and related issues; so good communication is essential but frequently lacking.

9 **Symptom surplus.** When one of you experiences severe depressive symptoms, there can be secondary effects long after the symptoms resolve. Symptoms that can lead to high levels of marital distress include: suicidal thoughts, negative intrusive thoughts, social withdrawal, and anger. Living with symptoms that are alarming wears down the most supportive of partners. It's like living in a heightened state of alertness day after day, minute by minute. It doesn't matter how much you love someone, after enduring weeks of relentless symptoms, nerves begin to unravel.

If you feel the weight of any or many of these pressures, the next step is to find a place in your heart for a deeper understanding. These nine factors listed above represent conditions that were out of your control and settled in between the two of you without your consent. Paradoxically, you will find that if you make room in your heart for a sympathetic response to those factors that were out of your control, you will experience greater control. For instance, *Honey, I just realized that all of those months of infertility made me hard to live with. The hormones made me feel so bad sometimes and even though I was living with it all day, you probably forgot some of the time and the two of us kept snapping at each other.*

Recognizing the impact of external variables can offer tremendous relief to the pressure you are both putting onto yourselves.

Are there things that took place in your recent past that have impacted the state of your current connection?

As we begin looking at the Tokens and how to apply them to your marriage, be sure to keep the underlying concept of connectedness in mind. Under any circumstances, staying well connected is a challenge that requires the attention and willingness of both partners. The connection remains paramount. When depression and shame disrupt the sense of belonging, the effort to restore connections becomes imperative. At times, it can feel like a biological imperative, often expressed as, *I need you.* Make no mistakes about it. This effort to reconnect on a healthy level is the origin of authentic love and affection. If you expose yourself in this way, and submit to the courageous work of moving forward with each other, you will find new meaning and authenticity to your relationship.

4

SECRETS OF A SUCCESSFUL MARRIAGE?
The Tokens

> *It is one of the most beautiful compensations of this life that no man can sincerely try to help another without helping himself.*
>
> —Ralph Waldo Emerson

I bought a new laptop that didn't work.

I've known, for a lifetime, that I should always keep the original box costly items come in, and I'm certain I did, but I have no idea where I put it. It's in one of those "I'll-leave-it-in-this-safe-spot-so-I'll-always-know-where-it-is" places. Right. Nowhere to be found.

So I started off irritated. *Why would a new computer not work, right out of the box? Who needs this aggravation?*

I asked my husband if he could help me send my bum laptop back since I didn't have the box and his office is filled with them. He said something like, *sure, just leave it by my stuff and I'll take it tomorrow.*

"I have tons of boxes at work," he went on to reassure me, "No problem."

"Can you really take it *tomorrow*?" I pleaded pathetically, "That would be great, I really need you to take it tomorrow. I need the refund processed so I can get the new computer. I'd love it if you could take care of this right away (yesterday?). Can you really take it tomorrow?"

That's when he shoots me one of those, I-am-your-husband-not-your-child looks, "Yes," he said calmly, but convincingly, "I will take it tomorrow."

I believed he would.

Unless he has an A.D.D. attack, which often sounds something like this: *What? When did you tell me that? You did? I don't remember. I never said I would do that. No, I did not. Really? I did? I don't think so. Well, maybe you're right.*

It's been 30 years of navigating around his always well-meaning, sometimes maddening efforts that are aimed to please all. I understand him pretty well.

Until I needed him to send back my laptop.

"Be sure to take the laptop tomorrow. Seriously, take it tomorrow."

"I will take it tomorrow!" he snapped with the exasperation of a man who was trying to please a wife who is hard to please.

When tomorrow came, I rushed downstairs, grabbed my work paraphernalia, and aimed for the door, when I saw the laptop. Sitting right where I left it, neatly piled with owner's manual, assorted discs and plastic packaging, awaiting my trusty husband to carry its defective self from whence it came. *OMG! I can't believe he left it here.* I asked him five times. He said yes five times.

I drove to work, imagining all the things I should, would, might (dare not) say to him. *I cannot believe you forgot it. After all that. You told me you would take it. C'mon. I ask for so little* (not true). *Why do you always do this?* And so forth.

My head was spinning with inconsequential nonsense, *I should have known better, I should never have relied on him to do this, so what, it can go tomorrow, but still, he's always so convincing when he "promises" he'll do it. Will he? Can I really depend on that? Should I call him, email him, text him, who really cares, what's the big deal? It's a stupid computer. Oh, I can't believe I thought that he actually would do this.*

You get the idea.

By the time my head stopped whirling, I entered my office, planning my assault. There, on the floor near my desk, I saw something. My brain took way too long to process what I was looking at, when I realized it was the power cord to the laptop. Yikes.

It's a good thing he didn't take the laptop.

So I emailed him with shameless sarcasm:

> Well, I know it's utterly shocking that you forgot, but it's a good thing you totally disregarded my urgent demand that you take that effin' laptop this morning, like you promised me, because I found the stupid power cord at my office on the floor by my freakin' desk. Ha. ☺

His response:

> I knew that. That's why I didn't bring it with me.

Yeah, right. Cute. We both knew he wasn't even aware that he had forgotten it.

The life lesson may be obvious, but it is one that I have shared with a number of clients since that day many years ago: In all good marriages, it is 50/50. Always. All the time. Sometimes you will mess up. Sometimes your partner will mess up. Sometimes it will be both at the same time. Sometimes you'll do the perfect thing. Sometimes you won't. Any way you look at it, it is a partnership of good efforts. After all, don't we all really do the best we can much of the time? Some times that's easier than others. Still, there are other times when circumstances force us to rely on our least desirable and weakest responses. This may be adequate in the heat of the moment, but it is not okay in the long run. We need to engage, have reasonable expectations, and then, close the gap by forgiving our partners at once when their best efforts aren't good enough. Because, it is likely that somewhere within the layers of all that hard work you are doing to preserve the integrity of your marriage, your partner is forgiving *you*, for your intermittent weak spot, or lapse in judgment. 50/50. That's how it works best. For every disappointment you might endure, there may be a power cord lurking.

Do not forget that.

This illustration is filled with relationship mistakes, most of them mine: don't expect others to do what you can do, don't presume, don't be lazy, don't be demanding, don't make promises you can't keep, don't freak out, don't lose perspective, don't be impatient, and there are more. The reason this story fits within the context of this book is this: we are all human and yes, we can expect to act and speak impulsively and not always in the best interest of our marriage. *But* the most salient message here is this: The key to your happiness is *how* you both navigate those awkward, rude, hurtful, or disrespectful urges and repair the moment. Together, and with gentleness. Or, humor. Or, admiration. Or, appreciation. That's how things get resolved. That's how you keep things from being buried along with other emotional residue waiting to explode.

Compassionate Negotiation: Finding a Middle Ground

You know that feeling when you and your partner are totally in sync with a decision or you are both on the exact same page regarding a something of significance?

Do you know that feeling when the two of you support each other even if you don't agree with each other? Or when you are proud of each other in front of friends or family?

Do you know that feeling when you understand how the other one feels before they tell you or you know what they are going to say before they say it?

Do you know that feeling when you laugh at the silly things your partner says or does that you know no one would laugh at because it's really not funny to anyone but you?

If you recognize and can actually feel these feelings, the goal here is to hold on to that sweet spot of connectedness. If you remember those feelings from the past, but cannot access them in your current married state, the goal here is to wiggle the wedge between the two of you just enough to make a little room for reconnection.

It has been shown that compassion predicts better conflict resolution (Fincham, Beach, & Davila, 2004). Although the research points out that this does not necessarily imply relationship well-being, I presume this is more true than not, in the real world. Compassion, with a bit of negotiation skills sprinkled in, is a key concept when discussing the use of the Tokens of Affection.

Compassionate negotiation refers to a skill that if you are not gifted with naturally, you can learn. It requires three things:

1. You know your partner and understand what he or she wants and needs.
2. You understand what is at stake and the value of what is being discussed.
3. You use this knowledge with kindness.

Remember that central to good negotiation is getting what you want. Or, put another way, persuading your partner to see things your way. That may or may not be the actual end result, but in the language of marriage, you are both getting what you need, no matter what the outcome, as long as you both feel heard, respected and cared for. Negotiating is a process where the ultimate objective is to settle, or manage a dispute or disagreement of sorts.

We are always negotiating in a marriage. Your turn this time, my turn next time. It is a talent that requires constant fine-tuning. Once one of the partners feels it is lopsided or unreciprocated, tension or bitterness may set in. The weight of postpartum depression unsettles the equilibrium of a marriage to say the least. Negotiations break down, dismantling all good intentions. As you become more comfortable applying a particular Token, you will become more effective at communicating what you need.

Remember that every time a Token is given, a new connection is made.

The Spirit of Tokens

As described in Chapter 1, Tokens of Affection refer to gestures, thoughts, feelings, and behaviors between partners that will enhance the connection. The underlying principle here is that affection and responsiveness to each other will help build and repair bonds. Commonly, a token refers to a tangible object, most often used as a voucher of sorts, in exchange for entry, authorization, or gift-giving. In this way, the Tokens of Affection represent access to something you want or need, within the context of your marriage.

Sharing a Token to build on your connection is as if you were saying:

(Esteem) *I know this is important to you, so I will give you _____.*
(Collaboration) *I believe you need my help, so I will offer this to you _____.*

(Compromise)	*I need you to do this for me; therefore, I will do this for you _____.*
(Selflessness)	*I see that you are feeling _____ How 'bout we _____?*
(Sanctuary)	*I miss you. Let's go _____.*
(Expression)	*You haven't talked to me about _____ in a while. Tell me more.*
(Tolerance)	*I'm trying to do better at _____. Will you try to _____?*
(Loyalty)	*I wish we felt more of that, so I will _____.*

Sharing the Tokens, or the skills you learned by reading about the Tokens, is the gift you are giving yourself on behalf of your marriage. Sharing Tokens is a way to interact with affection. Regardless of what it is you want or need to say or do. With the Tokens in mind, you will be able to say, or do it better. If this is a bit confusing at this point, you might want to return to this section after you have read the individual chapters on each Token. These examples of how to use them may be clearer then.

This is why it is important to ask yourself throughout this book, how badly do I want this? How important does this work feel? What am I trying to recapture? Because unless you are motivated by a longing to reconnect, unless you are willing to make sacrifices on behalf of your marriage, this work will feel tedious and incompatible with what you hope to accomplish.

Although some of the skills you will learn may seem routine or commonplace, there are many opportunities to make ongoing, daily investments in your relationship. According to marriage experts, daily positive interactions between couples hold great significance with regard to intimacy, as well as, health symptoms. People tend to be happier and experience fewer negative health symptoms when they feel understood in their intimate social interactions (Lun, Kesebir, & Oishi, 2008). Finally, investments such as these in your marriage will provide a safeguard against future problems that will invariably arise (Lambert, Fincham, Gwinn, & Ajayi, 2011).

When you apply the Tokens of Affection to your relationship, both of you will feel better. It is that simple. You will feel better because you have made the decision and taken the time to invest and to understand each other better. When this happens, you will be in a better position to extend these gifts to your partner. The reward will be amazing. It might seem too intuitive to mention, but maintaining the connection between the two of you is not something you should take for granted. It will not magically sustain itself just because you love each other. The power of connectedness comes from the positive and healing energy you contribute on a regular basis. The Tokens of Affection will be most beneficial when they are used in the spirit of generosity and appreciation for each other.

If you and your partner are now attempting to neutralize the fumes of depression, the lasting health of your marriage may hinge on your understanding of the concept of connection. It is not always enough to hope that things will relax into a familiar comfort zone on their own. Moreover, comfort does not necessarily imply contentment. Sometimes, we can get so comfortable with each other that we become emotionally lazy. You cannot sit on a couch all day in sweats and expect things to change. Sure, it may be comfortable, but contentment requires legs. You've got to get up and keep moving toward each other if you hope to maintain or enhance the connection.

Okay, we agree that all of this is easier said than done. We've seen that affection is hard to come by when personal resources are depleted. It's challenging to express fondness when you are angry or warmth when you feel wounded. There are other things that get in the way, too, metaphorically, and quite literally, such as clutter, garbage, messes. In your home and in your head. The ultimate challenge here is to temporarily open your heart and your mind to the possibility that good things will come from this work on which you are embarking. Expect a good outcome. Your belief in a rewarding end result will go far to motivate you and help regulate your emotional response. During any difficult time in your marriage, the Tokens of Affection hold the power of engagement and the prospect of connection. In this way, the spirit that drives the use of Tokens should evoke a shared vision of renewal.

Behaviors That Sabotage

Is it possible that the Tokens won't work?
Are there couples who are not ready to use the Tokens?

The answer to both of these questions is yes.

All marriages experience conflict. This is normal, to be expected, and considered to be a vital component of healthy partnerships. Attempts at conflict resolution can make things worse or make things better. Be assured that the Tokens are tools which extend beyond the gift-giving nature of affectionate gestures and will, hopefully, breathe new life into your marriage well into your future. Even if your marriage feels strong, perhaps even better than ever before, the Tokens have the capacity to secure the bond between the two of you. It's an ongoing process, to be sure. And like anything that is good for you, it takes dedication, motivation, and consistency.

Most importantly, you can rely on the Tokens for support during arguments. Contrary to previously held beliefs, we now recognize that the healthy expression of anger or discontent can be useful to a marriage. In fact, when approached with care, disclosure of painful feelings can be a good way to get out emotions that would otherwise continue to escalate. Again, care needs to be taken when addressing painful emotions. Spewing out negative words and feelings only sets the motion backwards.

Consider some of these behaviors that will impede your effort to engage in Token sharing. As you read this list of barriers, think carefully about how pieces of some of these nine warning signs might resonate for you in any way.

Dabbling in any of the negative interactions mentioned below may not be fatal for your marriage, but your marriage will take a serious hit if one or both of you find yourselves lured by these toxic temptations. Once either of you directly or indirectly decides to no longer contribute positively to the relationship, interactions become contaminated.

Here are some definitions of obstacles that are certain to interfere with the use of Tokens:

- **Stonewalling.** This term was coined by Gottman in his research with couples to refer to delay or stall tactics (Gottman & Silver, 1999). This occurs when either partner tries to dismiss the other by avoiding the issue, changing the subject, retreating to silence, or physically removing themselves, for example. Gottman points out that while partners may think they are behaving in a neutral manner, stonewalling always conveys disapproval or arrogance.
- **Uncoupling.** This is the result of focusing only on your list of negatives. It refers to a time when the bad in the marriage outweighs the good; when it feels like there are more problems than solutions and when a preference for separateness prevails.
- **Secrets.** It is not recommended that a couple keeps secrets from each other. A good rule of thumb is: *If I can't tell my spouse, I probably shouldn't do it.* This should be distinguished from issues of privacy or personal information that does not pertain to the marriage, such as confidences shared between friends.
- **Infidelity.** Betrayal in a marriage is one of the deepest wounds. Some couples emerge with renewed strength; others cannot survive the collapse of trust.
- **Suspiciousness.** Whether it is based on actual misbehavior or whether one of you is misreading cues—if you feel like you are walking on eggshells or you find yourself questioning over and over again whether or not you should remain in the marriage, there may be a serious lack of trust.
- **Manipulation.** Hurtful communication includes unfair fighting (see communication skills in the next chapter), constantly dwelling on past issues, name-calling, insulting, personal attacks. These tactics shut down communication and any hope for a healthy resolution to a conflict.
- **Abuse.** Any and all forms of abuse: emotional, physical, verbal, mental, sexual are deal-breakers. Hitting, slapping, shoving, threatening, forcing, stalking, degrading, and intimidating are just a few examples of unacceptable behaviors.
- **Lying.** Cheating, stealing, behaving in any dishonest manner will critically compromise the heart of any relationship.
- **Addiction.** When an activity, substance, or behavior has become the center of someone's life to the exclusion of other activities it is considered

addictive behavior. Some examples include: alcohol, drugs, compulsive gambling, sex, work, exercise, shopping, or eating disorders.

Any one of these barriers can be detrimental to the process and can derail efforts of constructive problem-solving. For this reason it is strongly recommended that, as a couple, the two of you directly address these issues if they exist in your current relationship.

Apply Yourself

For those of you who feel that your marriage is emotionally in sync, we have described how the Tokens will reinforce your bond and secure your progress. For those of you who are worried about the way your marriage feels at times, the Tokens can revive lost affection. Finally, for those of you wonder if your marriage is past the point where the Tokens will be helpful, it is recommended that you seriously consider professional support either prior to or in conjunction with this work before proceeding. Going forward, the presumption here will be that you have done this preliminary work and that the two of you are now poised to present and accept gestures on behalf of the marriage.

The following chapter is a crash course in preparation for your Token work. Here we provide tips that you can study and draw upon in order to sharpen your relationship skills and maximize your effectiveness. The chapter is divided into two parts. Part I: Communication 101 presents basic guidelines for good, healthy communication skills. Part II: CBT 101 outlines the link between your thoughts, your interpretations, your feelings and your behavior, and how you can learn specific techniques to feel better and relate to your partner more successfully. It is recommended that you review this chapter even if you feel you have a good handle on your communication, your underlying thoughts and assumptions, and your emotional responses.

5

CONNECTION STRATEGIES

Feelings of worth can flourish only in an atmosphere where individual differences are appreciated, mistakes are tolerated, communication is open, and rules are flexible – the kind of atmosphere that is found in a nurturing family.

—Virginia Satir

Communication is one of those things that we regularly take for granted; we do it effortlessly and often without much thought. That is, until things go awry. Suddenly, under great pressure, you might stammer with uncertainty and your mind may race wildly with random thoughts that make could possibly make things much worse. Good communication is an asset in any relationship and it is especially important during conflict, when speaking and thinking tend to be more impulsive and reactive. It is never too late to learn basic skills and practice them so they become habitual.

As mentioned, this chapter provides a review of skills that will augment your ability to get your point across and help you gain control over some of the emotions that might be getting in the way. Part I covers basic communication skills to call attention to ways you might be making things worse and how you can rectify that. Part II presents an overview of cognitive behavioral therapy (CBT) strategies to help you understand how your inner monologue influences the way you feel and respond and how you can actually learn to modify the way you think and feel.

PART I: COMMUNICATION 101

Every couple has their own style of relating. Some talk a lot, some don't. Some are warm and loving, some are not. Some are loud and boisterous, others are passive. When I am asked to share that sacred space with a couple in my office, I am often intrigued by the incredible range of communication skills that either make things better, or make things worse.

This chapter was included to introduce or reinforce some tried and true communication techniques. You may find you already use them. That's great. It will be a refresher course. For those of you who are less familiar with these skills, please take the time to read about them and practice, practice, practice! They will be helpful to know and use in many areas of your life.

If you were to ask 100 random people what's the one thing marriages need to survive, the majority would say, "good communication skills." Many marriage therapists might respond similarly, although most would also agree that communications skills are not enough. It doesn't matter how well you listen or how well you express yourself or what techniques you use, if you don't care about the other person. Makes sense, doesn't it? Even so, it will be useful to review some of the time-tested, communication skills so you can be armed with this information going forward. Your use of the Tokens will reap greater benefits if you are equipped with these basic rules of thumb.

By definition, communication involves both of you. It is the blanket that envelopes the (you + me) equation. It is what keeps you warm and cozy and together. Communication can be verbal or nonverbal, through words or signs. It is how you share your thoughts, messages, and desires. Only you know if your communication style is working for you within your marriage. If it is, that's wonderful and you can rest assured that the exchange of Tokens will likely offer gentle reinforcement for the foundation of your marriage. If, on the other hand, your communication skills could use a tune-up, I suggest you review the guidelines below and pay close attention to the areas that cause most difficulty for you. The goal here is to provide an overview of skills that will help you communicate more effectively, especially during stressful situations and conflicts. Remember that the escalation of conflict situations is generally linked with less relationship satisfaction, whereas greater conflict resolution is associated with higher levels of satisfaction (Gottman, 1979; Pike & Sillars, 1985). Learning how resolve conflicts effectively is sure to make you both feel better.

Keep these two things in mind:

1. Communication strategies need to be practiced. Reading about it is not enough. It has to be put into action. Anytime you practice something over and over again, it becomes habitual and when that happens, it becomes easier. Some of these strategies may seem awkward at first, but keep practicing. Once it becomes more natural for you, it will also become more meaningful.
2. Disclaimer: Postpartum depression can erode communication patterns. You are turning that around now. While some of these skills may seem too obvious to mention and practicing them may feel too monotonous to possibly make a difference, you might be surprised to find out how much better things begin to feel when you take the time to think about how you

are expressing yourself. I am aware that the combination of having a baby to care for and recovering from depression make the use of "I" statements or listening skills seem comparatively trivial. But you will see that this investment in the details of your marriage will directly improve the quality of both your childcare and your recovery.

TOKENS OF AFFECTION COMMUNICATION CODE

When your partner indicates (or when you perceive) a genuine or urgent need to communicate, with a look, a word, a cry, a motion, an utterance, or an outright request, you should:

Stop what you are doing.

Pay attention.

Respond with an expressed and loving intent to address or postpone.

The Set Up

How you begin a discussion, especially a hot button topic, can have as much impact on the outcome as the points you raise and the direction the discussion takes. Here are some tips for the set up:

1 Find a time when you are both available. Ideally, you are both alone, without distractions.
2 Ask if this is a good time to talk. If it's not, agree on the best time.
3 Be clear about what you want to talk about.
4 Be gentle and composed. According to Gottman, 96% of the time, the way the conversation starts can predict the way it will end. When one partner begins the discussion with what he calls a *harsh startup*, such as being negative, accusatory or using contempt, the discussion will circle down the drain. On the other hand, when one partner begins the discussion using what he calls a softened startup, the discussion will likely end on a positive note (Gottman & Silver, 1999). This statistic was determined from the first 3 minutes of a 15-minute interaction!

   Harsh start up: What's wrong with you?! (Tense facial expression, abrupt tone, accusatory)
   Softened start up: Are you okay? (Gentle voice, loving tone, sincere intent)

5 State your complaint or dissatisfaction in terms of how it makes you feel. Avoid shaming your partner or placing blame.

After the set up, there are two primary skills that are particularly helpful to keep in mind when highlighting techniques associated with successful communication, "I" statements and active listening.

"I" Statements

The use of "I" statements is easy, if you do it right. It turns a conflict into a productive discussion by focusing on what *you* want, rather than what your partner is doing or not doing. Thus, there is less chance of a defensive response, which could potentially escalate the situation.

"I" statements should be used when:
- You are troubled by the way your partner is treating you or if he/she is behaving in a way that causes you any degree of distress.
- You have been put in a defensive position.
- You want to reach out and make a connection.
- You are upset or need clarification.
- You do not like the way you are being treated or the way you are feeling.

Examples of "I" statements with proposed alternatives:
A You never called and dinner is ruined!
B *I get worried and upset when you are late and don't call. I wasn't sure when to feed the kids. Can you call me before you leave so I have an idea of when you will be home?*

A You're being an ass. Stop talking that way.
B *I feel frustrated when you talk to me like that. Can you please lower your voice so we can continue this conversation?*

A You are so disrespectful.
B *I'm upset about the way you talked about me yesterday.*

When using "I" statements, start your sentences with:
    I feel ... *(I feel sad when you prefer to be alone)*
    I need ... *(I need to know that you want to be with me)*
    I want ... *(I want to spend more time with you)*
    I wish ... *(I wish the days were longer so we had time together after work)*
    I love when ... *(I love when you leave work early and spend time with me)*
    My concern is ... *(My concern is that work is more important to you than me)*
    When ... *(When you don't respond to me, it makes me feel sad and alone)*

Keys to using "I" statements:
- Express the feeling you have.

- State the behavior that is troubling you.
- Propose an alternative:
  It would be helpful if...
  I would like it if...
  I would feel better if...

Words of caution:
- **Be careful when attaching the word *that* or *like* or *you* after stating *I feel*.**
  It can work,
  I feel like we haven't been as close lately.
  But it can also only focus on the behavior and less on how it feels to you,
  I feel like you don't want to be here with me.
  Or worse,
  I feel you are selfish and immature when you act that way.
  This is a "you" statement, not an "I" statement.
- **Avoid the use of words like *always* and *never*.** *You are always late!*
  They are always part of a "you" statement and are certain to put your partner on the defensive.

Active Listening

For years, the counseling community promoted the use of active listening skills inspired by the work of renowned psychotherapist Carl Rogers and his work with client-centered therapy techniques. When I was in graduate school, I remember being divided into groups of two to role play active listening techniques (Rogers & Farson, 1987). One of us was the speaker. One of us was the listener. The objective, we were told, was to restate or reflect back, the words, meanings and feelings of what was spoken. You can't help but feel self-conscious, at first. It can feel stiff and artificial. But paraphrasing your understanding of the message and asking for verification from the sender is important feedback that exemplifies active listening.

It looks like this:

1 Speaker sends message.
2 Listener restates or reflects message and sends back for verification.
3 Speaker confirms or not.
4 If not, feedback loop continues with clarification from the speaker.

You both might want to practice this, for fun, so you can get the hang of it, switching roles from speaker to listener, so you have a good understanding of how it works if and when you might need it. The problem is that some experts now suggest that active listening doesn't really work. That is not to say it isn't valuable and, surely, couples who utilize this technique are probably doing a good job communicating. Still, we are discovering that couples who are happily married are not using this technique and using it is not associated with greater satisfaction or longevity of the marriage. It isn't that active listening is bad. It's just that it's may not be enough.

In addition to summarizing your partner's statements, be sure to continue to listen with a commitment to the process.

In order to completely engage in a listening posture, you can use verbal affirmations or responses, such as:

- I see …
- Hmmmmm …
- Really?
- I understand …
- Go on …

You can use non-verbal responses, such as:

- Concentrate your attention.
- Dismiss distractions.
- Nod your head in agreement.
- Use your eyebrows or cheeks or mouth to express your position.
- Use body language that suggests you are present and engaged.

Perhaps most important,

- Always, always, do your best to maintain eye contact.

Overall, whether or not you restate or reflect back your partner's words, your capacity to listen well, will directly influence the efficacy of your dialogue and ultimately, the outcome. This refers to the ability to speak with love and listening with an open heart. Trying to understand your partner's internal experience is a key component of generous listening. In this way, speaking and listening becomes a true team effort, turning contention into a mutually-empowering dialogue.

Banned Behaviors

Please note that these attempts to communicate will instantaneously disqualify you from any constructive exchange. Avoid them at all costs.

1 **Yelling, screaming, shouting, shrieking, you name it.** You may not think you are yelling, but if it feels that way to your partner, you probably are. Lower your voice and maintain a calm, even tone. If you are not careful, the tone and volume of your voice will sabotage whatever message

you are trying to get across. Take a deep breath. Remove yourself from the room, temporarily, if you need to.
2. **Hurtful teasing, name-calling, abusive language.** Mean-spirited language is a deal breaker. You lose credibility and the point you are trying to make becomes irrelevant. The discussion is over.
3. **Silent treatment.** Refusal to participate is often a passive-aggressive and unhelpful tactic that is extremely hurtful. Depending on the circumstances, a severe retreat of this nature is typically controlling and demonstrates absolutely no reconciliatory effort. I am not referring to an individual's temporary desire to regroup or abstain from dialogue if emotions are running high. However, silent treatment is an act of exclusion—it refers to an individual's desire to shut out his or her partner, rejecting an attempt to smooth things over.
4. **Bringing up the "D" word.** Unless you really want a divorce, stop saying it. Take the word out of your vocabulary. It's manipulative, not a nice thing to do, and undermines your attempt to resolve issues.
5. **Contempt.** This is a toxic contributor to the death of a marriage. It implies the absence of any admiration or respect. Instead, there is disdain and disgust. According to Gottman, contempt puts a relationship on a doomed trajectory and is the single greatest predictor of divorce (Gottman & Silver, 1999). Examples of contempt include hostile humor, mockery, name-calling, insults, and even facial expressions. Gottman equates eye rolling with contempt. Reminder—you need to be very careful with your non-verbal responses!
6. **Fighting in front of the children.** It goes without saying that disputes will pop up at the most inopportune times, and disagreements do not make appointments to fit neatly into your schedule. However, both you and your partner need to take responsibility for this and resist the inclination to slide into a heated quarrel when your children are present, no matter what their age. This is not to say you should avoid any conflict in front of your children. They can see and hear you argue if you do it with compassion, respect, and appropriate boundaries. Here, I am talking about trash-talking, down and dirty fighting. That is not okay for your marriage and it is totally unacceptable in front of your children, babies and all. You have control over whether this happens or not. Make the right choice.

12 Dos and Don'ts of Effective Communication

Don'ts
1. Don't assume.
2. Don't blame.
3. Don't judge.
4. Don't use words like "always" and "never."

5   Don't do all the talking.
6   Don't insist on having the last word.
7   Don't interrupt.
8   Don't jump to conclusions.
9   Don't be sarcastic.
10 Don't walk away.
11 Don't roll your eyes.
12 Don't play the martyr.

Dos
1   Do find the right time and place for your discussion.
2   Do use "I" statements rather than "you" statements.
3   Do listen well.
4   Do maintain eye contact.
5   Do be honest and direct.
6   Do express yourself with clarity and support.
7   Do focus on the present issue.
8   Do check your tone and the words you use.
9   Do begin with a statement of good will.
10 Do acknowledge how your partner might be feeling.
11 Do give your partner the benefit of the doubt.
12 Do take a time-out if needed.

Effective communication can soften the edges of day-to-day dialogues and better prepare you for conflicts that arise periodically. Study these skills. Practice them. Apply them continuously until they become fixed in your brain. You will find that the implementation of these skills will lead to more satisfying discussions and more productive outcomes.

PART II: CBT 101

It's really a wonder that people communicate as well as they do, especially when they are mad at their partner, or when they are hurt by something their partner did. We say this because everyone has his or her own unique way of viewing the world. Or put another way, everyone has "baggage" that colors the way he or she interprets, judges, and generally makes sense of interactions with others. Because everyone has his or her own personal history that shapes the way the interactions are approached, it follows that no two people will think about an interaction exactly alike. These different vantage points create a ripe context for misunderstanding, frustration, and hurt feelings.

This means that effective communication skills are only half the battle. The other half of the battle is an understanding (accurate interpretation) of the interaction itself, the motives for saying what was said, and the meaning that the interaction has. We classify these interpretations, understandings, viewpoints, judgments, and so on as being representative of *cognition*, or thinking. When we approach an interaction with our partner with cognition that is as accurate and as helpful as possible, then the likelihood that the interaction runs smoothly, productively, and positively increases. On the other hand, when we approach an interaction with our partner with cognition that is biased, inaccurate, and/or otherwise unhelpful, then the likelihood of conflict increases.

A large part of cognitive behavioral therapy (CBT) involves the acquisition of skills to help you identify cognitions that are associated with emotional distress, evaluate their accuracy, and, if necessary, modify those cognitions. The formal term for this process is *cognitive restructuring*. In most instances, people who go through the steps of cognitive restructuring realize that they are interpreting situations in their lives in an overly negative manner, forgetting to acknowledge the positives or even aspects that are neutral. This means that the manner in which they think about the situation is biased in some way. When people take into account *all* important pieces of information when interpreting a situation—both the positive and neutral—they usually find that they feel less distressed than they did when they were focused exclusively on the negative. That's not to say that the emotional distress will disappear; after all, when someone is going through a difficult time, many negative thoughts and feelings are entirely accurate and understandable. However, applying the cognitive restructuring process will take the edge off of the emotional distress, instilling hope and putting the person in a better position to think through his or her reactions, make good decisions, put the brakes on self-defeating (or relationship-defeating) behavior, and take care of oneself (and the relationship).

When applied to relationships, the understanding of biased cognition and its effects has two important implications. First, it implies that each person must take responsibility for (a) catching oneself when he or she makes an interpretation of the interaction and (b) evaluating its accuracy and usefulness before taking it as fact and acting upon it. Second, it implies that each person must have at least a cursory understanding of his or her partner's filter by which he or she views the world. When you understand your partner's filter, baggage, and triggers, you can choose appropriate language and take care not to unnecessarily activate those triggers.

Here's an example that illustrates the power that baggage can hold on the basis of past experiences. To this point in the book, we have referenced Hallie and Andrew, who had a fragile and volatile relationship by the time they sought couple's therapy. Hallie grew up in a household in which her father either worked long hours or traveled out of town for business. When he was home, he played golf on weekends or was glued to the newspaper tracking the stock market. Hallie's mother, dissatisfied with the marriage, turned to alcohol and often took long naps after having had a few glasses of wine. Hallie perceived that she and her brother were on their own, left to fend for themselves, and she developed the message, *People who should be there for you will fail you*. This was Hallie's baggage, or the filter through which she interpreted some of Andrew's behavior and statements toward her.

Andrew, on the other hand, grew up in a "Brady Bunch"-like family, such that his mother did not work outside the home and was extremely involved in the rearing and activities of Andrew and his three siblings. When he came home from school, a snack was waiting for him. His mother chauffeured not only Andrew and his siblings, but also most of the neighborhood children, to sports practices and games. When his first girlfriend broke up with him, his mother held him, assuring him that everything would be okay. These experiences shaped Andrew's beliefs about family, such as *Family members are supportive of each other no matter what*, and *Good mothers are strong and available*. Although these messages, which compose Andrew's "baggage," might not seem negative at all, they nevertheless color the manner in which Andrew views the world and his subsequent reactions. For example, when something happens that is inconsistent with Andrew's previous experiences, he responds with confusion, alarm, and even anger. When the connection between Andrew and Hallie dissolved following postpartum depression, Andrew's expectations for the role he expected Hallie to play in the family were violated, and he struggled to make sense of what was happening with his family, given that it was so foreign to what he had experienced while growing up. As their connection continued to deteriorate, it seems like they were viewing nearly every interaction with one another from completely different foundations.

This is where CBT 101 comes in.

Each partner in a marriage has the responsibility to check him- or herself and to ensure that his or her own baggage isn't inadvertently biasing the manner in which an interaction with the partner, or even the partner him- or herself, is viewed.

Here are some steps to help you achieve healthy thinking:

1 **Notice when you have a negative emotional reaction toward your partner.** This emotional reaction can emerge when planning for, during, or following an interaction, or it can come about even when you are simply thinking about your partner. Cognitive behavioral therapists believe that if you are experiencing some negative shift in your mood, then you are having some sort of thought, interpretation, viewpoint, or judgment (cognition).

2 **Ask yourself, what was just running through my mind?** What cognition truly underlies the emotional distress you are experiencing? The first thought might very well be something like *He's an ass* or *She's selfish*. And you can certainly evaluate this thought using this cognitive restructuring process. At the same time, in our experience, something even more

profound is going on that can explain even better why you are so angry, hurt, discouraged and so on. If this is the case, you might follow up with questions like, *What does my partner's behavior really mean? What does it mean about their love for me? About our future? About our family?* These questions evoke cognitions such as *He doesn't care about me* or *She is trying to hurt me*. Very powerful cognitions, indeed, that would be upsetting to almost anyone. The trick is to make sure that they are grounded in fact, rather than in the emotion of the moment.

3. **Critically evaluate the accuracy and or helpfulness of the cognition.** This is the pivotal juncture of CBT 101. You must question the thought, uncover all of the pieces of information that go into the thought, before you take it at face value. It might just be your emotions talking. Here are some specific questions that you can ask yourself to gain some perspective on these cognitions.
   - What evidence supports this thought? Is this evidence factual, or is it speculation? What evidence does not support this thought?
   - Are there any other explanations for my partner's behavior? Is he stressed at work? Is she stressed from taking care of the children? Does he really mean to hurt me, or is it his baggage that was triggered? Is she struggling and having a hard time, not meaning to take things out on me?
   - Does ____ have to lead to or equal to ____? Are you reading too much into the situation or the things your partner said or did? For example, is not taking out the trash equivalent to failing the family?
   - What's the worst that can happen? But what's the best that can happen? And the most realistic? We usually find that the most realistic outcome is much more closely aligned with the best case scenario than it is with the worst case scenario.
   - In the greater scheme of things, is ____ really so important or consequential? Remember the phrase, *choose your battles wisely*. Is this a battle worth choosing?
   - What's the effect of believing these interpretations and viewpoints? What might be the effect of changing my thinking?
   - What would I tell a friend who is experiencing similar problems in his or her relationship?
   - If our relationship must be tested in this way, what wisdom can we gain? How can we use this experience to achieve growth in our relationship?

4. **Construct a balanced response.** A balanced response is a new thought, interpretation, viewpoint, or judgment that is more accurate and helpful than the original cognition. The word, balanced, is critical here. Cognitive restructuring is not about positive thinking! To suggest that you blindly think positively when your partner is saying things that feel hurtful is simplistic and has the potential to invalidate your feelings. The goal

here is to achieve balance by acknowledging the objective negatives while, at the same time, acknowledging the other pieces that are also at work and that might soften the edges of the negatives. To construct a balanced response, simply piece together the answers to the questions that you asked yourself in Step 3 when you evaluated the accuracy and usefulness of your thoughts.

5. **Note what is different as a result of constructing the balanced response**. Has the intensity of your emotional distress decreased? Are you in a better position to use the Communication 101 skills, rather than approaching your partner in an aggressive or otherwise unhelpful manner? Do you feel more hopeful about your marriage than you did before constructing the balanced response? It is important to acknowledge the benefits of using cognitive restructuring, as it will remind and motivate you to use it in the future.

Let's take a look at how this works in action. During a couple's therapy session, Hallie exclaimed, exasperated, "Andrew's *never* there for me. He just checks out!" Not surprisingly, she admitted to a great deal of anger and hurt. As the session progressed, Hallie was gently encouraged to objectively evaluate whether it was true that Andrew was never there. She easily identified evidence to support this notion, such as the fact that Andrew usually came home from work and ate dinner in the basement, rather than eating with Hallie and the kids. However, when she slowed down and thought for a moment, she was also able to acknowledge many times when Andrew *has* been there for her, such as when he let her sleep and got up with the new baby in the middle of the night during the period of time in which her depression was at its worst, even though he might have complained about it. She was also able to acknowledge the many things he is currently contributing to the operation and well-being of the family. Toward the end of the session, Hallie was able to come up with a balanced response, "Right now, it feels like Andrew isn't there and has checked out because we don't have productive conversations very often. But he is doing a lot for the family, and he was there for me in the depth of my depression more than I give him credit for."

And the result of this balanced response? Hallie's anger and exasperation decreased, allowing her to turn to Andrew and express herself with more kindness. Because the intensity of her emotional upset had lessened, Andrew was able to let go of some of his defensiveness, take ownership over the behaviors that really were indicative of checking out, and agreed to be more attentive to what she needed from him. Thus, the construction of effective balanced responses has the potential to reduce your emotional upset, which not only allows you to feel a bit better about your partner and the relationship, but it also allows you to make good choices as you proceed with conversations about delicate topics. In addition, it creates a calmer, more balanced context for your partner to respond to you, which will decrease the likelihood that your partner will perceive that they are being judged, accused, or otherwise put on the defensive.

So far, we've illustrated how to deal with your own negative thoughts about your partner and the relationship. You can also apply cognitive restructuring to understand the source of your partner's comments and even anticipate how your partner might respond to certain communication approaches. Hallie knew that Andrew cherished his family of origin and sometimes struggled with the fact that their family life was different. Throughout the course of therapy, she began to learn that when he lashed out, it was often because he was working through this struggle rather than intentionally trying to make her feel badly. Although it certainly did not feel good to be the recipient of his anger outbursts, she became much less agitated and less likely to retaliate when she remembered that his anger stemmed from this source. In turn, she could respond in a way that was helpful (such as, "I understand that this is not what you had expected life to be like right now"), rather than in a way that fueled an argument (such as, "God, why are you always such an asshole?").

Andrew also found it helpful to understand that Hallie's reactions stemmed from her view that those close to her would inevitably fail her. Sometimes when he came home from a long day at work, the last place he wanted to be was in the kitchen with screaming kids. All he wanted was some down time in the basement. However, because he knew that Hallie's previous experiences led her to often interpret such behavior as letting her down or checking out, he learned to stay upstairs for a while, help with the kids' dinner, and look forward to some time alone later in the evening. When he had a particularly bad day and felt that he desperately needed some alone time before diving into family time, instead of simply disappearing, he learned to let Hallie know what was going on with him. He would check in to make sure she would be okay without him if he took 15 minutes to himself. When he took this approach, Hallie was able see both sides and respond with more empathy.

As you will see in the following chapters, understanding, catching, and responding to biased or otherwise unhelpful cognition is crucial in implementing every single Token of Affection. It's about understanding your triggers. It's about giving your partner a break regarding his or her triggers. And it's about viewing your relationship in a balanced light, flaws and all.

6

TOKEN OF ESTEEM

Coming together is a beginning, staying together is progress, and working together is success.

—Henry Ford

We are taught to believe in the sanctity of marriage. Traditionally, couples strive for the romanticized vision of a lifetime of mutually fulfilling and abundant love. Storybooks promise it. Hollywood depicts it. Society promotes it. Yet, when we sit behind the closed doors of our own marriage, we discover, some earlier than others, that it doesn't always (ever?) closely resemble that representation. The endless passion has swapped places with urine-soaked diapers and long fretful sleepless nights. Infatuation with each other has been buried underneath piles of laundry and mounting bills. The stability you craved has been stunned by random waves of panic that seem to originate from nothing. The bliss you were promised when the two of you decided to have a baby? Alas, the depression wiped out early dreams of happily ever after and now you occasionally wonder where in the world the two of you will end up.

Psychologist Michael Vincent Miller portrays a bleak picture in his book, *Intimate Terrorism: The Crisis of Love in an Age of Disillusion*. He writes that the wedded love we expect to be plentiful is in fact, quite scarce. Moreover, although we are told that the more we give, the more we will get in return, what in fact happens when marriages are "plagued by emotional famine" (Miller, 1996, p. 93) is that both partners find that the more they give in the relationship, the more they are asked to give. Our central goal here is to disprove that assertion.

Our purpose is to reframe the notion of abundance in terms of emotions and bank on the wealth of feelings from which both of you will benefit. As long as your emotional reservoir has room for memories and expectations of love, you should find that giving more, as we propose, will *not* lead to more giving on the part of the giver. Giving more will, in fact, bring back to you, more of what you seeking. The only way giving more leads to an imbalance of giving is when one partner automatically acts in ways to maintain this imbalance. (We will further discuss over-giving in Chapter 8.) An example would be when one partner is continually choosing to be the one in charge because of their own perfectionistic or controlling tendencies. That partner may be unintentionally enabling the relationship and reinforcing the helplessness of the other. When that happens, the constant giving and giving may indeed lead to more giving. The outcome of that effort, needless to say, is not a healthy dynamic.

Create a Community of Respect

The first Token is the Token of Esteem. Esteem reflects the regard and value you have and is best understood in terms of self (self-esteem) and others, as in this case, esteem for your marriage. Whether you've been married for less than a year or for 20, whether it feels like you've been together forever or still on your honeymoon, esteem is the first and fundamental principle that underlies each subsequent Token. There must be genuine regard for the relationship, your partner, and yourself, before you can look further inside and do the work.

Esteem is also one of the first things to vanish when depression captures all the attention. It's hard to feel good about yourself or your relationship when everything else feels so hopelessly dark. It's hard to feel good about yourself when you are using every last bit of energy just to go through the motions and would rather be sleeping or crying or withdrawing or running away. Once the depression has lifted, the shot to your self-esteem is likely to reverberate and things don't bounce back as quickly as you would like. Women say that once they start to feel like themselves again, they find success from positive affirmations, such as, *Everything will be okay, I'm okay, my marriage is okay, I can feel good about myself again, I can begin to focus on things that are going well, and so forth.* Until then, though, imagine the effect your self-esteem has on your relationship. It's hard to separate the two.

Without a community of respect, there is no room for healing or growth.

Token of Esteem Inventory

Low self-esteem is associated with isolation. Put another way, the better you feel about yourself, the more likely you are to engage in meaningful relationships. This inventory will help you identify feelings and behaviors that may contribute to your self-esteem as well as the regard you have for your relationship. At the same time, it will help you recognize areas that you might need to address further. Remember that how you feel about yourself is directly proportional to how much you have to give to the relationship and how much you can expect to receive in return.

With each item below, check the ones you think are characteristic of how you feel most of the time and put a circle around the box around the ones you would like to improve. See how many of the items resonate for you. By reviewing these questions, you are initiating the process of building a community of respect.

Self-Esteem
- ☐ Do you accept yourself for who you are, even if there are ways you hope to grow and change?
- ☐ Do you grow from your mistakes rather than punish yourself or let the mistakes prove your unworthiness?
- ☐ Do you forgive yourself when you do something of which you are not proud?
- ☐ Do you manage your critical self-talk?
- ☐ Do you believe you are good enough?

If you have more circles than checkmarks, consider the fact that low self-esteem may be contributing to how you perceive your relationship right now.

Relationship Esteem
- ☐ Do you like who you are when you are together?
- ☐ Have the two of you been behaving, thinking, and speaking in ways that demonstrate mutual regard?
- ☐ Do you try not to control your partner or not allow your partner to control you?
- ☐ Do you feel respected by your partner?
- ☐ Do you feel good about how you've been contributing to the marriage?

If you have more circles than checkmarks, consider the possibility that your regard for your relationship is suffering. If you feel this is a temporary state, in response to the recent depression, you might find that some of this evolves into a more comfortable state as you proceed through the book. If, on the other hand, you feel that your disregard for the relationship is a chronic state with deep roots, I would urge you to take a serious look at how you feel about your relationship and assess whether you are committed to doing this work.

The Peril of Low Self-Esteem

Self-esteem is understood as a person's overall self-appraisal of their own worth. Specifically, how much you value yourself, how willing and able you are to identify your good qualities. Self-esteem is bidirectionally related to depression, creating a chicken-and-egg scenario. It is not always clear, in any given situation, whether a person's low self-esteem makes him or her vulnerable to depression, or whether the depression makes it hard to feel good about him- or herself. Most of us who work in this field believe both sides of this circular pattern reinforce the problem. Practicing the skills introduced in the previous chapter will go a long way to help enhance your feelings of self-esteem as well as confidence in your relationship.

If your self-esteem is low, it can affect how you perceive and respond to aspects of your relationship. One study showed that individuals who had low self-esteem (as measured by a self-esteem questionnaire) projected their self-doubts onto their partners, creating uncertainty regarding their partners' affections. It seemed, therefore, that occasional self-doubts might lead to relationship insecurities (Murray, Holmes, MacDonald, & Ellsworth, 1998). For example, imagine one partner comes home upset about a job interview that didn't go as expected. If this person had low self-esteem, they might fear their partner's disappointment, rather than turning to the partner for support and reassurance.

In this way, individuals with low self-esteem are caught between what they need from their partners and their own sabotaging beliefs. In some cases, people may value their partners more than they value themselves, perhaps viewing them as a source of ongoing affirmations. However, with self-doubt and fears looming, this seems to leave that person open to all kinds of risks and potential rejection. In other words, if you are feeling insecure, you might be in need of your partner's affirmation, but you might be less likely to perceive it as such. You probably are familiar with that feeling from time to time.

Consider this simple example:

Two women are getting ready to go out to dinner with their husbands. One has low self-esteem and one has high self-esteem. Each of them says aloud, "I don't like the way this outfit looks on me."

Each husband turns to look at his wife and responds sincerely with, "I think you look great. Really."

The woman with high self-esteem thinks, *oh, good, thanks, let's go!*

The woman with low self-esteem thinks, *no I do not, I look fat and frumpy, you're just saying that.* She is unable to accept his affirming response, thus, devaluing him as a resource for support. You can see how this dynamic is isolative by design and can disrupt connections. In the absence of a secure sense of self, individuals are less able to feel secure in the interactions within the relationship. Therefore, without sufficient regard for oneself, regard for the relationship remains elusive.

Change Your Perspective

Let's start with this basic question: How do you view your relationship? Do you see it in terms of *me*, as in, *are my needs being met?* Or, in terms of *you*, as in, *am I getting what I want out of this?* Or, do you view it in terms of *us*, as in, *how are we doing as a couple?* This concept of *us*, as introduced in Chapter 1, has interesting implications that has sparked considerable research in this area of relationship dynamics.

Linda Acitelli, a psychologist and researcher, talks about the distinction between explicit (expressed) relationship awareness and implicit (implied) relationship awareness. Explicit awareness refers to thoughts about the relationship, for example, *We have a warm and loving relationship.* Implicit awareness is more of a mental representation. The implicit awareness is more automatic, more of a viewpoint; it's how two people fundamentally see themselves (Acitelli, 2008). The couple's view of the relationship as one entity (such as, using "we," or "us" rather than "me") helps maintain a positive, unified view of the relationship (Wegner & Guiliano, 1982). During times of conflict or stress, *couple identity* increases the tendency for couples to view themselves as working together as a team rather than individuals with opposing viewpoints (Acitelli, 2008). We are not forgetting about the singular "me" and "you" aspects, nor are we undervaluing the needs of each individual. What we are looking at here is the benefit of the united perspective and the impact it has on the functioning of the relationship.

It is also interesting to note that gender differences do play a role here. It may not be surprising to learn that for women, explicitly talking about the relationship seems to be more natural, and is viewed as positive maintenance on behalf of the relationship's well-being. In contrast, men tend to view explicit talking about the relationship as beneficial only within the context of problem solving (Acitelli, 2008). They see it as a means to an end. According to Gottman (Gottman & Silver, 1999), although there is this gender difference regarding implicit awareness (how the couple is viewed), this difference does not have the same meaning as it does for explicit awareness (expressed). For instance, most men do not feel as threatened by their wives' reference to their identity as a couple as they might be by their wives' preference to speak explicitly about the relationship! In fact, when a couple adopts a relationship perspective, it actually helps men view their relationships and their partners, in more positive terms. Implicit awareness seems to be beneficial for both partners.

The bottom line is that taking a relationship perspective and speaking in terms of "us" or "we" is good for the relationship. Simply talking about the relationship from an "I" perspective, without engaging the couple identity or "we" perspective, may not necessarily lead to the desired outcome. Throughout this book, you will find alternative ways to express yourself when talking is not the best course of action to take. The point is that the relationship needs to be the focus of this work. It is not just what you need or just what your partner needs. Going forward, you should be thinking in terms of *us*, which reflects the esteem you hold for the relationship.

Integrity: Yours and Mine

There is a natural process that takes place within a marriage, one that continually checks the balance between each individual's integral sense of self and that individual's commitment to the couple. To a large extent, the integrity of your relationship depends on the ability to focus on each other's strengths, while maintaining healthy interdependence, is paramount. A crucial element of esteem, *integrity* also refers to how you feel about yourself and your partner, separate and together. It is honest, is it trustworthy, is it real?

Relationships are always changing, by definition, but we need to ensure that the dynamic nature of the relationship does not threaten individuality. Consider this: A number of couples tell me they have a healthy "co-dependent" relationship, supposedly referring to the give-and-take nature of their relationship. The incorrect reference to this way overused term (which actually refers to co-addictive relationships) implies that the couple "depends on each other," *I need him for that, he needs me for this*, so that feels "co-dependent" to them. But it's the wrong use of the word.

The word *co-dependent* refers to a need-based reliance that, in fact, is not healthy and it is not merely, *I need you*, it's more, *I need you to need me*. In this way, the co-dependent partner defines him or herself in terms of how the other one makes them feel. When one out of the partnership is co-dependent, there is typically little regard for his, or her, own needs or desires.

Interdependence, on the other hand, is a term that refers to a healthy alliance that is strength-based. While co-dependence undermines power and self-esteem, interdependence enables a couple to rely on each other's strengths without sacrificing their own values and needs. Having a couple identity, as we discussed above, is also referred to as cognitive interdependence, when couples view themselves as a collective unit (Agnew & Etchenberry, 2006). Understandably, this notion of interdependence is under attack during the arduous course of depression and treatment. We've seen how needs and priorities shift dramatically to accommodate the extraordinary pressure. Emotional needs, physical needs, psychological needs, yours, his, hers, ours, all wrestle for survival in recurring fashion.

While we move forward from this concept of relationship awareness and set the groundwork for affectionate interaction, we must not lose sight of preserving your sense of self and individuation relative to self-esteem and self-integrity. As mentioned earlier in this chapter, without a strong belief in yourself, it is difficult to achieve the positive relationship perspective. Even as we aspire to improve the functioning of *us*, ultimately, it is about uniting the independently strong *you* and *me*. This is not a new concept, but it's one that bears elucidation. In his book, *Passionate Marriage*, author and psychologist David Schnarch describes his theory of differentiation and how vital this delineation of self is to the success of any marriage. One of his initial exercises for couples is his "hugging till relaxed" technique (Schnarch, 1997). On its most simplistic level, it involves partners standing close to each other, focusing on themselves, standing on their own two feet, trying to have a relationship with themselves while also trying to maintain one with their partner.

He describes it this way:

> Hugging till relaxed is elegant and simple. It requires four sentences. Stand on your own two feet. Put your arms around your partner. Focus on yourself. Quiet yourself down—way down.
> (Schnarch, 1997, p. 160)

Schnarch recommends starting for a count of "Four-Mississippi," which he cautions can feel like a very long hug, about the time when someone will likely start to pull away. He also clarifies that he doesn't assume the activity is successful just if both partners relax. After all, one possible result of the exercise might in fact be the realization that one or both partners are unable to relax when they are that close to the one they love. That's important information to have.

I think this is a great exercise, one that seems so straightforward and still, so hard to do for many. What I love most about this exercise is how wonderfully it represents the paradox of connection. We begin to understand how two people can stand together, but independent, rely on each other for support, but have two completely separate internal experiences, and either merge, melt, or disengage. It's the perfect way to illustrate how important your sense of self is to your relationship. Try it.

Integrity, as a crucial element of esteem for the relationship, also includes the notion of self-integrity, similar to our discussion on self-esteem. When individuals are governed by strong principles that you hold near and dear to your hearts, your marriage becomes the channel for transmission and implementation of these principles.

Self-Compassion

Another component of the Token of Esteem and one of the best ways that I have found to foster self-esteem and self-integrity is self-compassion. I've been told by skeptical clients that this can seem a bit too touchy-feely at first, especially to those who have always been more comfortable taking care of others than of themselves. Ironically, many people who are naturally supportive and empathic toward others often score surprisingly low on self-compassion tests (Neff, 2011). Regardless of the resistance, self-compassion is a subject worth exploring and a practice in which you should consider investing your time and energy.

Kristen Neff is a psychologist who studies and teaches the concept of self-compassion. She describes self-compassion as involving three components: (1) being kind to oneself in instances of suffering or any perceived inadequacy, (2) a sense of common humanity, recognizing that suffering of any kind or personal failures are inevitable aspects of the shared human experience, and (3) self-compassion entails an objective awareness of one's own emotions—the ability to identify one's personal hardship or painful thoughts and feelings (Neff, Rude, & Kirkpatrick, 2007).

Neff developed a self-compassion scale of 26 statements (which can be found on her website at self-compassion.org) designed to determine if people are kind to themselves and whether they recognize that ups and downs are simply part of life.

Consider this short sampling of items on her scale:

- *I'm disapproving and judgmental about my own flaws and inadequacies.*
- *When I'm feeling down I tend to obsess and fixate on everything that's wrong.*
- *I'm intolerant and impatient towards those aspects of my personality I don't like.*
- *When I'm feeling down, I tend to feel like most other people are probably happier than I am.*
- *I can be a bit cold-hearted towards myself when I'm experiencing suffering.*

Can you relate to any of these?

In her work, Neff points out that unlike self-esteem, the feelings associated with the development of self-compassion are not derived from a sense of worthiness. Rather, they come from caring about yourself, without judgment or critique. When you are truly self-compassionate, you are able to sustain these good feelings about yourself even when things don't go the way you plan or want them to. Self-compassion protects you from feeling inadequate when you mess up. And we all mess up from time to time.

The research also shows that self-compassion and self-esteem tend to go hand in hand. If you are self-compassionate, you will likely be less critical of yourself and thus, you are more likely to have higher self-esteem. Furthermore, like high self-esteem, self-compassion is associated with significantly less anxiety and depression (Neff et al., 2007). Self-compassion has also been found to be a strong predictor of mental health, in general, as it is positively associated with life satisfaction and feelings of social connectedness (Neff, 2003). As people get better at cultivating a sense of self-compassion, it appears they also experience improved psychological health and less stress.

Think about it. People who are more anxious or tend toward depressive thinking are considerably more likely to be hard on themselves. The inner critic is noisy and persistent during episodes of anxiety or depression. Self-blame or similar *I suck* tapes that run in our heads sometime are simply not compatible with self-compassion. The two cannot co-exist. Therefore, when people learn to become more self-compassionate, they learn to feel better about themselves. Yes, you can learn this. Self-compassion is a prerequisite for relationship esteem. How could you possibly respect your relationship if you are constantly beating yourself up? Take the time to learn how do to this. Then practice it.

Here's one way to become more self-compassionate, according to Neff's work. Pay particular attention to the sound bites so you can memorize the phrases and refer to them easily:

Neff suggests you start with a physical gesture, such a crossing your hands, one on top of the other, across your heart and pressing gently into your chest, say or think the words to yourself.

1. "This is a moment of suffering."
   Be mindful of the moment of suffering. This would be any time you are overcome by feelings of pain, sadness, failure, defeat, inadequacy. Keep in mind that a moment of suffering can run the gamut from a serious personal loss to being upset in traffic.
2. "Suffering is part of life."
   Remind yourself that suffering is universal. Imperfection is part of the shared human experience. You are not alone. Recognizing that adversity is part of life may sound trite, but it is true and can help provide perspective in the moment of pain.
3. "May I be kind to myself in this moment."
   This calls in a sense of caring and gentleness toward yourself.
4. "May I give myself the compassion that I need."
   This statement affirms your worthiness and the value of self-compassion.

Repeating these sound bites, in combination with the self-compassionate posture of hands crossed over your chest, has been shown to be associated with the development of self-compassion. Once this practice becomes a habit, the kindness toward yourself will trickle into your relationship. Self-compassion is likely to inspire positive emotions during any conflictual moment with your partner, making it easier to access the affection instead of the irritation. According to the research, self-compassionate people report greater satisfaction in their marriages and are described as more caring, connected and affectionate (Neff et al., 2007). Isn't that really what we are working toward here?

Letting Go and Letting In

It's a bit early in the book to tackle any huge emotional obstacle that may be interfering with your ability or desire to connect, yet, if we don't address this challenge, it is likely you will inadvertently sabotage the outcome by not putting your whole self into this process. We have seen how negative emotions poison the connection. For the moment, accept that your ability to move forward relies on the strength of your belief in yourself (self-esteem) and your commitment to your relationship (esteem for the relationship). For now, that will be enough.

All couples have, at one time or another, deeply disappointed each other. The emotion attached to any hurt inflicted upon each other might be one of any number of negative emotions. Unless couples can learn to release some of these negative feelings, it becomes difficult to co-exist peacefully as a team. (We will examine this concept of letting go in Chapter 7.) As hard as it is to let go of anger or disappointment, for example, it is a necessary and quite affectionate gesture. Essential to the development of mutual regard and appreciation for the relationship is a sense of caring and concern toward the offending partner. It makes sense that a positive motivational state provides the foundation for reconciliation. And reconciliation, in this sense, is a first huge step toward forgiveness, which we will discuss in Chapter 11.

Nevertheless, kindness is hard to come by when you feel angry. Or, hurt. Or, betrayed.

Hallie said she could not forgive Andrew.

"I think he felt bad for me for about two hours. Then, it was back to who's making dinner, why are you still crying, why do we have to pay so much for all the goddamn doctors, get your shit together already, I need you!"

"Did this surprise you? Were you expecting Andrew to respond a different way?"

"Um. Yeah. Well, wouldn't any human being reach out to their wife if she is curled up in a corner sobbing and saying she'd rather be dead? I mean, c'mon. It doesn't take a rocket scientist to figure out that I needed support. He's a moron."

When hurt, anger, and other negative emotions remain unattended, they insidiously morph into monsters. When that happens, fangs come out, poison spews, and claws take hold of the unsuspecting partner. *What did I do this time*? Andrew wondered.

Another paradox related to the concept of letting go is how good it can feel to feel so bad. Sometimes people can feel entitled to be angry, and the unwillingness to let go feels like a badge of honor, in a way, *you hurt me so I'm not going to budge*. Clinging to the anger feels unconstructively gratifying. We hold grudges, we wallow, we wait for an apology with prickly anticipation. We vow never to let ourselves be that vulnerable again. In the meantime, we sidestep the opportunity to find relief and an open heart. When you blame others, you keep yourself locked into the pain. When you let go, you move from role of victim to taking responsibility for how you feel by taking control of yourself and your life again. Letting go can set the stage for a deeper understanding and effectively reduce anger.

Conflict in a relationship never feels good. When in the throes of it, emotions can run amuck and things can escalate or decompensate quickly. Either way, it can feel hard to escape from, even claustrophobic, for a marriage. Yet conflict plays an important role, particularly when you can harness the conflict on behalf of the relationship and make sense out of what is being disputed.

I asked Hallie why she thought Andrew had a hard time supporting her during the darkest days.

"I have no idea. How would I know? You mean, besides the fact that he's a dick?"

"Something like that. What do you think got in his way? Why do you think it was hard for him?"

"I'm not sure." She took in a swelling sigh while her eyes darted back and forth, trying to find an answer that made sense. "It's hard for him when I'm sick. Whenever I'm sick, even if I have a cold, he spazs out and gets angry."

"What does he do? How does his anger manifest when you get sick?"

"He storms around like he's 5 years old. He starts snapping at me and insisting that I take care of him when I'm hardly able to take care of myself!"

"What do you do when that happens?"

"I scream back at him. I know, that's not helpful, but it's all I can do when he's acting like a child."

"Why is that? Do you scream at your children?"

"Ugh. No. I try not to."

"Then why do you scream at your husband?"

"Because." She stops and listens to her words. "Because, um, I'm frustrated and I don't know what else to do?"

She stops talking. And hears that her responses to Andrew's behavior are indeed, not helping.

She also begins to realize that his regressive behavior has been channeled by whatever symptoms impede her ability to take care of the family. She discovers after further exploration that her illness remind him of when his mother was repeatedly sick and unable to care for him and his young siblings. So the slightest hint of Hallie's impaired capacity to care for the family instantly charges an emotional reaction. He feels abandoned, frightened, confused, and angry. Hallie's eventual appreciation of his emotions enabled her to respond more effectively. When she reframed his anger as an expression of an unmet need that scared him, she was better able to reassure him and ultimately, help him, help her.

When we insist on staking claim to a negative feeling in response to something our partner has done or said that was hurtful, we simultaneously block out any positive emotions that might accompany the process of letting go. We refer to this as letting in. When we let go of hurt, we let in relief. One of the worst things you can do in a partnership is beat the other side down. Whether it's ego-driven by unfulfilled needs, or simply because you've had a bad day, energy should be spent building each other up, not breaking each other down. To do so is to count on unsophisticated tactics that never feel good. It is not fair, it is not nice, and it is not helpful.

In order to create a community of respect, both partners need to want to do that. Respect and esteem do not come from power or anger or fear. They come from opening your heart to the possibility that good things will happen when you take care of each other and the relationship.

Esteem for your relationship, as the first Token, sets the foundation for affection on behalf of your relationship. Taking the time to look closely and how you feel about your relationship and yourself within the context of this relationship is an important first step. Learning how to reframe your perspective and move forward with new regard for your identity as a couple, gives you the essential tools to embark on this journey together.

Token Tools for ESTEEM

1 **Get past recent anger**

    He wasn't there for me. She wasn't there for me. This may be true. But it's getting in the way. "Get over it" has never been an acceptable psychological directive, but in realistic terms it works as an intervention for couples who have the ego strength as well as the momentum to move toward forgiveness.

    Try this:
    Letting go is as simple as your decision to do so. Tell your brain it is okay to let this go and make the decision to feel better. Help your body along by sitting still with no distractions, breathe in, slowly, then breathe out, slowly. As you release the air, repeat a mantra that feels right to you, *I can let this go. I can let this. I will be okay if I let this. Things will feel better if I let this go.* It just might work. It might not. If it doesn't, keep practicing it. If it does, it will be liberating.

2 **Check-in**

    I don't especially feel like thinking about how he's feeling right now. He owes me. Do it anyway. One of the things my clients hear me say, over and over again, is that you don't have to want to do something, to do it. You don't have to understand something, in order to be a part of it. You don't have to like something you are doing but you might still have to do it. Check in with your partner whether you feel like doing it or not. It's the nice thing to do. It's considerate. It's loving. And it's an important reminder to both of you that the lines of communication are opening up.

    Try this:
    Ask questions. Check out your intuition. Show interest. All of these are examples of uncomplicated, non-threatening conversation starters that make someone feel cared for. If you get one word answers, probe a bit more.
    Are you feeling better today?
    Or,
    What was the best part of your day?
    Or,
    What happened at your meeting?
    Or,
    How does your back feel today?

Or,
Did anything happen today that you want to talk about?

3 **Quiet your critical voice**

I suck. Try to replace negative self-talk with more realistic and balanced statements. It's not easy, but it's important. You don't have to actually believe what you are saying, for now, but inserting the realistic and balanced words will help your brain focus less on the negative claims that have been so all-encompassing. Remember that your self-esteem is a critical prerequisite for this work. Working on yourself, whether in therapy or by paying mindful attention to what you need to focus on, will greatly augment this process.

Try this:
- Most of you reading this book are probably too young to remember Stuart Smalley (n.d.), the character played by Al Franken on *Saturday Night Live* back in the early 1990s. He would sit in front of a full length mirror saying the following affirmation, "I'm good enough, I'm smart enough, and doggone it, people like me!" His fierce conviction, coupled with his quirky affectation got people's attention. Putting mockery aside, telling yourself that you are good enough or smart enough, or a good wife or husband, or great mother or father is an important part of this transition to parenthood. You can sit in front of the mirror and say it or you can say it in the car. However you do it, I suggest you pick an affirmation and say it out loud. More than once. And again later the same day. Then, back it up with evidence. What have you done, even if it's in the past, which makes you good enough, smart enough, a good wife or husband, or a great mother or father? The more you fill your head with balanced thoughts about yourself, the less room there is for your *I suck* tape to loop around and around.
- Practice the self-compassion posture described in this chapter. Refer to it anytime you beat yourself or find yourself in a situation that makes you feel bad about yourself.

4 **Change pronouns**

The use of the word *we* and *us* can help your partner feel the mutual regard. It indicates closeness and promotes teamwork.

Try this:
Simply add the words "we" and "us" into your vocabulary when the two of you are discussing things together. Be aware of how often you use these words. Believe it or not, using words like "we" and "us" can indicate the presence of shared long-term goals or life vision.

5 **Give back to your true love.** Remember the first time you met each other? Remember how that felt? Remember when you looked forward to seeing each other for a night out? Maybe you still feel that way, maybe not. As marriages move beyond recovery and readjust to the transition into parenthood, couples can easily begin to take each other for granted. The spark may be gone. Or, for some, it has fizzled. Couples can forget each other's special qualities and what drew them to each other in the first place, focusing instead on the annoyances. Reclaiming some of these thoughts and memories can make it easier to give. If on any level you believe that you have to give in order to receive, then start giving now.

Try this:
- Make a list of the qualities of your partner that you first fell in love with. Think about why you thought he/she would be a good life partner. Write them down. Now, take another look at the list. See if those qualities are still a part of your life together.
- Ask your partner to make a list of the reasons he/she fell in love with you. When both lists are finished, talk about it together. Share wonderful memories.
- Tell your partner what you love most about him or her. Or what you miss. Or what makes you feel good. Or why you married him or her. Or why you are dedicated to doing this work and finding your way back home. Give that gift to your partner.

7

TOKEN OF COLLABORATION

In the long history of humankind (and animal kind, too) those who learned to collaborate and improvise most effectively have prevailed.

—Charles Darwin

While most of us recognize the value of working together, it is easy to get in our own way by not recognizing some of the simple strategies. *Collaboration* is a term that is often used in discussion of corporate culture. That's because it refers to a process that is vital to the successful execution of any project or practice. It's hard to ignore the comparison between collaborations and marriages. Both involve a "partner-friendly" (Byrne & Hansberry, 2007, p. 80) relationship that involves shared responsibilities and mutual accountability and authority (Mattessich & Monsey, 1992). At first glance, collaboration invokes words like teamwork, cooperation and communication. But a closer look reveals an additional level of intimacy that is more likely to lead to success. It involves deep determination to achieve a shared objective.

Token of Collaboration Inventory

Read each statement and check the ones you feel are true for you. Put a circle around the boxes which reflect those you need to work on.

- ☐ It is easy for me to trust and accept my partner's opinions and judgments.
- ☐ My partner and I work well on projects together.
- ☐ When my partner and I join forces we each contribute our own expertise.
- ☐ I am good at identifying my abilities and potential to contribute.
- ☐ I am good at identifying my partner's abilities and potential to contribute.
- ☐ I generally do not let feelings of competition or power get in my way.

Any box with a circle around it means you should be alert to this when working together, especially in conflict. Check the Token Tools at the end of this chapter for specific tips on improving your ability to collaborate.

What Makes it Work?

When couples choose not to collaborate, in general, they may inadvertently set it up so that they win the battle but lose the war. True collaboration relies on one's ability to keep the larger picture in mind and act purposively toward the common good of the relationship. In lieu of this, we often see power struggles, hostility, and emotional distancing.

Accepting Influence

The concept of collaboration highlights each individual's unique abilities while sharing the authority. Think about doing any simple project together. Both of you bring your own strengths to it, and throughout the course of the activity, one or the other of you might take over the decision making. For example, you are hanging a large picture in your den. Your partner has been designated as the premier carpenter, with hammer and nail in hand, while you are the designer, deciding exactly where to place the new piece of art. Chances are good that you will each submit to the other's area of expertise, without much dispute. But with more complex issues, such as childrearing or financial decisions where the lines of authority are more fluid, couples can get stuck in the middle, fighting for position.

Sharing authority in this sense is related to another concept that Gottman refers to as accepting the influence of your partner (Gottman & Silver, 1999). In studying marriages, Gottman found that men who allowed their wives to influence them had happier marriages. So much so, that when a man is not willing to share the power with his partner, the research shows a whopping 81% likelihood that the marriage will implode. Furthermore, the research found that the most stable marriages with the greatest degree of satisfaction were those where the husband treated the wife with respect and did not resist power sharing and decision making with her.

According to Gottman, the unwillingness to accept influence is usually the husband who clings to the potentially destructive habit of always wanting to be one up. In his long-term study of 130 newlywed couples, he found that men who allow their wives to influence them have happier marriages and are less likely to divorce than men who resist their wives' influence. When a man is not willing to share this power with his partner, there is an 81% chance that his marriage will implode (Gottman, Coan, Carrere, & Swanson, 1998).

Accepting influence does not just mean one should acquiesce or simply agree for the sake of agreeing. It refers to the process of honoring what is important to your partner and accommodating that into the conflict resolution process. It means that you believe that your partner's opinion matters. Gottman calls this "yielding to win" (Gottman & Silver, 1999, p. 114), and views this as both an attitude and a skill that savvy men learn in order to ground them and keep their eye on the prize. His classic example is the classic toilet seat debate. A man who has the larger picture in mind understands how many points he gets by taking the second to put down the toilet seat and pleasing his wife in the long run!

Although this research clearly puts the onus men to accept partner influence as a primary collaborative effort, it should go without saying that women, who may intrinsically be more inclined to do so, should continue to accept influence from their spouse. Gottman's data indicate that the vast majority of women, even in unstable marriages, already do this. Without a doubt, both partners should actively engage in a give and take posture and let the other know that their opinion matters.

Andrew had a hard time accepting influence:

In one of his least shining moments, Andrew walked in the door and told Hallie he was playing tennis Thursday night. She sharply reminded him that her old friend was coming in from out of town and she wanted him to be there to meet her for a bit.

"Sorry, can't change my plans."

When she told him it was really important to her and he knew about it but must have forgotten, he replied, "Oh, well."

As you can imagine, Andrew is in big trouble. His inability to accept influence from his wife, to consider what is important to her, leaves them both in constant states of inflexibility and resentment. Gottman points out that women have been socialized to accept influence from men and are therefore better at it. Partnerships are enhanced when the men are able to do the same thing.

Attitude

In addition to this notion of sharing authority and accepting influence is another variable of good collaboration: attitude. In a 2005 survey, results suggested that attitude is more important than experience in collaborative work (Ditkoff, Moore, Allen, & Pollard, 2005). The authors concluded that most people preferred collaborating with others who were inexperienced with a positive attitude than very experienced people who lacked the positive attitude. The positive attitude was characterized by these qualities: enthusiasm, candor, commitment, open mindedness, and curiosity. They note that a positive attitude is critical for teamwork and it may even prevail over a lack of experience or skills. This is an innovative claim since so much of organizational research is based on specific skills and techniques.

We've all heard that you can't change your spouse, but you can change your attitude. For the most part, I agree with this statement but I reserve a tiny bit of disagreement in order to claim that if I didn't believe people could fundamentally change, I couldn't do the work that I do. I do believe that your spouse can learn to change some of his or her ways on behalf of the larger good, and so can you. That being said, you are wasting your energy if you focus primarily on your partner's behavior. Instead, your energy is better spent on yourself and your response to his behavior. Make sense?

It follows, then, that your attitude toward your relationship, how it feels currently, how it felt before the baby and depression, and how you hope it will feel in the days ahead, all play a role in your ability to work effectively as a team. Caring about your partner and your marriage is the cornerstone of collaboration. This is why, in couples work, one of the first tasks for the therapist is to determine the degree of commitment and caring. To reiterate our take-home message with the Token of Esteem, in the absence of mutual respect and care for the relationship, advancement is not possible. Even when the connection is shrouded by anger or when one or both partners have retreated in defeat or despair, it is possible to uncover the deep-rooted bond that attracted them to each other in the first place. This is what happened to Hallie, when she began to explore the reasons that Andrew was so reactive to her depression and recovery. His fear-based anger and her defensive retort spun them both around until they believed neither cared about the other. Without taking the time to examine this in therapy, it is possible that their bitterness would have continued to polarize them indefinitely.

C.A.R.E.

If you remember to C.A.R.E., you will be able to keep an eye on both the larger picture (your marriage) and the task at hand (whatever you are doing at the moment). Keep these principles in mind:

Common purpose. Collaboration is not about agreeing. It is about coming together to create a new solution or achieving a goal that is mutually beneficial. If you and I both want the same thing in the end, it is less important that we don't agree from the outset. Unfortunately, many couples get stymied along the way, stalling in the mess of the immediate content rather than the process, or the larger picture.

For example: We are both hungry. We both need to eat. I want Chinese. You want pizza. Couples can get lost in the content and quickly deteriorate into a contest of wills:

> *We had pizza the last three times!*
> *We always go where you want.*
> *Ugh, I'm sick of Chinese.*
> *You always get your way.*
> *You are spoiled-rotten and act like a baby when you don't get your way!*
> *I am so sick of you whining about what you want.*

This is a simple illustration of a larger problem but the bottom line is this: If you are keeping score, refusing to budge, pointing fingers, boasting victories, hitting below the belt, speaking off topic, or basically, not taking care of each other, you will not eat, metaphorically speaking, of course, and you will both stay hungry. The only way you will both be satisfied is if one of you takes the lead and, out of strength and love, says, "Okay, let's eat there (where you want to eat) tonight."

Attitude. The survey cited earlier reported that *enthusiasm* for the subject of the collaboration, and *open-mindedness* and *curiosity*, were rated as most important by almost all participants (Ditkoff et al., 2005). If we apply this to our work here, it makes sense that plugging into the relationship, or specifically, being engaged in whatever is being discussed, coped with, brainstormed or negotiated, is vital. A successful outcome is more likely if both of you care about the common purpose and both of you are committed to the subject at hand. Being open-minded is an enormous advantage as it increases tolerance and flexibility. Collaboration will fail if stubbornness permeates the air.

Respect. Not unexpectedly, the female respondents in the survey rated good listening skills, self-management, and tactfulness as more important in a collaborative team than the men did. The men identified courage and candor as more important than the women did (Ditkoff et al., 2005). What this means for our purpose is this: You should not forget, *ever*, how important something else—something other than what is important to you—may be to your partner. Whether it's a gender-related distinction, or a personality-related difference, or even just a momentary preference, how your partner feels about something is critical to the ultimate solution. Respecting what that means and how that feels will enable you to work *with* it and not *against* it. You can potentially hurt each other or harm the process if you operate from a perspective of self-interest. Remember that collaborating does not mean winning or being right. It means creating a new solution by combining your skills, desires, and aspirations for the project, event, or decision. Once you lose sight of this shared goal, it becomes a *yours-versus-mine* scenario, which is a fatal flaw.

Expectations. Your expectations are related to your attitude. Do you expect this to go well? Do you anticipate that your partner will work with you on this? Are you going into this with hope or with trepidation? Do you feel defensive right out of the gate or do you feel confident that the two of you will be able to find a workable solution? Your expectations have the potential to bias the outcome by influencing your language, your posture, your communication skills, and ultimately, your ability to contribute effectively. Keep your expectations reasonable and clear. Clarity of your expectations should be apparent to your partner, as well as to yourself. Do not expect your partner to act in a way that is not consistent with his strengths or who you know him to be. Opening up your heart to possibilities will unite your shared ideas toward a more meaningful exchange.

It is important to apply these elements of C.A.R.E. to all subsequent Tokens and connection-enhancing actions. Remember that you are both weary from recent pressure at home. Both of you may feel tempted to wait for the other to take care of things. But remember how important it is to be flexible as you move through this process. Our goal is to find common ground through genuine caring.

The Dance of Togetherness

We all know what it feels like to be in the same room with someone, but not really be *with* them. Or, what it feels like to work with someone on a project, but not really be involved in a meaningful way. There are countless excuses we can make to justify sharing space with someone without investing much of ourselves. Sometimes we do that with people we do not know very well and sometimes we do that with our intimate partners. You know that invisible wall that occasionally separates you from the person in line in front of you at the grocery store? Or, from the person next to you in the elevator? That arbitrary divider that defends us from strangers and simultaneously protects us from random contact with someone we do not know? People claim they are protecting their personal space. Uninvited closeness. Too much. Too soon. Everyone has his or her own comfort level for the relative placement of this shield and—depending on the circumstances and the mood we are in—sometimes we are more bothered by a personal space violation than others.

Most of us can relate to that feeling and the importance of relying on that shield at times in our marriage. There are hundreds of reasons why people might need to isolate themselves within the confines of their own personal space, *I'm not in the mood, I need some space, I'm tired, you're getting on my nerves, I have work to do, I cannot listen to one more thing, I'm overwhelmed,* and so forth. But the point needs to be made that while personal space is essential for too many reasons to list here, it can also interfere with progress if the space within the marital relationship is unsettled.

While researching this book, I came across an interesting differentiation between these concepts: cooperation, coordination and collaboration. According to the authors of *Four Keys to Collaboration Success* (Lukas & Andrews, 2006), many people mistakenly presume that if they are working together, they are collaborating. But the authors assert that the differentiating factor is the level of intensity. In other words, you can cooperate with someone with the least amount of emotional investment. Coordination of efforts implies balancing two or more people's needs or efforts. True collaboration entails the highest level (intensity) of interchange between the parties. Whether the differentiation of these three terms means anything in the real world, or not, the reason they are being mentioned here is that many people in relationships believe they are working together when they are not. For example, note the difference:

I guess I'll go to therapy with you this once, but I think it's a waste of our money. I would accept that as a level of cooperation, particularly when the option not to come is so tempting to so many people!

Or,

I'll go to therapy with you if you think it will help you. This shows an increase in commitment to the process, clearly cooperative, as well as willingness to bring together (coordinate) the (still separate) goals.

And finally,

Sure I'll go to therapy with you. Hopefully, it will help us look at the things we need to do to feel better. Here, we see the merging of shared goals.

It is worth noting that all of these responses have the potential to produce a constructive outcome. In all cases, both partners agree to attend a therapy session. But the likelihood is high that the couple in the third scenario, who begin with a mutual level of motivation and commitment to the process, are more likely to be invested in change and more likely to achieve better treatment results (Ryan & Deci, 2008).

The questions you need to ask yourself when you are involved in a joint effort with your partner, whether it is a menial task, or a family project, or a conversation, or a decision that needs to be made, is: How engaged am I in this process? Are my words consistent with my level of commitment? Am I sabotaging the outcome by resisting in some way? Am I really collaborating with my partner or am I merely a participant with no emotional investment? Am I standing behind my shield in an effort to preserve my personal space? Is my heart open? These are the variables that make it a true collaborative effort.

Separate But Together?

In any ensemble there exist separate entities. The successful collaboration of two hearts can only take place as a function of understanding ourselves and our own intentions. David Schnarch refers to this as differentiation, "a process by which we become more uniquely ourselves by maintaining ourselves in relationships with those we love. It's the process of grinding off our rough edges through the normal abrasions of long-term intimate relationships. Differentiation is the key to not holding grudges and recovering quickly from arguments, to tolerating intense intimacy and maintaining your priorities in the midst of daily life" (1997, p. 51). In other words, when we maintain our separateness and individuality *and* strive for emotional connection, we achieve differentiation. It involves the ability to maintain who you are while you are have a meaningful connection with someone you care about. Schnarch cautions that a lack of differentiation can create an overwhelming need for togetherness which can feel burdensome or excessively needy.

Token Tools for COLLABORATION

1 **Work toward a solution**
   When working together on a topic or a project, or a marriage or a conversation, you might be amazed at how often or how easily your default response is cynical or critical in some way. Ask yourself how flexible you tend to be, particularly when it comes to decisions and discussions between the two of you. Sometimes, agreeing to move forward toward a solution together is better than swirling around the drain, even if the decision needs to be modified later.

   Try this:
   Next time the two of you are involved in something together, try to *only* offer helpful comments. You might not even realize how easily you slip into nagging territory, or you might think you are being helpful when it is perceived as pestering by your partner! Try to resist the urge to offer constructive criticism. Notice how difficult that can be sometimes. See if you can sit back and let your partner make the decision for this project while you just offer your support. See if that feels comfortable or not.

2 **Check ego at door**
   One thing that helps is if you can begin to view any alliance as in your self-interest. As we will see in subsequent chapters, the more you invest, you more you get back. Questions like, "How will this benefit me?" are not productive. They break the momentum of teamwork.

   Try this:
   The sure-fire best way to transcend ego-driven thinking is to generously and unconditionally focus on doing something for someone else. Think of collaboration in a spiritual way and find a purpose that you can contribute to that is greater than you right now. It doesn't have to be big and powerful. Focus on your purpose, not yourself. Pay it forward. Any effort to take care of your marriage is an effort with the spirit of collaboration in mind.
   - Next time your partner asks you to do something, say "sure!" even if you don't feel like saying that or doing what was asked of you.
   - Next time your partner tells a story about work or something that happened that day, ask a question for more details, even if you're not particularly interested in the topic. Be curious. Extend that to your partner.

3. **Recalibrate expectations**
   As we've seen, with the shared vision of enhancing your relationship, anything is possible. Dial down your perfectionistic tendencies. Small steps in the right direction are significant in the long run. It doesn't have to be the way you want it. It doesn't have to be the way you envision it. It doesn't even have to look anything like the way you thought it would be. Having expectations is not bad. They just need to be realistic. If they are too low, you may not work hard enough. If they are too high, you may be disappointed.

   Try this:
   Take a look at these common expectations. Pick one that rings true for you. Then, write a few sentences about with the opposite stance, or why that expectation is *not* true:
   - My partner will never change.
   - This is just how my marriage is going to feel.
   - My partner should meet all my needs.
   - If my needs are not met, it is my partner's responsibility.
   - If my marriage doesn't feel good, it means I might be happier with someone else.
   - My marriage should look more like our friends' marriages, or those in the movies.

4. **Give up competitive edge**
   Competition in a marriage breeds aggressive interactions and potential contempt. Not that there's anything wrong with a fierce tennis match, but rivalries on the court or field do not translate well at the heart of this work. The desire to beat out the other one is counterproductive and will ultimately backfire.

   Try this:
   Think about how easy it is to collaborate with a stranger, like putting down the bags you are carrying to open the door for someone needing assistance. Then, that same person holds the door for you, as you enter behind them. You both acknowledge this with a word of gratitude, or a smile.
   Think about ways in which you are kinder to strangers than you are to your life partner. Do you always have to be first? Best? Right?

5. **Open to change**
   Your willingness to work together should be apparent in your voice, your eyes, your body language, your words, and your overall readiness to meet your partner halfway. By taking on this collaboration with an open heart, you are sending a message to your partner, to yourself, and to the universe

that things between the two of you can feel better and stronger. And that the time is now.

Try this:

Change your routine. Start with some concrete changes, like where you go out to eat, or the route you drive together to visit family. Confront the monotony that comes with every relationship and stir it up a bit. Find an activity that you enjoy and do it differently.

8

TOKEN OF COMPROMISE

When we are no longer able to change a situation, we are challenged to change ourselves.

—Viktor Frankl

One of the reasons I decided to write this book is because of how easy it seems for some couples to be unkind to each other. Not intentionally but, ostensibly, with reckless abandon. As if they are entitled to say what they are saying the way they are saying it because they themselves are hurt or angry. As if it doesn't really matter much. Of course it matters, to most partners in a committed relationship. So why do some continually behave as if they didn't care? Why does it seem so hard to find a middle ground? Or, simply, be nice?

In general terms, the ability to compromise refers to a couple's tendency to agree to agree or agree to disagree. Here again, the content is less important than the process. The specifics of what are being discussed are less relevant than the couple's proficiency at negotiating the discrepancy. Compromising in a relationship does not mean you are giving something up. It means you care enough to reconcile. It means that a healthy surrender is more powerful than a nasty altercation. The decision and ability to compromise also implies that you feel good about yourself and the relationship (esteem) to work together with your partner (collaboration) toward a solution that is mutually satisfying.

Token of Compromise Inventory

Read each statement and check the ones you feel are true for you. Put a circle around the boxes which reflect those you need to work on.

- ☐ When disagreeing, I am comfortable letting others be right.
- ☐ In instances when I truly believe I am right, I can still see my partner's point of view.

- ☐ I am good at controlling my emotions when I believe I am right and my partner is wrong.
- ☐ I am able to uphold my view of our partnership even if we are disagreeing.
- ☐ I am able to settle with the outcome of any disagreement and I do not let my negative emotions linger.

Any box with a circle around it means you should be alert to this when working together, especially in conflict. Check the Token Tools at the end of this chapter for specific tips on improving your ability to compromise.

Stick with the Process, Not the Content

I started seeing Carrie and Jon after the birth of their second child who was now 3 years old. Carrie recovered well from her acute symptoms of depression, but her strong family history of severe depression left her feeling vulnerable. It didn't help that Jon believed as long as she was still taking medication, then *she* was the sick one, thereby practically discounting her authority before anything was ever said. Clearly, since she had the symptoms, she had less clarity, he would rationalize. The two of them did a little cha-cha every time they would come into my office. Whatever the subject was at the time, it would invariably turn into this: *I did not. Yes you did. How do you know? I saw you do it. You did not. I did too. No you did not!*

Unlike Hallie and Andrew, this couples' confrontational style was characterized by more back and forth bickering. It felt less outwardly spiteful to me, but more insidious. Rather than assaulting each other's character, Carrie and Jon focused on the details of the moment. Although it is tempting to liken this to a playground dialogue, it feels very serious to the two people involved.

"Why are you mad? I told you'd I'd be home at 6:30!"

"You did not. You said 6:00. I know you said 6 because I remember thinking, why can't he leave the office earlier? He usually can leave by 5:30, so what's the problem? And you know it's hard for me to be with both kids all day, I know you said 6."

"I did not. I distinctly remember saying 6:30. I was in the goddamn meeting until 6:15 how could I have been home by 6:00 for Christ's sake?"

"How should I know? You're the one who said you'd be home by 6:00!"

"You are so wrong. You say whatever you think will help make your point. You can say whatever you want. I said 6:30. And that's that."

"Ha. No, actually, you did not. You were probably too busy at work to remember what you said."

"Will you listen to yourself? You're the one who was too busy to concentrate on what I said? I guess the kids were making too much noise or something. I said 6:30. I'm not late, you should not be upset."

"Whatever."

Soon, they don't even know what they are fighting about. I certainly don't know what they are fighting about. We have all lost sight of the content of their discussion while mesmorized by the process itself. They have bypassed whatever meaning the content held (for example, the expectation that he be home by 6:00 pm) and are now playing a game of tug of war to see who wins.

When I bring this to their attention, they instinctively try to suck me in.

"Can the two of you hear what I'm hearing? Are you able to listen to how you sound?

Jon face is red and his eyes radiate a look I've seen often that tells me he'd rather be anywhere but here right now. He jumps in, "Yeah, she sounds like she always does. She's right. Doesn't matter what I say."

Carrie rolls her eyes and smiles at me in an attempt to conspire against him.

"Jon, what's happening here?" I ask, hoping he can help draw them away from the content and back to the process.

"I have no idea what you are asking me."

So I help.

"Does this feel good? Fighting this way? Do you think it's productive?"

"Well, if she...."

"Jon." I interrupt his flow to stay on point. "Forget what Carrie said or did. Just stay here with me for a minute. Does this feel good?"

"No."

"Good. It should not feel good. Do you like this dance that you do? Do you want to continue to fight this way when the two of you disagree?"

"Well, if she ... um, I guess not." He conceded.

"Good. Then why don't the three of us have a conversation about how to do this better? Let's start with a discussion about why it's so important for each of you to be right. When, frankly, it doesn't really matter, does it? What matters is that you are both speaking in circles, with words that will not help you find a happy medium."

Remember in the previous chapter, you read about Gottman's assertion that couples do better when the man learns to accept influence from his wife? Here, we see Jon's reluctance to do so. It doesn't matter who is saying what, he simply refuses to let her be right and will fight to prove that on a regular basis. Compromise is not in his vocabulary. Thus, their dance persists.

Win-Win

Carrie counted how many times each week Jon went out without her. She started doing this after she began to feel better. She knew that her depression interfered with Jon doing some of the things he loved to do and now believed he was taking advantage of this. So she counted. It could be for tennis, for dinner with colleagues, or a football game with friends. She categorized the nights out as "pleasure" or "work" and pleasure outings received twice as many points. This way, could she try to "keep things fair" by balancing her data with her desire to go out with the girls. It also made it convenient for her to use this information against him, "You went out twice last week, so I'm going out again tomorrow." Although the initial intent might be one of fairness, the score keeper ends us wielding inflated authority. There is no supreme command in a marriage. Remember, it's you and it's me and it's us. You can either poison the relationship or you can contribute to it. By keeping score, you are setting up a competition of sorts, and you compete, there is always a winner and a loser.

In the previous chapter, we concluded that the key to collaboration is the common goal. Without common goals, partners would be parallel playing like children in the playground, each doing their own thing with their singular objective. While collaboration is the larger framework which should ideally administrate the direction of each dialogue, compromise is the manner in which that is accomplished. Compromise is the road to collaboration; it is how you get there. With this in mind, balancing what you want with what your partner wants is not easy. But when we break it down to its most simplistic "me" vs. "you" structure it becomes easier to see that the couple has lost sight of the "us" in the equation which inevitably leads to power posturing.

Insisting on being right is probably one of the greatest stumbling blocks to effective communication. Remember that Gottman's research reveals that the happiest marriages were those in which the husbands treated their wives with respect and were not threatened by the loss of power when compromising to reach a common end. He further describes a gender differentiation here. His finding shows that women tend to be better addressing a conflict without escalating the negativity. Even when they do, his data show that the marriages are more unstable when the husband reacts with negativity than when the wives do. He points out that this disparity may be accounted for because, as pointed out in the previous chapter, women tend to be more open to their husband's influence than the other way around. Again, as off balance as this may appear at first glance, it is worth repeating: The research supports the notion that men need to be mindful that this resistance to letting their wives influence them may put their marriage at risk (Gottman & Silver, 1999). Men who are unable to accept this dynamic as worthwhile are stepping in their own way. Remember there is an 81% chance that the marriage will self-destruct. That's an extremely high number.

Most agree that compromise is a win-win situation; some things are given up and some are gained. It is a solution that involves movement from individual competing interests to a combined and mutually beneficial result. If either one of you feels slighted, or deprived, or denied, compromise has not been achieved. That doesn't mean that there won't be times where you are the one giving something up on behalf of the relationship. Sometimes you will make the sacrifice, sometimes your partner will make the sacrifice and sometimes it will be both of you at the same time. If the problem is solved or resolution is accomplished, it will no longer feel as though you have given something up. Instead, it will feel like you both have made positive strides.

What's Getting in Your Way?

When asked, most partners would claim that the way they resolve conflicts is the only way they know how. In other words, they act in ways they have been taught, or modeled, or with which they are most familiar. If it's bad enough, they are likely to know it is bad. But more often than not, I am told by couples that this is just the way they do it. All the time. As if they never considered the possibility that they could learn more efficient and effective ways of managing their disagreements.

Consider the following list of actions that might be impeding your ability to compromise:

(Note that compromise must never hurt nor should it dishonor your core beliefs *and principles*.)

1 **Are you a black and white thinker?** Black and white thinking is best characterized by the use of the words "always" and "never." This is a great time to review the CBT skills in Chapter 5 if you think you could benefit from more work on this. For example:
That will never work!
You always do things this way!
You never understand me.
You never appreciate me.
Why do we always go where you want to go?

Any unwillingness or lack of ability, to sit in the uncertainty of any moment, will delay progress. Things that are gray are hard to define and things that are hard to define can make us anxious. Black and white thinking is easier in many respects. It is a convenient way to accept things the way you want them to be, rather than consider possibilities that exist in the grayness.

Without a doubt, depression has spread all kinds of grayness in your relationship. You want things to make sense. You want things to be the way they were. Some things will, indeed, go back to the way they were, but some things will be different going forward. Living with the ambiguity inherent in this transition is vital. It is what leads to compromise.

Trust in your partner and in the relationship will help make this doable. Relinquishing old habits and beliefs will enable you to practice better listening tactics and to be a bit more gracious about the "other side" of the difference of opinion.

2. **Are you being overly reactive?** Watch your intensity. When emotions run high, communication will not be productive. This is when you are more likely to submit to nasty attacks or be overly defensive.
3. **Are you fighting fairly?** As was stated in Chapter 5, the rules of fair fighting are universal and critical to each Token. Compromise is virtually unattainable if the rules are violated. Even one. Remember: No fighting in front of the children. Or, anyone else. Pick a good time and neutral place when neither of you are too tired or hungry or angry. Stay focused on the present issue. No character assault. No name-calling. No cursing. Be kind. Carefully review Chapter 5 and be sure to practice any particular skills that you are not as strong in.
4. **Are you afraid of confrontation?** Fear of confrontation can misguidedly prevent you from taking care of business that may be important to your marriage. Disagreement does not mean confrontation. Confronting an issue does not necessarily mean confronting your partner. Does that make sense? Just because you want to deal with an issue head on, does not mean you need to be confrontational. You can leave the provocative language out of the discussion and replace it with a sincere desire to address the issue at hand.

    Say what you need to say. Then wait. By demonstrating to your partner that you want to understand his or her feelings and thoughts on the subject, you will project an attitude of respect and increase the probability of a good outcome. Stephen Covey, author of *Seven Habits of Highly Effective People* states in habit number 5, "Seek first to understand, then to be understood" (Covey, 1990). He says that most of us typically seek to be understood first; making our case, listening with the intent to reply. We don't spend enough time listening and trying to hear the other person's perspective. I suspect this is true for most of us, in many of our relationships. Though challenging, to be sure, it defines the heart of compromise.

    If any kind confrontation is an area of vulnerability for you, remember that your disagreement can lead to a discussion, not a confrontation. Either way, begin with small steps by expressing yourself in ways that are most comfortable for you. You might start with writing down some thoughts, so you have a script, of sorts. You can practice with this or you can use it as a cheat sheet if you are on the phone. I'm not a fan of emailing or texting when things get heated or serious. I worry that intentions will be misinterpreted or misconstrued. I realize, though, that many young couples find this to be the most efficient and acceptable means of communication and, if that's the case, you can certainly use those avenues to augment the dialogue, but I would emphasize that face-to-face dialogues will ultimately be more sincere and effectual.
5. **Are you indiscriminately bickering?** It's important to stay tuned in to what needs to be discussed and what doesn't. This is not as easy as it might sound at first glance. And of course, you might think something warrants

a conversation and your partner might not. Surrender is not a bad thing; we discussed this at the beginning of this chapter. This is particularly true when it comes from a position of strength and confidence in the relationship. Look at it this way: I can surrender by not raising an issue if I'm afraid to bring something up that might make you mad, or I'm afraid you won't like what I have to say. In that case, I just don't bring it up. That wouldn't be a terrible thing, but it's a form of retreating as a result of anxiety over what I perceive might possibly happen. Avoidance might feel good in the short term, but in the long term, it creates an unhealthy interactional pattern. If, on the other hand, I see that you're in a bad mood from work and probably are not feeling up to what I want to talk about right now, I might decide to wait until another time and defer the conversation. That decision not to bring it up is out of strength, and my regard for the relationship. We can truly pick our battles. We can make choices about how we fight, what we fight about and what rules we follow. Learning to yield under the right circumstances is not a weakness. It's about sharing the power.

6 **Are you forgetting the larger, common goal?** We all get swept up by the incidental diversions from time to time. Sometimes we can get so caught up in the moment that nothing else seems relevant. But this shortsighted thinking can dig you into a hole of unrewarding returns. You are much less likely to get what you want if you stubbornly cling to your position. Regardless of what that position is. When compromise is the intent, letting go is the manner in which that is accomplished. Again, letting go in this sense is not reckless submission or acquiescence for the sake of simply keeping the peace. It is an act of affection and a token of compromise.

These tendencies to be a black and white thinker, be overly emotional, fight unfairly, fear confrontation, randomly quarrel, and lose sight of your identity as a couple will continue to fuel the negative energy. In order to shift the balance in favor of your relationship well-being, your decision to take care of your marriage has to prevail over the temptation to give in to the emotional residue.

Token Tools for COMPROMISE

1 **Calm down**
Keep in mind that both of you are semirecuperating, no matter how much time has passed since the actual treatment of depression. Emotions remain raw for some time, particularly, as we've discussed, if one of you is harboring unresolved resentment. Bringing all those emotions into the discussion of the moment will be incredibly counterproductive. Stay present. Stay focused. Stay in line with the common goal.

Try this:
- **Take a break.** If your gut tells you this isn't a good time to discuss something, it probably isn't. Wait. Go do something else. Distract your brain so when you return, you can have more clarity. But, at the same time, remember that there is never going to be an absolute perfect time to talk about something, either.
- **Take a walk.** There is tons of science to support the benefits of exercise (Petruzzello, Landers, Hatfield, Kubitz, & Salazar, 1991). If you are too stressed or upset to talk about something, walk around the block and come back before you initiate the discussion.
- **Take a breath.** Like exercise, there is science to back up the advantages of deliberate breathing exercise. Pulling more oxygen in and becoming aware of your breathing calms both your body and your mind. Notice your breathing, both the inhale and the exhale. When you are anxious or stressed, your breathing becomes shallow. The goal is to slow your breathing down, engage your belly, instead of your chest, and pay attention to it as your body relaxes.

2 **Renounce your right to be right.**
You've heard it a million ways: it's better to be kind than be right. It's better to be happy than be right. Every time you cling to your ego-driven need to be right, you are declaring war. Sometimes, we criticize others so we can feel better about ourselves. That's not a conscious decision, but in doing so it can inflate our ego or sense of self. When you insist on being right or argue for the sake of arguing, what you are really doing turning away from your partner (Gottman & Silver, 1999), potentially weakening your relationship and inserting a wedge of arrogance or self-righteousness. None of which encourages compromise. If you think about it, wouldn't you rather choose to be strong enough to yield your position in order to pave the way toward reconciliation? Compromising is another way of saying you prefer to behave in ways that are more effective in the long run, than triumphant in the heat of the moment.

We have seen that in healthy marriages, it is not necessary for couples to agree. Resolving the point of contention does not mean you end up agreeing. It might be that you end up agreeing to disagree.

It's worth mentioning that if you feel you are always the one who is conceding and the balance of power feels totally inequitable, then we are probably talking about a relationship that needs more work than this book has to offer. Please make sure you are always feeling that things are in balance between the two of you. Whenever emotions feel consistently disproportional, it's time to take a close look at those underlying dynamics with the help of a professional. Being a martyr or resenting how much you are giving up is a sign that the compromise is not healthy.

Try this:
- Identify the times when it is hard to give up being right. Pick a specific incident when you and your partner could not agree and you had trouble letting go of your position. Write this down. Next, ask yourself how important this position is to you. How would things have turned out if you did not cling to that position? What would the worst scenario be? Are there times when you really could consent to another position if it weren't for your inflexibility? When does it matter, and when doesn't it matter? Can you distinguish between those situations?

3 **Suspend negativity**

When dilemmas arise while the marriage recovers from the blow of depression, it is possible for suppressed resentment to bring a level of negativity to the situation that may be inconsistent to the level of conflict. It's possible, for example for partner to be totally blindsided by the extent to which the other is upset. So how do you suspend negativity when you might be holding on to so many hurtful emotions? You just do. For now. One incredibly influential spiritual leader and author, Eckhart Tolle, in *The Power of Now*, responds to the question, "How can we drop negativity?" He writes:

> By dropping it. How do you drop a piece of hot coal that you are holding in your hand? How do you drop some heavy and useless baggage that you are carrying? By recognizing that you don't want to suffer the pain or carry the burden anymore and then letting go of it. (2004, p. 79)

My clients love this analogy as it offers them an almost tangible metaphor. Imagine the hot coal in the palm of your hand. What should you do to stop the pain of the burn? Open your hand, let it go. Drop it. It's not easy to do that with negative emotions, but it certainly is your choice to try. Sometimes, old emotions are hot coals. Drop them. Your marriage will be better if you make a serious effort to stop fighting.

Try this:
- Take your hand, open it up and look at it. Now, picture yourself holding the hot, burning coal. Quickly let it drop. Say aloud, "hot coal" as you let it go. Keep this image in your mind and use it the next time you find yourself holding on to something that you'd really rather let go of! Drop it. Hot coal.
- Another trick for your brain is to keep a rubber band on your wrist. Every time you notice that you have a negative thought, you snap the rubber band. If you really snap it, it will sting! When you pair the

pain with the negative thought you are training your brain to make the association between the negative thoughts and the snap, or the pain that comes with it. As with the classic example of Pavlov's dog, when two stimuli are paired together, learning takes place. Thus, if your brain learns that pain occurs with each negative thought, in an attempt to avoid that pain, you might respond by having fewer negative thoughts. Whether or not this really works is up for debate, most agree it may just be a distraction for the brain, which has value in and of itself. Most people tell me it makes them more aware of their negative thinking which may in and of itself, increases one's ability to manage it.

4 **Stop keeping score**
As Carrie demonstrated in her relationship, do you find yourself keeping track of who's right, who did what when, who compromised last time? If you are, chances are good that you are tallying up ammunition with which you can use against your partner. Friendly fighters do not count. You can imagine how dangerous keeping score can be for the integrity of a marriage. It implies a lack of trust and an unfounded perspective that the numbers really count. It's an irrational way of establishing control which is meaningless at best, and possibly harmful to the wellbeing of the relationship.

Don't be surprised to discover that you or your partner might be keeping score by counting who wins and who loses without realizing it. Have you ever caught yourself saying, "Hey, you did such-and-such last time, now it's my turn!" That's keeping score. Stop counting.

Try this:
- Identify this behavior as something you and your partner might be doing. Discuss this concept with your partner. See if you can come up with ways that you both see this unfold in some of your conversations.
- When you are aware that you have said something that constitutes scorekeeping, admit it, and acknowledge right away that you are sorry and that is wasn't fair.
- Suggest a ceasefire. Ask for your partner's help instead of pointing the finger.

5 **Don't presume**
When we make assumptions without checking things out, we are taking a risk that we might waste mental energy on something that is not based in truth. True compromise cannot be based on presumptions. Good communication consists of the honest exchange of heartfelt positions, not conjecture or speculation. We may not want to hear what is being said,

but we certainly owe it to ourselves and each other that we know exactly what we need to deal with.

Try this:
- If you and your partner experience a disagreement that is making you nervous to discuss, find a trusted friend and rehearse the potential dialogue with a friend. Practice what you will say. Have your friend rehearse a variety of possible scenarios so you can feel better prepared and reduce your anxiety.

9

TOKEN OF SELFLESSNESS

After the fire, when I'd tried to express my gratitude for their kindness to our customers, they'd been awkward, uncomfortable. My father had to explain to me that giving thanks is not a common practice in India. "Then how do you know if people appreciated what you did?" I'd asked. "Do you really need to know?" my father had asked back.

—Chitra Banerjee Divakaruni, *Queen of Dreams*

I am a walking paradox. On the one hand, I am generous and compassionate, both at work and at home. I am self-sacrificing and, give or take intermittent lapses, usually in sync with the needs of others. Readers who can relate to this degree of sensitivity in themselves know very well it can be both a blessing and a curse. I tend to allow myself a certain degree of personal suffering when there is suffering anywhere on the planet. My nerve endings stretch endlessly, which makes my bones hurt when someone across the world is in pain. At the same time, I am well known for my unreasonable expectation that others instantly respond to what I want. I expect prompt answers to my questions and efficient responses to my requests. That doesn't mean I always get that. It just means I expect it. Patience is not my strong suit. I am impulsive and eager to get things done. My way. This tendency is partly what fuels my ambitious nature. It is also what frustrates people who work and live with me.

To be fair, it is also extremely easy for me to be lazy. I can curl up with my iPad for long periods of time when I should be writing or cleaning or exercising. I can get in bed at 8 in the evening and watch *Dancing with the Stars* when I have a deadline I should be working on. There is a sign in my home office, a huge metal, cut out letters that read: "It's All About Me." We laughed about it when my husband first brought it home, but we also knew there was nothing funny about it. It is true. Most of the time I am absurdly comfortable asking for things that I want, or need, or think I might want or need. And serendipitously, or perhaps with great intent from the Universe, I am surrounded by loved ones at home and at work, who respond to me with impressive grace and devotion.

So why bring up my own complicated ego-driven impulses and other self-involved tendencies? I do this to outline one major point. None of that matters when it comes to the well-being of my marriage. I am uncomfortable at the slightest hint that my husband is not okay with something I have said or done. I am careful to protect his interpretation of my momentary foolishness or impetuous demands. Therefore, when I bark orders or whine about something, I simultaneously become aware of how that made him feel. I can see it. I can feel it. This is the paradox that regulates a majority of our interactions. No matter what it is that I think I want, I soon realize that I do not want it at the expense of our relationship or his happiness. It's not always easy for me to let go, to drop the hot coal, but I try. I do my best to see things from his perspective.

This is why the Token of Selflessness involves a transformation of the heart.

Token of Selflessness Inventory

Read each statement and check the ones you feel are true for you. Put a circle around the boxes which reflect those you need to work on.

- ☐ I am able to consider the needs of my partner without getting defensive.
- ☐ I feel confident in myself enough that I can forfeit what I need in support of our marriage if it is for the better for both of us.
- ☐ I am able to distinguish between giving up something out of strength versus out of weakness.
- ☐ I am patient and understand that by giving to my partner I will increase the probability that my partner will have more to give me back.
- ☐ I am able to control my emotions and first consider the needs of my partner if we are both stressed.

Any box with a circle around it means you should be alert to this when working together, especially in conflict. Check the Token Tools at the end of this chapter for specific tips on improving selflessness.

Give to Get

Selflessness is basically the opposite of being selfish. It is putting aside what you need at the moment in order to take into consideration, the needs of someone else. Partners who exclusively put their own needs first quickly lose sight of the greater needs of the relationship.

In Chapter 3 you met Shelby who missed Matt and wanted her life back the way she knew it before the birth of her second baby, before her depression swirled around them, and before all her expectations of how perfect this was all going to be, vanished. We talked about how close they used to feel and how distant Matt was now. She resented the fact that she always felt in charge of fixing that. That the relationship counted on her remedial action.

"I wonder how long it would take Matt to notice that something wasn't right if I didn't bring it up? Why do I always have to be the one to fix it? Why does he wait for me to come to him if we 'need to talk'?"

"Does it work when you do that?" I probed. "Do things get better when you initiate the dialogue?"

"Yes."

She heard the ridiculousness of her protest.

"Okay. I get it. But, still. Why is it always me? How did I get designated the executive of every squabble, the administrator of marital bliss?"

"Because you're good at it. There are other things in the marriage that Matt does better than you, right? He's good at some things. You're good at some things. That's how this works. This is the gift that you bring to your marriage. He brings his own strengths to your marriage."

According to Gottman's research, women are usually the ones who most often bring up difficult topics for discussion with their spouses and men are more easily overwhelmed by marital conflict than their wives (Gottman & Levenson, 1992). It stands to reason that if women tend to be the emotional caretakers of the relationship, they need to take on this responsibility without resentment. That's not easy, even in the happiest of marriages, because sometimes, quite frankly, it's hard to be the one to repair things if you're hurt or infuriated.

We've seen how quickly things can deteriorate when depression shares the space designated for a new baby. We've seen how joyful expectations rapidly dissolve into frantic life-altering deprivation. And when we factor in the probability that women are more likely to be the depressed partner during the postpartum period, it puts them in a precarious position. They may find themselves trying to juggle their emotional vulnerability with their perceived role as nurturer. This is one of the reasons I believe postpartum marriages heal better when the woman is in therapy.

There's a timeless principle that has made its way across borders and into the hearts of many—It is more blessed to give than to receive. We've all heard it. Many of you already lead your lives by that philosophy. Nowhere is this more true than in relationships where both partners are feeling depleted. Remember that with depression comes a host of associated emotions that undermine recovery of the self and of the marriage. Often there is an increase in perceptions of rejection, low self-esteem, and anxious inadequacy. These perceptions can seep into the healthy day-to-day functioning and put a damper on all your hard work. When they surface, they are often accompanied by a neediness that is uncomfortable for women who have been working hard to reclaim control of their lives. The prevalent need is a persistent need for reassurance. *How am I doing? Am I a good mother? Are we okay? Do you still love me?* These are fairly ego-centrically oriented concerns, which bring us to the difficulty of taking care of a marriage when one partner is uniquely self-absorbed.

The instruction to reach out, or give to, or take care of a partner when you are feeling the need for attention and appreciation can be maddening. This is perhaps where the concept of Tokens of Affection is most illustrative. After all, true affection is not only made of kind moments and positive sentiments. Affection is a state of mind. When those kind moments come from heartfelt ease, such as hugging a puppy or cradling a newborn, it's easy, it's natural, it's awesome. But when affection comes from deep inside a recovering soul in an effort to spread goodwill throughout the partnership, it is effortful and has lasting, significant returns.

In Chapter 5, we discussed that giving too much is not okay. All relationships consist of a natural give and take dynamic that shifts frequently according to the needs and circumstances. But in general all efforts to give and take should stem from a state of homeostasis; that is to say there should be an internal stabilizing mechanism that reboots in response to intermittent disturbances. In conflictual relationships, this doesn't always happen. Instead, things can escalate quickly, even from minor infractions. If your giving is one-sided or if there are conditions to your generosity and it feels out of balance with the rest of your relationship, it would be helpful to have a professional help the two of you sort through this.

Over Giving

Giving for the wrong reasons can be detrimental to both your marriage and your self-esteem. Women often report that they give and give and give and receive little in return. Giving can come from a generous place, which implies that you have taken care of your own needs and can put forth energy toward others. It comes from a full heart. Over giving, on the other hand, is not the ultimate form of selflessness. Instead, it essentially comes from an inability to receive. That means you give, give, give because you think (hope) it will be appreciated or it makes you feel good about yourself, or you feel morally obliged to. The truth is, if you are unable to take in the love, or attention, or help from others, and accept it completely, you are giving from an empty heart. Think about some of your relationships and try to be honest about whether your giving is from a generous place or a depleted one. Over giving feels burdensome, because it is a one-way flow of energy. Generous giving feels light and joyful.

Consider the following points to help you determine whether you might be giving too much:

1. It feels so good and important for you to be the giver in almost every relationship.
2. You feel guilty when someone gives something to you.

3 You put the needs of others before your own.
4 You apologize excessively if you are not able to "give" the way you would like to.
5 You avoid or are uncomfortable at the thought of asking for something.
6 You have considered the possibility that your giving could be the result of some insecurity.
7 You find that you give because you want to feel loved, liked, or admired.

If you have identified yourself as an over giver or can relate to any of these examples of over giving, you are probably exhausted. Sacrificing your need on behalf of others is an unsustainable state. If you are not sure whether you give for the right reasons, it is likely that your giving is based in negativity of some sort. You know that feeling when someone gives you an inappropriately intimate or generous gift? You know how uncomfortable it feels when it is unjustified or just plain awkward? It feels, at that moment, that it is way more about them than it is you, right? Keep that in mind if you are tempted to give from a place of need, rather than generosity of spirit.

Consider how over giving can take the form of self-sabotage.

- Isn't it funny how you seem to attract the wrong people? Do you find that you are surrounded by people seeking to exploit you in some way, or take advantage of your good nature?
- You are working too hard. The balance is off. You are probably thinking too hard about it. Most people can tell, they can feel, when you are giving from a place of pressured desire for something in return, rather than an open and kind heart.
- It can lead to a detrimental sense of entitlement. I gave this to you, so now, you owe me.
- If you are giving to get something, it will backfire. If you are giving to prove something, you will wind up on the losing end. If you are not sure if this is what you are doing, you need to take a closer look at your motivation.
- You compromise your health and recovery. Giving at the expense of yourself or your own needs is another way you deplete yourself. Remember that recovering from depression requires a balanced approach. You are both already depleted of resources.
- In a worst-case scenario, you end up not extending your best effort to your partner or your relationship either because you can't (you are exhausted), or you don't want to (you are angry and resentful). It will increase the likelihood that you will feel disappointed, taken advantage of, and constantly frustrated.

And finally, it's important to see how the tendency to over giving can result from depressive thinking and can also *keep you feeling depressed longer*. The distorted thought can be something like, *I will be a better person and you will love me more if I give this to you.* This is not the same as *I love you and feel loved by you, and therefore, I will give this to you.* Do you see the difference? Giving in the hopes of getting something back can boomerang and leave you feeling uncared for.

Sometimes, overdoing it can be a futile attempt to overload the other side in the hopes of reciprocated attention. *If I give and give again, surely I will get something back for this.* If it backfires, though, you will feel undervalued and unappreciated.

WARNING SIGNS
WHEN OVER GIVING BECOMES PROBLEMATIC

- You continue to give in situations that leave you feeling emotionally empty.
- You are feeling alone in your relationship and barely able to take care of your own emotional needs.
- You are afraid that if you stop excessive giving, your partner may be unhappy, or admit that he or she is more interested in something other than you.
- Are you constantly bankrupting yourself to rescue your partner?
- You are afraid that if you stop giving your partner will leave.
- If you are giving to your partner instead of communicating what you need and how you feel, you are giving too much.

If you identify with any of these warning signs, your over giving is not helping. It is keeping you in an unrequited relationship that, whether you know it or not, is not feeling good to you. It is time to call this to the attention of your partner, either through serious conversation or with the help of a therapist.

To offset this inclination to over give, start thinking in terms of what you are actually doing. A bit of honest introspection is called for. Most over givers have exceptionally kind hearts and are incredibly caring by nature. That's the good part. The trouble comes when you have difficulty setting limits and attain ego-satisfaction or personal gratification from others seeing how gracious you are. Think about it. If this is something you find yourself wrapped up in across the board, at work, in your neighborhood, with your friends, you might want to learn to delegate and set limits as an attempt to release yourself from this tendency to over give. With respect to your marriage, review the Token Tools at the end of the chapter to find ways to put boundaries on over giving.

A Model for Selfless Support

There is one reason to give in a relationship—to make your partner feel better. To help them feel better if they are sick. To help them feel happy if they are down. To help them feel proud when they have accomplished a goal. To help them feel loved if they are sad. Giving comes from a genuine desire to help with no expectation for anything in return. No thank you. No reciprocation. No acknowledgement of sacrifice.

However ...

There is an incredibly powerful trade off that takes place when generosity extends beyond the giver and into the heart of the receiver. When I hear someone report to me, especially in front of their partner, that a particular need is not being met, I ask what they have done for the other one lately. Carrie and I had such a discourse:

"I feel like it doesn't matter if I'm here or not. I mean, I know it matters, but he doesn't act that way. He's downstairs playing on his iPad. I'm upstairs putting the kids to bed. By the time I go downstairs, he's snoring."

"What is it that you would like him to be doing instead?"

"Ha. Anything but snoring. Or he could at least come up to bed and snore there! We're like an old couple who doesn't sleep in the same bed anymore. We're like friends who share the same space."

"Is this the way you want it to be?"

"No! This is not at all the way I want it to be. I want him to come to bed with me. I want him to help me put the kids to bed. I want him to want to help me and be with me. I want him to smile and tell me he misses me."

"Those are good things. What have you done to help those things happen?"

"What do you mean?"

"What have you done, for him, to help him want to do those things?"

"I still don't know what you mean."

That's when I realized Carrie really didn't know what I meant.

What does it mean that you can reach your goal by appearing to move in the opposite direction? The answer is the fundamental practice of *selfless support*, or, the mutual demonstration and appreciation of acts of selflessness in the service of the marital connection. Selfless support is based on the premise that if I behave in ways that make you feel good, our marriage feels better. Likewise, if our marriage feels good, I feel good and you feel good. The math is simple. Again, it's *you + me = us*.

Make a Pledge for Selfless Support

Generosity, unconditional acceptance, determination, restraint, and self-worth; these are the components of selfless support that make it work. The selflessness that underscores each edict is the Token that makes compromise and collaboration work best.

TOKEN OF SELFLESSNESS

Remember these rules of selfless support and the underlying principle upon which they are based:

- *I will act in your best interest at all times.* (generosity)
- *What is important to you is important to me.* (unconditional acceptance)
- *I will do what I say I will do.* (determination)
- *I will refrain from asking or wondering what I will get out of this.* (restraint)
- *I will let myself be loved.* (self-worth)

I will act in your best interest at all times. This statement is one of spirit. A generous nature is one that balances a belief in the partner with a belief in oneself. It does not imply a forgoing of self-interest. Rather, it's a sense that if you are okay, then I am okay. And vice versa, of course.

What is important to you is important to me. This statement implies an unqualified, nonjudgmental position. There are no absolutes, as there will surely be times or circumstances when life gets in the way and positions must shift to accommodate the moment. The components of this pledge entail the heart, not the head. Sometimes the heart can override the details of the moment, and sometimes, for sure, it must not.

I will do what I say I will do. Follow up is crucial. Words don't always hold value if they are not followed up with action to support them.

I will refrain from asking or wondering what I will get out of this. Restraint is a form of bigheartedness, especially if you are restraining from anger or contempt. Having control over negative responses is a gracious and selfless stance.

I will let myself be loved. When you allow others to support and give to you, you are at the same time, giving them the pleasure of doing something good for you and allowing yourself the pleasure of receiving it. This is not easy for everyone to do but it is a win-win situation. Our brain's pleasure centers respond positively which turns the act of giving and receiving into a mutually gratifying experience.

Keeping the principles of selfless support in mind at all times will help you focus on the core of your relationship, rather than the emotional residue. It will help you consolidate your individual and mutual efforts while you continue to secure your connection.

Awareness: The Other, First

When we wait for our partners to understand our emotional needs, without telling them what we need or how to do that, we set ourselves up for grand disappointment. For the most part, this is true across gender lines. Many couples insist that the other should just "know" what they want, so they rely on old patterns or idle expectations. Expecting the other to be a mind reader, or being emotionally lazy in a relationship makes everything harder. This isn't easy work. But it is, surprisingly, easier than you might think, once you learn the magic of giving, in order to get.

> *C'mon, we've been married for five years! Why can't she figure this out already?*

Or,

> *Why do I have to tell him the same thing over and over?*

Or,

> *I tell her what I think she should do and then she goes and does something else!*

These are examples of self-driven, frustrated expressions of unproductive communication. Yet, couples get quite cozy in these murky waters and do little but complain when it doesn't produce the desired results. Bear in mind that the heart of selflessness, the ability to take into consideration the needs of your partner without sacrificing your own needs, is an intricate balance. One that requires regular reflection on your part. Things begin to get complicated when external stressors occupy the space and tension rises. Suddenly, all the nice things you learned about being kind to each other fly out the window! Baby needs to be fed, house is a disaster, promises were broken, and being sweet and loving feels like, well, another chore.

Imagine the mother of a toddler and baby, frantically trying to get dinner on the table. Everyone is tired and cranky. The toddler is busy getting in the way and baby is sitting in a high chair whining for more Cheerios. The dog is barking. Television is blaring. Mom's head is pounding, her face, wincing with pain. She is exasperated. Dad is on his way home from a long meeting that didn't go the way he had hoped. He was sure to lose the account after all his late night preparations. Both are frustrated. He walks in the door and Mom hands the baby off to him, "Here. Take him. I cannot stand the screaming one more second."

Can you relate to the tension? Can't you feel how awful it is for both of them in that instant? Now, imagine this same scenario, only this time, when Dad walks in, Mom leaves the screaming baby in the high chair, greets her husband and says,

"I know you're tired. I know you've had a long day. I could really use 10 minutes without the baby screaming in my ear. Do you want to go up and change and then come relieve me or do you want to do it now?"

In this way, she has

1. First, acknowledged his emotional state.
2. Clearly stated what it is that she needs.
3. Offered him a choice so he can pick what feels best to him.

The bottom line—she gets 10 minutes away from the screaming so she can refresh.

Here's another example:

She wants to go to the mall. He doesn't.
"Let's go to the mall" may or may not get the desired results.

Instead, "I know you don't really like going to the mall, but there is something I need there and I would love your company. Maybe we can grab lunch together while we are there? That would be fun!"

The take-home point is this:

Recognize the emotional state of your partner, first. You increase the probability that you will get what you need or want if you first acknowledge how the other is feeling. Then state what it is that you want or need.

In doing so, you will be effectively integrating the previous Tokens. With esteem for your marriage, a collaborative effort and a compromising heart, you validate the emotional state of your partner first.

If you accept the premise that depression is a self-absorbing experience, it makes sense it will take some recalibrating to move out of the "me" frame of reference and into the "you." Indeed, it's not easy to shift that mindset. Not only do the symptoms of depression give rise to self-centered thinking, it's also easy to understand how the depressed spouse could really feel entitled, as it were, to extra attention because there has been so much suffering. While this is understandable, it is also not helpful in moving away from the depression and toward the health of the marriage.

People are less likely to get defensive if they believe their needs or emotional states are understood. Sometimes selflessness can be disguised as something else. You have to know your partner well and know when your partner is stretching past his or her comfort zone on your behalf. You have to watch for it to find it in its purest form and not take it for granted. For example, when one of my clients reported that her husband put aside his natural tendency and preference to avoid any and all conflict and reluctantly came to her and said, "Okay, so we need to talk now, don't we?"—she knew this was an act of selflessness.

When asked for an example of selflessness, some clients shared their personal experiences:

When my husband sits and listens to me rattle off nonsense that made me nuts that day when I know he would prefer to go outside with the dogs and not have a conversation.

When I'm tired and cranky and my husband asks me to rub his back. And I do.

When my wife sits with me and watches football just to be with me when I know she can't stand watching the game!

When my husband puts the kids to bed and tells me to go down and read so I can relax and I know he was tired from his day

Giving, with proper boundaries and intent, is the fundamental aspect of selflessness.

Can I Be Selfless If My Partner Is Acting Like a Child?

Of course you can. And you should. Everyone is allowed to regress occasionally. You can excuse a transient lapse in good behavior; a mood or moment overcome by a passing bad day or snarky attitude. This is precisely when you should resist your inclination to snap back or roll your eyes (contempt, remember?). This is when you should pull in your resources, do your best to listen, observe what is going on, and help your partner find a more comfortable spot when immature behaviors set in. It takes extraordinary compassion to meet pettiness head on but it is an affectionate act of ultimate selflessness.

You can achieve this by:

1 Identifying how impenetrable your partner is at the moment.
2 Acknowledge the behavior or words that are making things difficult right now.

3 Monitoring your own emotional reaction. Responding with anger will not be helpful.
4 Offer a gentle redirect. Either one specifically about the behavior in question (oh my, maybe you didn't get enough sleep last night?!). Or, a one that postpones the moment (*perhaps we should try this again later, after you eat something*). Sometimes, your readiness and willingness to overlook temporary jerk-responses can be your greatest act of selflessness and support. Accepting your partner when he or she is at the worst is a lovely compliment to both of you.

Tokens Tools of SELFLESSNESS

1 **When in doubt, give first.** Always, always, be aware of how your partner is feeling. Both of you will benefit when you identify how the other is feeling prior to saying or doing something that may be perceived as "taking," particularly if the other is depleted.

For example, your husband is watching a football game. The baby is snuggled in his crib. You have found a moment to respond to some emails. Then, you remember your husband forgot to change the light in the laundry room that the two of you have agreed needs to be done. The ceiling is high; the ladder is there, in place and in the way:

Worst: You didn't change the light bulb! It takes forever for you to do anything around here! I can't do anything in there without a light and the ladder in the middle of the room!

Better: Hey, you forgot to change the light bulb.

Best: I know you are enjoying the game right now. When it's halftime, would you please take care of that light bulb so we can see in the laundry room?

Try this:
- Before expressing what you need, identify and label the emotional state of your partner
  I know you are _____(tired, busy, frustrated), but I need _____ (you to, go and, take a).
  Or,
- Express how your partner might perceive your request, thus, disarming him or her.
  I know I am getting on your nerves, but would you mind _____.
  I know you hate to hear this, but I would love it if you could _____.

2 **Tiny gestures are huge.** Acts of generosity, sprinkled freely throughout your relationship, will enrich your connection. If this feels overwhelming or a bit too demonstrative, remember that even small signs of affection go a long way. We are social beings and even when we think contact with another is the last thing we want, it is often the first thing we need.

Try this:
Non-verbal gestures of these sorts, exchanged between partners, are affectionate overtures. Any small gesture will do.
- A look
- A nod
- A smile
- A touch
- A caress
- A cuddle
- A pat on the back

3 **Accept acts of kindness.** When you receive a compliment or a gesture of compassion, or an accolade of some sort, it can dishonor the giver if you are unable to appreciate it.
If this is hard for you, try it in baby steps.

Try this:
- Start with "thank you" when someone says something positive to or about you.
- Or simply smile.

4 **Do not over give.** If you have identified yourself as one who tends to over give, take the time to examine what implications this might have for your marriage. If you are always cooking for your neighbors and volunteering when you don't have time, or the first in line to help out when you would rather be home sleeping off your bad cold, you might be at risk to be an over giver, but none of these things are bad, they are, in fact, what makes you so wonderful. There are many legitimate reasons as well as cultural expectations as to why some people are prone to over give. However, at the end of the day, your relationship needs to entail mutual giving.

Try this:
- Write down everything you did for someone else in that past 24 hours. Even if it is something you *wanted* to do. You might be surprised to find out how hard this is and how much you are doing for someone else.
- Learn to say, "Let me get back to you," or "this isn't a good time," when you find yourself bombarded by requests from others. With

regard to your marriage, talk to your partner and get a sense of whether over giving is a problem for either one of you. If so, what do you both need to do about that?

5 **Don't wait for thank yous.** True acts of selflessness rise from deep within our core with pure and unconditional motivation. Expecting a thank you spoils the intent and sets you up for disappointment. Offer it freely from your heart. You will know whether it makes a difference or not and how it is received. The only recognition you need is the recognition from yourself that you are doing the right thing.

- Do something anonymously for someone you care about, or for a stranger. See how good it feels to just give. Pure and simple.
- Judith Orloff, author of *Emotional Freedom* (2011) and frequent blogger, says one of her favorite random acts of kindness is to leave a $5 bill in some public place so a stranger can find it and feel lucky.

10

TOKEN OF SANCTUARY

It must happen to us all ... We pack up what we've learned so far and leave the familiar behind. No fun, that shearing separation, but somewhere within, we must dimly know that saying goodbye to safety brings the only security we'll ever know.

—Richard Bach, *Running from Safety: An Adventure of the Spirit*

Like it or not, women tend to be better at this relationship stuff than men. As mentioned, research supports this notion that men, as a whole, tend to be less emotionally self-aware (Levant & Pollack, 1995) and less proactive than women when it comes to raising difficult issues for discussion (Gottman & Silver, 1999). However, a recent study has shed light on the association between relationships and the emotional well-being of men and women, highlighting that men are more reactive to the quality of ongoing relationships. Somewhat surprisingly, results showed that men also received greater emotional benefits from the positive aspects of a relationship, challenging the longstanding stereotype of men who are unaffected by emotional ups and downs of a relationship. The authors suggest that for men, romantic partners may be their primary source of intimacy, in contrast to women who may enjoy numerous intimate relationships with friends and family (Simon & Barrett, 2010).

Regardless of what the research shows, engaging men in this process of personal reflection is often met with resistance or out and out refusal. This reluctance may be partly social, partly biological, and partly personality based, but regardless of its origins, understanding the male reticence is crucial to the successful exchange of tokens.

Understanding gender differences will help you discover the most efficient and effective means with which you can carry out this mission of improving connectedness. Failure to understand what might stand in the way will sabotage your best efforts. The Token of Sanctuary refers to finding just the right place, the sweet spot in which you both feel safe and cared for. This includes a physical space and all that that entails, as well as an emotional space, and how to carefully create such a safe haven.

Token of Sanctuary Inventory

Read each statement and check the ones you feel are true for you. Put a circle around the boxes which reflect those you need to work on.

- ☐ My partner and I have one or more places that we feel comfortable openly discussing hot topics that may be difficult or upsetting to us.
- ☐ I am able to let my partner spend private time in a space that does not include me, without feeling threatened or excluded.
- ☐ I respect my partner's need for alone time, but if need be, I know how to carefully and effectively reach into that space and get their attention.
- ☐ We are good at reserving our disagreements for the right time and place.
- ☐ I am good at reading my partner's signals if I have overstepped a boundary or mistakenly spoken, picked the wrong time and place to talk about something.

Any box with a circle around it means you should be alert to this when working together, especially in conflict. Check the Token Tools at the end of this chapter for specific tips on creating a sanctuary.

Is There Room in Your Cave for Me?

Social expectations have historically appointed women as chief executive of emotional, family, and relationship issues (Pace & Sandberg, 2012). Over time, men have largely been encouraged to find satisfaction at work and be in control of their emotions. Unfortunately, after a while, evolutionarily speaking, this can lead to repressed emotions with long-term negative effects, such as the development of over-controlled, overly-cautious behaviors which may restrict receptiveness to their own needs and to the needs of others (Walters, Carter, Papp, & Silverstein, 1988). Regardless of the specifics, if men and women are hard-wired to respond to emotions differently, it would be prudent to take that into consideration when you are entering an emotionally-laden dialogue or topic.

In my book, *Therapy and the Postpartum Woman,* I make reference to a remarkably perceptive comedian named Rob Becker (n.d.) whose Broadway one-man smash reveals some of the more entertaining differences between men and women. His spot on humor reflects the sometimes funny, sometimes painful, always accurate, gender-related preferences that play out on the home front. The pivotal theme for his show rests with his caveman reference, which blends Becker's study of anthropology, psychology, and sociology, and with astute precision, makes us laugh about our differences. First and foremost, we should all be laughing in our relationships (more on laughter in Chapter 11). Second, and most vividly, he creates a storyline that draws from prehistory days with imaginings of primitive hominids wielding clubs and retreating to their cave dwellings. Ah, the cave. Today, there are websites, TV shows, specialized furniture lines, and urban dictionary definitions—all referencing today's civilized version of prehistoric desires. Wikipedia describes it this way: "Man caves have multiple purposes: they're a place to be alone, to be away from women and from female sensibilities, to indulge in hobbies, and to hang out with male friends. It is, loosely, a male-only space to retreat to" ("Man Cave," n.d.). It's a great metaphor, and this manspace is hugely relevant to our work here.

Without belaboring the point, (some) men desire time and space for private thought, work, and play, and so do women, of course. For instance, the place I feel most comfy and cozy with regard to alone time is my home office. I've been known to hunker down there for the better part of a day, losing all sense of time passing. Sometimes, my aching shoulders and neck are the only signals I have to alert me to the dwindling daylight. I love the comfy chair, I love the space heater that emits warmth and white noise that keeps me mesmerized and focused. I adore the pictures of my too-far-away family members who are never far from view. Everyone knows not to disturb me when I lose all sense of time and space in there. It's my cave.

A second place I crave alone time in is my kitchen. I love my private time twirling between ingredients and appliances, creating masterpieces out of scant offerings. So much so, that I ask (rather, insist) that this space be respected and that things will go much more quickly if everyone else scatters. But when all is said and done, although I rudely claim ownership of this room, ultimately, it feels comfortably neutral to both of us. That feature makes it conducive to sanctuary possibilities.

For years, our culture has provided men the opportunity to retreat to their man caves in which they can hibernate while engaging in sports or gaming-related activities. Now, more than ever before, women are carving out their own nook for privacy and self-nurturing. Rooms with candles, fresh flowers, sewing machines, computers, books, music, peace and quiet, whatever best soothes the female soul. Of course, it's different for everyone. Still, whatever the décor, the design is the same: to provide a personal space in order to retreat and replenish.

Hunting

Back to Rob Becker and his caveman play. The magic of his work is not in his humor, but in his insight. He says that when a man is sitting in front of the television watching football, for example, he is "hunting." Because he is hunting, he is single-mindedly focused on one thing: Football. He must concentrate. He must not waver. If he does, he might lose sight of his kill, or dinner for his family. Thus, he remains keenly fixed on his prey. Hears nothing. Sees nothing else. Oblivious to everything and everyone. Especially, his wife.

"Honey?" she sweetly calls from the kitchen.

No response. Nothing.

"*Honey???*" she repeats with wonder and determination.

No movement. *Shhhhhhhh. He's hunting.*

"HONEY!!!!!!!!!! ARE YOU *DEAF*??!"

"*What??* Why are you screaming?"

Not the best communication.

Becker dramatizes that the key to bridging the gender gap in relationships is, in this illustration, for the wife to understand that he is hunting. Really. It's not that he is ignoring her. It's not that he is being a jerk. He does not care more about football than he cares about her. He is hunting. It is primitive. It is instinctive. It is real.

Becker then guides the amused audience to the next step, how the wife should proceed. He says something like, *she needs to enter his cave.* He suggests she come over to the couch and sit down next to him (his peripheral vision can only grab her image when they are side-by-side! After all, he is hunting!) Sit down. Touch him. Get his attention, then, when making eye-contact (eyes off target), tell or ask him what you need.

Yes, this is an exaggeration to make a point. And no, this is not to imply that women should arbitrarily submit to the whims and primal needs of our ancestors. However, the message is a solid one; one that we mentioned throughout earlier chapters of this book:

Unless and until you consider the emotional state of your partner, you will only be communicating halfway and are more likely to be met with resistance.

Gathering

While men are zeroing in on their targets, as described by Rob Becker, women are the gathers, busy collecting information, or things, or sensory input. Having evolved from gathering stones and material for warmth and food, they are now busy reflecting, organizing, planning, and essentially gathering what they need to make sure everyone else has what they need! Women joke about it—*My husband can only do one thing at a time, if that!*—they claim; when it comes to the art of multitasking, women typically lead team. While early men were indeed responsible primarily for hunting, we presume that women tended to the children, the home, and other tasks of daily living. This ability has likely evolved to enable them to successfully manage more than one task at a time. The myth of who multitasks better, which is certainly up for debate, has recently been addressed by a small study which demonstrated that women tended to perform better than men when asked to carry out a number of functions simultaneously (Laws, 2010).

Regardless of who is better at what, the main point here is that men and women may approach tasks differently, with distinct agendas and distinct processes. Keep in mind that the reason we are exploring these differences between men and women in this area is to find some common ground, the sanctuary, that both can settle into to insure a meeting of the minds. This can only be achieved if we close ranks and find middle ground.

Finding a quiet place when there is literally stuff all over the place is no easy assignment. It's crowded everywhere. Laundry isn't done. Toys are strewn across the floor. Clothes are piled up in the corner and bills are collecting on the desk. There's no place to think, and peace and quiet are out of the question. Both of you are working hard to keep things moving in the right direction. You're both busy. You're both tired. We've seen how keeping score, as in who is doing more, is not only helpful, but it can be harmful to the spirit of your mission. Right now, it's probably safe to assume that *both* of you are multitasking pretty much on a regular basis, which is why you need to stop and pay attention to how best you can follow through with your intent to maximize understanding and connection between the two of you.

To shed light on this notion of multitasking, take note of the following conclusions drawn by recent research (Offer & Schneider, 2010) which studied the activity of families trying to balance work and family life.

1   Mothers multitask more than fathers when they are home.
2   Fathers multitask more than mothers when they are at work.
3   Both multitask more at home than when they are at work.
4   Multitasking at home takes place more often when children are around.
5   When mothers multitask at home they are significantly more likely than fathers to carry out these tasks for the express purpose of being with their children.
6   Multitasking appears to peak at 8 a.m., when the family is getting ready for work and school, at 4 p.m., when school is over and afternoon activities begin, and in the early evening, at 7 p.m.
7   Mothers are more likely to report feeling productive when multitasking than fathers.
8   Multitasking appears to help mothers accomplish tasks but it comes with a gender-related emotional toll. Multitasking is associated with higher levels of frustration, irritability, and stress (Offer & Schneider, 2010).

Although this particular study focused on working parents, the implications are interesting; particularly #6, which states the hours of peak multitasking in families. If we link our two premises, that men are inclined to "hunt" and that women are the primary multitaskers at *home*, we begin to understand how the foundation of a sanctuary is built. The foundation is based on finding the right place (away from distractions), finding the right time (avoid peak children or task times), and always honoring the inherent differences between men and women, between you and your partner.

A New Cave: The Sanctuary

In our attempt to bring the marriage back to center stage, our goal is to create a space, a physical comfortable space where the two of you join forces with no competing attractions. Ideally, there should be no cell phones, no access to any electronic device, no children, no pets, no TV on, no radio in the background. Door closed, light on, sound off.

As an empty nester, the distractions in my house have dropped off considerably, which would lead one to believe that there should be much more focus on each other, which may be true to some extent. Still, when we factor in busy careers, tired brains, hectic schedules, two dogs, and oh, that attention deficit thing, I find myself competing for my husband's time and especially, attention. One night when our children were very young, I discovered an entry point into my husband's preoccupied brain. I don't remember the specific topic, but I do recall it was something about our daughter that I did not expect him to agree with right away or I anticipated some dismissive response. I started with the vulnerable spot in his heart, our daughter:

"Mel is upset. We need to discuss such and such."

As expected, he responded with concern, "Okay, sure, what's up?" leaving me still questioning his ability to sustain interest while he was feeding the dogs. Keeping in mind my own very strong requirement for undivided concentration, I needed more.

"Can you come here for a minute, we need to talk." (Bad choice of words, it can work, or it can backfire, big time.)

"What's going on?" he stayed focused after putting the dog bowls in place and washing his hands. Then, I saw magic unfold. He leaned back onto the kitchen counter and hoisted himself up, finding a spot right in the corner; legs dangling, hands at his side grabbing the granite. Nowhere to go. I had him trapped in the corner of my kitchen! Suddenly I realized, I had just what I wanted: presence, attention, focus, and the most important for me—eye contact. Enduring eye contact. I had discovered gold. He sat. We talked. We listened. We problem-solved.

This is an example of pulling my partner into my space. My domain. My comfort zone. Then, finding a way to help make him comfortable there, and subsequently, able to listen intently. The difference between a cave and a sanctuary is that the cave is "me" oriented, while the sanctuary is for "us."

Remember, the sanctuary will refer to both a physical and emotional space. In addition to finding the right spot where you are both comfortable, you must also feel free to express yourself, verbally and non-verbally, good feelings and negative feelings, without fear of judgment, ridicule, mockery, criticism, or any other disrespectful reaction. The spirit behind the sanctuary is drawn from the very basic belief that marriages need a neutral place to hide out and refuel.

Rituals

My husband and I later laughed when I would command him to the kitchen counter when we needed to discuss something, and, fortunately for him, we discovered additional ways to satisfy the same conditions. Still, the lesson learned was important. Find the way, the place, and the time to increase the likelihood that the subject to be discussed will be captivated by your partner, rather than avoided. Granted, the kitchen counter was not the most comfortable spot for a sanctuary but it provided the structure with which I could better understand the components of this special place. It also allowed the conversation to be the central activity without distractions. Securing a sacred space that can shut out the world is vital to the wellbeing of your marriage. We have discussed how important rules are to a family system and how when things are predictable, couples tend to feel safe and more grounded. When you create the sanctuary, you are offering a loving rule based on your commitment to the relationship. Rituals can reinforce the philosophy behind the sanctuary and provide much desired structure.

For instance, Shelby and Matt (introduced in Chapter 3) described their "mini-Sabbath," alluding to the Jewish practice of honoring the end of the week with rest and reflection. Each Friday evening, they sit at the kitchen table, with relaxing music in the background. They turn dial down the dimmer so the lighting is soft, doing their best to create a romantic moment while both children are by their side or on their laps. Shelby makes some yummy treats to munch on. This is when they discuss the day, the week, the children, their relationship. They tell stories; they state and restate what is important to them and how they think they are doing. They talk about how much better Shelby is feeling and how the two of them have come through such a difficult time with great love and renewed hope. Sometimes these times together are deep and meaningful, but most of the time they described them as lighthearted and peaceful. This is their sanctuary.

Couples who have regular, meaningful conversations are more likely to remain emotionally connected. Find a spot. Make it safe and cozy. Lure your partner in with a voice or words or actions that speak to him or her. Unlike the example used above, this works best when it is not in *his* cave or in *hers*. Usually, those designated caves are appealing precisely because the other one is not in there!

Rules of Operation

1. The exact location of your sanctuary can change but it's best to try to be consistent to establish predictability will have a soothing effect.
2. It is not necessary to discuss the terms of this sanctuary in any overt way. It can just be experienced.
3. The place you choose is what is most meaningful to you. The Postpartum Stress Center surveyed women online regarding where the sanctuary was in their marriages, some responses were:
"The kitchen. That's where we always are. We both feel good there."
"The bedroom. It is the only area of the house that is exclusively ours, plus, it is one of the few areas where we can shut the door."
"The beach. At night time we can walk or stay in the car and talk and its always secluded."
"On the living room couch with a bottle of wine. We call it the 'state of the union' talks."
4. The sanctuary should be closed at the following hours: 8 a.m., 4 p.m., and 7 p.m. These are high stress points which will increase stress and decrease productivity (see research reference earlier in this chapter) and therefore should not be the designated time to "meet."
5. Remember you cannot just show up. Participation is essential. Talk. Listen. Validate. If talking is not required, share the space together and let yourselves experience what you need to experience in a quiet, loving way.
6. Find a phrase that you are comfortable with to use as an introduction, if there is not a set time to meet. This phrase should always have the emotional state of the other in mind (that is, enter their cave for a moment) and should always be framed as a possibility not as an expectation.
For example,
> *If you're not too tired, I'd love it if we can make some time tonight to sit and talk.*
>
> Sounds better than,
>
> *We have to talk.*

Never lose sight of why this effort is so important. Your lives are busy. It's crowded everywhere. Laundry is backing up. Toys are strewn across the floor. Mail is piled up in the corner and bills are collecting on the desk. There's no place to think and peace and quiet are out of the question. It becomes clear that as things begin to resemble routine life again you and your partner need a place you can call your own. This is particularly important if you feel a bit estranged or emotionally distant from your partner. Although it may at times be tempting to put your relationship on the back burner while everything else is bubbling over in the background, we have seen why this is not a good idea. Creating a sanctuary will help you preserve, restore, or create a break from the rest of the world; a space you two call your own, where distractions are minimal and attention is maximized.

Token Tools for SANCTUARY

1 **Revere the sanctuary.** Above all, follow the above rules of operation. Never ever fight unfairly within this space. Review the good communications skills in Chapter 5. If things begin to unhinge, it's time take a deep breath and recalibrate. Either modify your tactics or move out of the sanctuary. Be clear about your intentions or needs. No mixed messages. No mind-reading. Speak openly about what you want or need during this quality time. This is the time and spot for loving and productive interactions.

Try this:
- You and your partner should separately write your top two ideas for where your sanctuary should be. Make a list of places in your home or elsewhere that you find soothing and comforting, and where you would like to have your relationship conversations. What feels like a safe, neutral, cozy spot? See what you each come up with. If you both pick the same spot, it's a done deal!
- Next, both of you should separately write two topics that you would like to discuss in your sanctuary. They can be practical decisions that need to be made, events that are affecting your relationship right now, or perhaps a more abstract exchange of ideas.
- Now, make a list of the distractions that you would need to reduce or eliminate so you can have meaningful conversations within the sacred walls of your sanctuary.

2 **Safeguard the friendship.** We hear this often because it's true. Friendship is the foundation of any good marriage. Gottman writes, "Happy marriages are based on a deep friendship" (Gottman & Silver, 1999, p. 19). He tells us that this entails knowing each other intimately, understanding each other's idiosyncrasies, and expressing affection in small ways on a regular basis. These are the qualities you should bring into the sanctuary with you whenever you need to address private or personal issues. Remember who what you mean to each other. Remember how much you care.

Try this:
- Write down the three things you like most about your partner. Have your partner do the same.
- Next, write down the three things you think your partner likes best about you.
- Exchange your lists and share what your each wrote.

3 **Carve out time without guilt.** Guilt spoils any party. It is by far the greatest enemy of this endeavor you are undertaking. The only way the notion of a sacred space will work is if you proceed with an open heart. This refers to both individual time in your respective caves, and time together in your sanctuary.

Try this:
- If you find the two of you do better with structure, it's a good idea to schedule a meeting in the sanctuary. These meetings can have two (separate) purposes. They can be business meetings, where you meet to discuss any subject that is on the table. Or, these meetings can be a date night in, where the two of you meet, alone, with no children, no distractions, and share alone time, together. Both meeting types are a statement that the marriage is high priority.

4 **Honor alone time.** Each of you should create, make use of, and revisit your own private caves. Work, hobbies, outside interests, friends, etc., all contribute to the well-being of your marriage. These are separate but equally important pathways to greater satisfaction all around.

Try this:
Make a list of some of the things you already do or would like to start doing that would make you feel good. Include all kinds of activities or indulgences that you might have put on the back burner since having a baby. Watch a lecture online of something that interests you. Play a game. Learn to knit. Learn how to say "I love you" in a new language. Whatever it is, spend time alone in your cave, enriching your life and breathing new life into your head, heart, and soul. You have been through a lot. You have been tired and weary. It is time to refresh.

5 **Respect each other's cave.** Remember, if you are going to enter the cave of your partner, which is not the same thing as your shared sanctuary, you must always be mindful of their current emotional state, what they are doing in there and how best to advance without interfering. Joining that particular space requires grace and deference.

According to Gottman (1994), 96% of the time the way a discussion begins can predict the way it will end. Remember that when one partner begins a discussion with an accusatory or condescending tone, the discussion is destined for disaster.

Asking your partner to enter *your* space, however, is simply a matter of requesting gently.

Try this:
- Next time your partner is cozy and snug in their cave, practice approaching the cave with a specific and courteous request. See what script works best for you and your partner. Discuss the pros and cons.

  For instance:

  Honey, I see that you are busy, would you mind if _____?
  Excuse me, can I ask you a quick question?
  Can I bother you for a minute?
  Babe, I need you for one minute, is now a good time?

11

TOKEN OF EXPRESSION

Courage is what it takes to stand up and speak; Courage is also what it takes to sit down and listen.

—Winston Churchill

Poor communication is the issue most often identified by couples who seek therapy (Broderick, 1981). Ask anyone who is in marital counseling why they decided to go, they will likely say, "We don't communicate well." It's the go-to rationale that most couples present as the basis of their current discontent. What do they really mean? If couples learn to communicate well, is that all they need to do?

In Chapter 5 we introduced some fundamental communication skills. Hopefully, you have kept these in mind throughout the book. In this chapter, we will explore additional ways you may or may not be expressing yourself and learn how some very subtle gestures can make a very big difference. In this chapter, expression refers to any outward manifestation of a mood or emotion toward your partner. This can be represented through words, movement, voice, touch, action, art, gestures, looks, language, intonation, or silence. It is, to be clear, any way that you convey any and every thing to your partner.

Token of Expression Inventory

Read each statement and check the ones you feel are true for you. Put a circle around the boxes which reflect those you need to work on.

- ☐ I am able to express myself with clarity, with words and without words, without provoking my partner.
- ☐ I feel confident that my partner understands me when I express what I need or want.
- ☐ I am able to understand what my partner needs or wants.

☐ My partner and I enjoy playful activities together and find it easy to laugh together.
☐ I am a good listener and I feel listened to when we talk.

Any box with a circle around it means you should be alert to this when working together, especially in conflict. Check the Token Tools at the end of this chapter for specific tips on improving your ability to express yourself.

Satisfaction and Communication

Though there are diverse perspectives on how much emphasis should be placed on communication by itself with regard to marital satisfaction, there is agreement that satisfaction in marriage declines when couples fail to engage in constructive communication and problem solving. More often than not, negative communication patterns involve criticism, blame, and contempt, which can then lead to personal attacks. On the other hand, couples who communicate with empathy and positive qualities are expected to be more content in their relationship (Gill, Christensen, & Fincham, 1999; Jacobson & Margolin, 1979). Basically, they are saying that marriages that respond to conflict with positive communication find their relationships more rewarding in the long run. Certainly makes sense, doesn't it?

You might be thinking that this is all well and good when things are going smoothly at home. After all, it's easier to be thoughtful and empathetic when everyone is happy. The challenge comes when you are being asked to be kind and considerate when you are still stumbling through the rocky post-depression patterns of relating. Of course, couples who communicate with positive qualities are expected to be more content in their relationship! Not so easy when both partners are recovering from the aftermath of depression. Once more it raises the circular query: Are they happy because they are using positive communication styles or are they using positive communication styles because they are happier? I suspect both are true. Let's take a closer look.

Other researchers profess the value of a different model of communication referred to as a "negative confrontation model of marital interaction" (Gill et al., 1999). This means that being empathetic is not enough; that the conflict can actually be good for the marriage, as long as it is handled in a constructive manner. As a case in point, Gottman and Krokoff (1989) say that engaging in conflict may lead to improvements in marital satisfaction. In fact, they claim that women should be less concerned about being compliant and positive and instead, focus on helping their partners deal with and discuss areas of disagreement. They point out that the wife's anger specifically may mobilize improvements, indicating a strong commitment to the marriage, which yields better results long term. When you think about it, it makes perfect sense that a wife's discontent, coupled with her propensity to express herself, could thrust the couple in an upward momentum if the timing and technique are effective.

If we combine these two approaches, we conclude that conflict is an important feature of any marriage; the key is to approach the conflict with skill and effective implementation.

In case you are wondering if any of this is relevant to how you are feeling right now, take a minute to review the literature on the transition to parenthood. Some consistent and important themes emerge:

1 There is a *decrease in marital satisfaction* during the transition to parenthood (Cowan & Cowan 1988; Shapiro, Gottman, & Carrère, 2000; Tomlinson 1996).
2 The *amount of communication between spouses decreases* during the transition to parenthood, with reduced communication associated with decreased marital satisfaction (Cowan & Cowan 1988).
3 In addition to the quantity, the *quality of communication also changes* after a baby arrives. An *increase in arguments or less openness* over childcare or relationship issues can arise (Cowan & Cowan 1988).
4 When couples *are unprepared for communication changes* and prefer spontaneous and frequent interaction with each other, some of these abrupt changes can become problematic (Cowan & Cowan 1988).
5 The most significant factor to impact marital dissatisfaction after couples have a baby is the *quality of their relationship before the baby* (Cowan & Cowan, 1992).
6 Couples who experienced less tension *and better problem-solving and conflict strategy skills had higher levels of satisfaction in their marriages* (Cox, Paley, Burchinal, & Payne, 1999).
7 All of this is amplified by depression, as depression, without considering any other factor, affects marital distress.

Think about these points—they are worth repeating. Always keeping in mind how depression by itself can disrupt marital satisfaction, remember that after you have a baby: There is a decrease in marital satisfaction. The amount of communication decreases. This decrease is linked with lower marital satisfaction. The quality of communication changes, more arguments, less frankness. When unprepared for these changes, more problems arise. Your previous (before baby) level of functioning affects your current level of satisfaction. Better problem solving skills will lead to greater satisfaction.

As mentioned previously, it's not always possible to tell whether poor communication caused a couple's marital distress or whether their marital distress caused the poor communication, but we know that depressed partners are more likely to engage in negative interactions, such as blame, withdrawal, or anger, than non-depressed partners (Beach, Fincham, & Katz, 1998). Moreover, there is less predictability in the communication of depressed partners (Biglan et al., 1985) and depressed partners are probably less likely to rely on positive modes of communication, such as ingenuousness, smiling, and good eye contact. Therefore, in this chapter, the goal is to reconstruct some of these details of expression that have been cast aside during the treatment of depression in the hopes of rekindling the connection between the two of you.

Putting the theories aside for a moment, think about how your own marriage and how the two of you communicate now. During those times when communication is difficult, when you don't understand each other, or when tensions are high:

- Do you think you make things better or worse?
- What frustrates you the most when you don't feel listened to?
- Do you honestly think you use your kindest repertoire of words when you speak?
- Do you take into consideration how your partner is feeling when you say what you need to say?
- Are you able to choose your words carefully when stress levels are high?
- Do you know what to do when your partner doesn't communicate well with you?

It *is* possible to develop good communication skills whether you are knee-deep in emotional residue, or not. Imagine, for example, that you have a job interview. You woke up with a migraine and got 3 hours of restless sleep the night before. You are miserable and just want to crawl back into bed. If you wanted this job and felt motivated for the interview, I presume most of you would pull it together in order to do what you had to do to get through the interview with flying colors. Especially if you knew you could crash soon thereafter! This is exactly the principle behind effective communication between partners. If you want this marriage and feel motivated to preserve its integrity, you need to fight for it whether you are irritable, sleep deprived, disillusioned, or anything else for that matter.

Are You Nice to Each Other?

The reason I repeatedly refer to this notion of being nice to each other is because this concern that couples are simply not being nice was the catalyst for this book. When feelings are hurt or needs are not met, people tend to express themselves more impulsively and without filtering what they say. When strong emotions, such as anger, enter the picture, they need to be carefully introduced into the dialogue. Interactions based on hotheadedness, whining, defensiveness, or offensiveness, will quickly incapacitate any communication attempt.

Therapy is often the place where these heated exchanges play out. From time to time, couples describe their negative interactions by retelling an event from the week, and sometimes I find myself smack in the middle of the mud-slinging. When that happens, after the insults begin, I begin to lose sight of the content and retreat into the process. *What are they doing? Why are they talking this way? Why are they both perpetuating it? What is the secondary gain?*

I do my best to conceal my reaction; that is my job, certainly, to remain impartial and objective. I am certain, however, that there are times when my eyebrows hike upward in disbelief, or downward in furrowed disapproval. *Why are you both being so unkind*, I think to myself or, sometimes, say aloud. Isn't there a better way to say what you are saying? In other words, can't you say it in a way that will increase the likelihood that you will be heard and get what you want? And not alienate your partner, and estrange his sensibilities?

Problem solving is a process that is best achieved by the acceptance of a common goal and a kind heart. That does not exclude the expression of painful emotions. You can love someone and be very, very angry. Again, it's the *way* you express it. It's *how* you express it that matters. The success of your interactions is directly related to your awareness of these communication nuances.

I learned this when our daughter was about six years old when her father was making her an omelet. He loved making breakfast for her. She would sit at the table with eyes wide open watching him spin from sink, to refrigerator, to stove, all the while, singing or making silly faces. In the meantime, I was busy with my own uneasiness relinquishing my mommy duties and kept strolling back and forth monitoring each phase of the omelet creation, stalking his every move.

"That's a lot of cheese you're putting in there,"

My husband has always been good at not hearing me. He stayed focus on his task; chopping, cutting, singing.

"Seriously, she doesn't like that much cheese," I insisted.

I paced back and forth, finding all kinds of ridiculous reasons to supervise his handiwork.

"She doesn't like green peppers." I added, just in case he thought he knew what he was doing. "Hey, really, take the green peppers out." I instructed.

And then, in a moment that would be forever branded in my brain, he shot me a look. It was a brilliant look. It was piercing. It was calculated. If looks had words, it would have said: *Really? Are you for real? I know how to make an omelet. Go away. Leave us alone. Let me enjoy this. You're getting on my nerves, leave the kitchen!* Though none of those words were spoken. Nothing was said. Only his eyes spoke. Immediately, when I looked into his eyes, I heard the words that were not uttered.

That was the moment I learned how to listen to what was not being said. I learned the role that common courtesy plays in a relationship and when to step back and let things be. I learned when to take a deep breath and, quite literally, leave the room if necessary. I realized how indispensable my husband's happiness was to me and how easily I could get in the way, if I weren't careful. I learned how important it is to accept responsibility for my part when making things worse and above all, when to say I'm sorry.

More to the point here, I learned how successfully one could express one's discontent with a single gaze. How two people can communicate effectively, sometimes without words, when they stop what they are doing or thinking and tune in to what the other is doing and thinking. It can be a moment of awakening for your marriage when you discover your ability to make that happen either as the initiator or the recipient. Learning to successfully convey and accept the expression of negative emotions is a vital element of your marriage and a skill worth perfecting.

Being nice to each other is more than good manners. It is a prerequisite for healthy connections. When you reach out on behalf of your partner, it obliges you to simultaneously look within yourself.

For example, do you:
- Say "thank you"?
- Say "please"?
- Say "I'm sorry"?
- Say "I miss you"?
- Look into your partner's eyes and try to understand what is being expressed or not being expressed?
- Pay attention to the subtle hints your partner sends you whether they are positive or negative?
- Appreciate the small things your partner does or says?

These gracious phrases and gestures may seem too basic to even take notice, but if you are not already exercising this muscle in your marriage, it is never too late to start. We have discussed that good marriages are more at ease with the mutual expression of respect. Sadly, people are often more considerate of strangers than they are with the people closest to them.

A recent study suggests that saying "thank you" may be a direct and simple way to improve marital happiness. The cycle of appreciation and expressing gratitude out loud has been shown to be linked to more enduring satisfaction (Gordon, Impett, Kogan, Oveis, & Keltner, 2012). Many times, in a relationship, we wait for the other person to make us feel good, or repair a broken moment. Rather than passively expecting your partner to make things better, you can actively start focusing on what is good, and what you appreciate. This, in turn, makes your partner feel appreciated which encourages them to feel more appreciative of you.

> ### A WORD OF CAUTION
>
> Some couples report they use email and texting as a way to intersperse bits of romance into their day. A simple text of "I love you" can certainly take the edge off of a prickly day.
>
> Beware of email and texting as a means of communication during conflict. If the two of you are used to expressing yourself by email or texting, I would urge you not to rely on these words-only forms of communication when disputes arise. You may find that you open yourselves up to misinterpretation and misunderstandings which will interfere with problem solving.

Proceed with Care and Curiosity

It's time to get reacquainted with each other. It's time to reclaim your place in this marriage that has been temporarily seized by distractions, both loving (your baby) and distressing (depression).

Until recently, it's likely that much of your communication has centered on those two things, your baby and the depression. Childcare and related topics and recovery from depression, although tremendously important, are not the sexiest things to discuss together. It is probable that you picked up this book because you are feeling ready to take back your marriage. Good. Priorities are shifting and the energy to follow up with that is close behind. What's your next step? Communicating with the one you love is not always as easy as it might seem. Sometimes the rash, knee-jerk reactions people have can shift things in the wrong direction. Depression and love are not particularly compatible. It's not out of the question that one or both of you have come out of this depression doubting your love for each other or at least, wanting answers or reassurance. Wanting reassurance about your love is another way of saying you are looking to reconnect.

In your effort to reconnect, keep these points in mind in order to fortify your communication skills that you learned in Chapter 5. As mentioned, couples who are unhappy frequently cite poor communication as the culprit. Yet it's more than that. Poor communication is generally not the problem. Poor communication is the symptom. Couples have poor communication because they are disconnected. Working on the connection, as you are doing in this book, will help with communication. Likewise, learning to communicate better, will improve your connection.

Consider the following guidelines:

1 *What you say*
2 *How you say it*

3 *Be curious*
4 *What you do*
5 *Really listen*

What You Say

Try starting with something like, *I miss you*. This is only one example of how the choice of your words can offer a peaceful bridge back to each other. Everyone has, at one time or another, felt alone, even in the presence of other people. Depression robs couples of intimacy. One of the primary reasons for this is that lack of pleasure and loss if interest in things previously enjoyed is a hallmark symptom of depression. What follows is that relationships can feel hollow, leaving some people hungry for more, while others lose motivation to change the way things feel, even if they are sad or frustrated. Remember we have learned that a whopping two-thirds of couples experience an increase in marital dissatisfaction after the birth of a baby (without factoring in depression!) and also a rise in conflict and hostility (Gottman, 2007).

Finding the words to briefly convey a desire to connect can be powerful:

- Do you miss your partner?
- Do you miss specific things about your partner? Or how you both felt before the baby arrived or before depression upstaged your marriage?
- Do you miss your old self? Do you miss the way you used to think, and feel, and talk, and act?
- Do you miss the space the two of you occupied before so much of life got in the way?

If you do, it's time to say so. Saying *I miss you*, aloud in those words, or writing it in a card if that is easier, can be the opening to a space you both long to revisit. It is a sweet invitation to the past, one that was shared by only the two of you. There are many other ways to express this same sentiment, of course. Find the words to attach to the feeling. Find a way to let your partner know.

How You Say It

Never underestimate the old adage, *it's not what you say, it's how you say it*. Nowhere is this more pertinent than when two partners are negotiating in a personal exchange. Again, this refers to our major premise that relating with affection is a more effective means of reconnection than negativity. When couples are in conflict, emotional reactiveness is common. Unfortunately, it does not bode well for a constructive resolution.

Think about it. Pick almost any sentence and imagine saying it with a positive spin or a negative spin. For example, take a look at some of these common phrases below and see how easily that can be interpreted as positive or negative, depending on your intonation.

First, say each one with a positive inflection, as if you wanted to communicate your readiness to reconcile or resolve things. Then, say each one with a negative inflection, indicating annoyance or displeasure:

We need to talk.
I don't agree.
Why are you doing that?
What's the matter?
Thanks a lot.
What are you doing?

Notice how your voice quality changes and the emphasis on different words. Notice even your facial muscles change. If you generalize these simple phrases into some of the statements we all make when we are hurt or angry or frustrated, you can imagine how easy is would be to send out the wrong message if you are not careful. Watch how you speak. Your words should not only reflect an underlying affection for your partner, they should also reveal a fundamental strength and belief in what you are saying.

What You Do

How do you express your love and affection for someone without words? There is evidence that shows couples who are more satisfied are better able to code and decode nonverbal cues (Gottman, Markman, & Notarius, 1977; Hall, 1984). This is partly attributed to the fact that they understand each other's quirks and signals more clearly than couples who are discontented.

Women tend to initiate touch more often than men (Guerrero & Andersen, 1994; Hall & Veccia, 1990), which may or may not be useful information to you, but for the women who are reading this book, if you are the one who does most of the repairing in your relationship and if conflict resolution often depends on you doing the facilitating or compromising, the power of touch, quite literally, is in your hands. Although there are some inconsistent data, most studies have shown women to be shown to be superior in decoding nonverbal messages, particularly positive ones (Noller, 1980). This information puts women in the preferred position to take charge of the communication process at that level. The touching, the eye-contact, the body language should be attended to and perhaps, interpreted in order to deepen the mutual understanding. Keep in mind that people send out a barrage of signals—some good, some bad—often without even being aware of it. Your posture, your hand movements, your shoulders and micro-expressions made with your eyes, your eyebrows or your mouth can speak volumes. Be aware of these discreet yet compelling means of expression.

Be curious. Be honest with yourself for a minute. With so much going on right now, how interested are you in the day-to-day activities of your partner? How interested are you in what your partner is thinking or feeling when it doesn't impact you or your family directly? How much do you know about what your partner is doing throughout the day that may have significant influence on the development of self-esteem, or job performance, or sense of self-worth? When was the last time you asked a question, just for the heck of it, about work, or outside activities, or a story about past adventures, or life before you? It's very easy to slip into self-centered thinking, for most people, much of the time. Postpartum depression can persuade the sufferer to remain locked in self-absorbed thoughts. It becomes difficult to see much else beyond the borders of the distorted thinking that accompanies depression. People describe it as being in a bubble or behind glass walls, where they can see the rest of the world out there functioning as normal, but they cannot grasp it or engage with it.

As difficult as it might be, it's time to break the bubble. Step forward, reach out, and reach toward your partner. Ask questions. Learn something new about your partner. If you are not particularly interested, pretend that you are (yes, really). Pretending that you care about details that may disinterest you in the moment will create empathic pathways that make this easier in the future. Try it; you'll discover that this can work in other areas of your life as well.

Really listen. The first step in being a good listener is to remove all distractions. It's hard to pay attention when the TV is on, or music is blaring, or dogs barking, or children are crying. Listening requires the ability to focus which is hard to do when your brain is busy filtering out interruptions. Many people claim they can multi-task and listen while they are doing something else, but if emotions or stakes are high, listening will require more than hearing the words.

When you truly listen you are sending the message that:

- *There is nothing else I need or prefer to do at this moment.*
- *I care about what you are saying.*
- *I can accept and tolerate the feelings you are having right now.*
- *You are entitled to feel this way, even if it makes me feel uncomfortable.*
- *I can help you make sense out of the feelings you are having.*

In Chapter 5 you learned that listening is not merely a passive activity but rather one that requires deliberate attention. If this is an area that you feel you are weak in, please review the chapter on communication skills. Really listening to your partner is an underrated skill that takes perseverance and practice to develop. It is a prerequisite to empathy.

What's So Funny?

If a man speaks in the forest, and no woman hears him—is he still wrong?

(unknown)

My apologies for gender-biased humor, but the underlying message is mocking the very point being made in Chapter 5 on how misinterpretations can lead couples off track. Let's proceed by stating the obvious: it feels better to laugh than to fight. It's hard to disagree with this statement. The healing power of humor cannot be disputed. However, it does not feel good to be made fun of, or patronized, or made the recipient of a sarcastic retort or a hostile joke. Of course, what's funny to one person is not funny to another. Once again, we rely on the mutual and tacit appreciation of each other and each other's idiosyncrasies. When couples can draw upon, but not make fun of, their history of playful stories and experiences, they then have access to a wealth of exit material when conflicts arise. To reiterate our earlier point, conflict is not the problem. It's *how* you fight and how you *resolve* the conflict that predicts the longer term level of satisfaction.

Although it is generally agreed upon by husbands and wives that humor is one of the most important qualities of a successful marriage, the casual role of humor in relationships has been studied with mixed results. The degree to which humor is valuable in a marriage depends on many factors, such as who is using it, how it is being used, and of course, the timing. The research does point to humor as a desirable characteristic associated with greater enjoyment, though it may not necessarily correlate with marital satisfaction or stability (Martin, 2007).

It's interesting to note that one study found that when husbands expressed humor during times of high stress, the couples were more likely to experience significant marital discord. Apparently it wasn't appreciated! The authors concluded that although the humor could be perceived as a deflection of anxiety and reduce the stress in the short run, it may also have interfered with the couples' ability to problem solve (Cohen & Bradbury, 1997). Conversely, in Gottman's research, it was found that when wives expressed humor during the discussion of a problem it was associated with greater marital stability. This was only true when the humor led to a reduction in the husbands' heart rate during the dialogue (Gottman, Coan, Carrere, & Swanson, 1998). Here again, we see evidence of women having influence in navigating the intricacies of problem solving.

Not surprisingly, positive emotions such as humor, affection, and validation were more likely to be present in happy marriages than in unhappy marriages, even in during conflict (Carstense, Gottman, & Levenson, 1995). Notably, husbands in satisfied marriages tend to use strategies to decrease negative emotions when involved in a low-conflict discussion, whereas wives in satisfied marriages deescalate negative emotion in high-conflict discussions; both spouses relinquish the de-escalation role in unsatisfied marriages (Gottman & Krokoff, 1989). In other words, when the marriage is strong, men are more successful at diffusing negative emotions when the degree of conflict is low and women are better at smoothing out the negativity when emotions are high.

Have you seen this to be true in your own marriage?

Have you noticed that one or both of you try to reduce stress by interspersing bits of humor? Does it work? Why or why not?

We've seen that humor can be used positively to diffuse tension, or it can be used negatively, such as hostile humor during a conflict. Again, this raises an issue with bidirectional association. That is, do satisfied couples use humor more often, or is the use of humor linked to greater satisfaction? In agreement with Gottman's work, another study showed that regardless of whether the couple was in a conflict situation or a pleasant encounter, partners who were more satisfied with their relationships reported great use of positive humor and lower levels of negative humor use than did individuals who were less satisfied with their relationships (Butzer & Kuiper, 2008).

The degree to which humor is effective is likely a result of how each partner perceived the use of humor in their own families of origin. In many ways, humor might reflect the traditions and characteristics of your family, which can be a good thing (the appropriate use of humor associated with a reduction of tension), or it can be deleterious (the use of sarcastic or hurtful humor). For example, if your family successfully used humor to deflect a high stress moment and you are comfortable doing the same, your partner, if not used to this, might misinterpret your use of humor and believe you are simply avoiding the issue. It boils down to this: the use of stinging humor is associated with relationship distress. Couples that are happy and stable use humor in positive, supportive ways.

Can't Get on the Treadmill? Have a Good Laugh!

WIFE: *"There's trouble with the car. It has water in the carburetor."*

HUSBAND: *"Water in the carburetor? That's ridiculous."*

WIFE: *"I tell you the car has water in the carburetor."*

HUSBAND: *"You don't even know what a carburetor is. I'll check it out. Where's the car?"*

WIFE: *"In the pool."*

Most of you already know that there has been much research on the health benefits of laughing. Did you know there was a word for this? Gelotology is a term coined in 1964 by Dr. Edith Trager and Dr. William Fry to refer to the study of laughter (Butler, 2005). As noted in our book on postpartum anxiety, *Dropping the Baby and Other Scary Thoughts*, laughter can hold the key to diffusing anxiety and promoting a sense of well-being (Kleiman & Wenzel, 2010). As we point out, Dr. Fry reports that after 1 minute of joyful laughter, his heart rate was equal to the rate he achieved after 10 minutes on a rowing machine (Fry, 1992). Incidentally, it doesn't seem to matter if it is real or fake laughter! Just think, laughter is as good as exercise. Dr. Fry explains that this is because when we laugh, we involve our entire body, and he considers the physiological effects to contribute significantly to the maintenance of good health overall (Fry, 1994). In fact, studies show that laughter has a significant impact on the body's immune system; shown to lower levels of adrenaline and cortisol—hormones that are released in times of stress—and to raise levels of endorphins (Berk et al., 1989). The humor response can be a coping mechanism to any uncomfortable situation. It can serve as a buffer, if and only if, both partners are on the same page. No one is suggesting you giggle your way through an argument. However, it is possible to gently redirect some of the immediate tension with loving and appropriate humor. Laughter is a completely different animal. Laugher, though not particularly relevant within the context of conflict resolution, should be high on your list of things to do to help the two of you maintain a general atmosphere of good will. Look for opportunities to laugh. *Really* laugh.

Did you know that a giggle has a 50% chance of reversing itself, which in turn avoids a full out laugh, in case you're in church or the library! Did you know that the sound of a giggle is amusing and contagious? Did you know that the efforts to suppress a giggle tend to increase its force (Berk, 2001)?

> *A man asked his wife what she'd like for her birthday. "I'd love to be six again," she replied. On the morning of her birthday, he got her up bright and early and off they went to a local theme park. What a day! They went on every ride in the park! Five hours later she staggered out of the theme park, her head reeling and her stomach upside down. Next, they went to McDonald's, where her husband ordered her a Big Mac with extra fries and a chocolate shake. Then, it was off to see a movie, with hot dogs, popcorn, soda, and her favorite candy. What a fabulous adventure! Finally she wobbled home with her husband and collapsed into bed. He leaned over his precious wife with a big smile and lovingly asked, "Well, dear, what was it like being six again?" With one eye opened, his wife said, "You idiot, I meant my dress size!"*

The moral of this story is: *Even when a man is listening, he's still going to get it wrong*. (Again, apologies to anyone who is offended.)

> ### TAKE TIME OUT FOR A GOOD LAUGH!
>
> The mental health and physical benefits of humor
> (Berk, 2001)
>
> **Psychological Effects**
>   Reduces anxiety
>   Reduces stress
>   Reduces tension
>   Reduces depression
>   Reduces loneliness
>   Improves self-esteem
>   Restores hope and energy
>   Provides a sense of empowerment and control
>
> **Physiological Effects**
>   Improves mental functioning, increases alertness, and memory
>   Exercises as well as relaxes muscles
>   Exercises the heart like aerobic activity
>   Improves respiration
>   Increases blood flow and improves function of blood vessels
>   Decreases stress hormones
>   Boosts immune system defenses
>   Increases release of endorphins (anecdotal evidence)

Are you laughing as much as you should be?
Here are two playful references to the influence women have over men.

There were two gates in heaven. One gate had the sign over it saying, "For Men whose wives ruled over them." The other had a sign saying, "For Men who were the head of their house." The line for the men who had been dominated was as long as the eye could see. The other line only had one man standing there. St. Peter asked the man, "Why are you standing in this line? The man said, "I don't know. My wife told me to stand here.

A wealthy and successful CEO took his wife for a Sunday afternoon drive near the little country town where she grew up. Noticing that the gas tank was nearly empty, he pulled in to the little country gas station. While the tank was filling he went to the rest room. On his way back to the car he noticed that his wife was talking and laughing with the gas station attendant. When they drove away, he asked his wife about it.

She told him that the attendant had been her boyfriend when she was in high school. He said, "Just think! If you hadn't met me, you might have wound up being the wife of a gas station attendant!" She replied, "No, if I hadn't met you and married him, he would have become a successful businessman and you might have turned out to be a gas station attendant."

Humor can effectively be used as one of a number of reparative strategies when used prudently. We see that the use of humor can be beneficial in the short run and in the long run, but couples need to be careful to understand each other well enough to know what will be perceived as a lighthearted and welcome diffusion rather than a manipulative and disruptive ploy.

Barriers to Expression

Although many factors can impinge upon a couple's ability to express themselves with positive intent and effectiveness, ultimately you are both responsible for the words and gestures you choose. In addition to the combined stressors related to childbirth, parenting, depression, and emotional residue, be aware that other external factors can also contribute significantly to the path a conflict episode will take.

Examples of common external influences that can potentially amplify an episode are:

- Too much caffeine
- Too much alcohol
- Not enough sleep
- Extraordinary stressful event during the day
- Being hungry
- Feeling ill or compromised physically
- Anything that interferes with your ability to be patient and objective

Expressing yourself when you are upset is never easy. Emotions take over; consideration often takes a back seat. Poor communication can result in emotional deprivation which leaves everyone feeling bad. This can be especially true for couples healing from depression. Often what we see is that the partner who suffered from depression tends to return to that pain and ruminate about how their needs were not met. When arguing, couples then regress and rely on impulsive reactions instead of more thoughtful ones. It's hard not to take things personally, when thoughts are distorted and symptoms are unchecked. However, as you move forward together beyond the depression, it's time to relinquish the pain attached to needs that were not met. Because some of those needs were direct functions of the depression, rather than accurate reflections of what you needed. Don't carry the distortions forward. Trust the recovery process and believe in your relationship.

Token Tools for EXPRESSION

1 **Say "Thank you."** It's easy to take things for granted when we are both so busy.

    Of course it is. Although just because it is easy, doesn't mean it is the best road to take to get to where you are going. It's time to put appreciation on top of your list of things to remember to do.

    Saying thank you is a way of complimenting each other, it says, what you are doing for me is not going unnoticed. You might be surprised by how good it can feel, to say it and to hear it from your partner.

    Try this:
    - Make a list of the five things you appreciate most about your partner. Remind yourself of these things when you feel quick to judge or criticize.
    - Make it a point to say thank you for one thing, every day, for a week. One thing. Each day. One week.
        - It can be in response to something your partner does—Thanks for waking me up on time.
        - It can be in response to something your partner says—Thanks for telling me how you feel about that.
        - It can be in response to something your partner is—Thank you for always knowing the right thing to say.
        - It can be in response to something silly—Thanks for making me laugh.
        - It can be in response to something serious—Thank you for loving me.
        - Pick one thing. Every day. For one week.
        - If you find this hard to do, keep doing it. If you find this easy to do, keep doing it.

2 **Find a common language.** This refers to the unique state of familiarity that exists between the two of you. Sounds silly, but it is true: No one knows the two of you as well you both do. We've discussed the fact that understanding how each other thinks and feels can actually help you intercept a surprise attack and get it back on track. Say things in a way you think your partner will be most responsive to. Try to dial the emotion down and enter the cave so you can speak the same language.

Try this:
Complete the following sentences, then, ask your partner to do the same:
- I love it when you _____.
- When you _____. I have a hard time understanding what you want.
- I know you have really heard me when you _____.
- It might seem silly, but when you _____ it makes me feel totally loved by you.
- I am trying to understand, that even though you know it bothers me, you still _____.
- I feel like we communicate best when we _____.
- Even though it's not easy for me, I might understand you better if I try to _____.
- When you are upset, perhaps it would be best for me to _____.
- However, when I am upset, I would prefer you to _____.

3 **Listen to what is not being said.** In your quest to find a common language, be attentive and read the cues in front of you. This is one of the best ways for you to understand what is not being expressed.

Try this:
- If what you are saying or doing is making things worse. Stop. Do something else or do it differently.
- Think about who your partner is and what he or she might be experiencing.
- Watch the body language (yours and your partner's).
- Pay attention to the facial expressions.
- Keep an eye out for emotions that may be difficult to access, or words that may hurt too much to articulate.
- Take the risk of checking out your intuition if you sense something that is not being articulated:
  Are you feeling sad?
  Are you thinking I don't make any sense?
  You seem upset.
  Did I make you mad?

4 **Be kind and stay curious.** This cannot be overemphasized. If you approach your partner with affection, you will increase your bargaining power as well as your partner's ability to participate in the dialogue. This is common sense, but it is often the first things people forget. Show your partner you care.

Try this:
- Try to find time to actively engage in the pursuit of something novel in your relationship. Admittedly, none of these suggestions are easy with a new baby in the house, but file them away in the back of your mind if the opportunity presents itself: Add a new hobby. Join a class together. Do yoga together. Take dance lessons. Play ping pong. Banish old habits in favor of new pleasures. Finding moments to spend together, especially when that time is at a premium, is key.
- Talk to your partner about something you have never discussed before. Discover new information. Tell your partner something about yourself that has never been revealed. Have fun with it.
- Every day say something nice to your partner. Pass along a compliment. Make a flattering remark about the way they look. Express admiration for the way they work. Every day. One thing.

5. **Laugh.** Pick a moment. Pick a reason. Make one up. Find a reason to laugh. Or learn to fake a laugh until your belly hurts. When you find yourself really laughing, try to make it last longer. Reap the benefits that a physically intense, breathlessly wonderful cackle can do for you.

Try this:
- Seek out and surround yourself with people and things you find funny. Enjoy the moment.
- Listen for laughter and search for the source. Share the chuckle.
- Practice smiling. A real smile. Use your eyes and your facial muscles, not just your mouth.
- Do something outrageously silly. Share it with your partner.
- Search for things that will make you laugh: buy tickets to see your favorite comedian, find an old funny movie to watch together, talk about memories that make you both smile.

12

TOKEN OF TOLERANCE

In the practice of tolerance, one's enemy is the best teacher.

—Dalai Lama

He #1: She is such a pain in my ass. She is always leaving things all over the place. Man, why do I always have to be the maid in the house? It's bad enough the kid's crap is all over the place. I have to clean up after her too?!

He #2: I have to admit I don't love coming home from work finding dishes in the sink and toys on the floor, but it's easier for me to clean it up than to fight about it.

He #3: We both work hard. Sometimes I clean up the mess. Sometimes she cleans up the mess. It works best that way.

There are many ways to learn to live with the things we don't like. There are just as many ways to drive ourselves crazy with irritability and loathing. Unfortunately, the experience of depression can expose us to all kinds of things we don't like about each other; some seemingly insignificant, like messy sinks, and some big and difficult to bear, such as emotional withdrawal.

Generally speaking, tolerance refers to an open-mindedness, a willingness to be fair when opinions, viewpoints, or behaviors differ from your own. Couples learn to tolerate things that get in their way by practicing. It is similar to using a muscle we rarely use. It doesn't make a difference right away; we have to persevere and keep performing the same action over and over before we can see it make a difference. Similarly, no one is suggesting it is easy to put up with irritations when you're not in the right frame of mind. It is a virtue that is perfected over periods of continual practice, lots of trial and error, and a bit of frustration sprinkled in!

In Chapter 8, we introduced the notion of kindness and compassion which underscores the purpose of this book. When we merge these concepts of compassion and tolerance with the premise that a strong connection is the key to marital satisfaction, we turn our attention to acceptance and empathy.

Read each statement and check the ones you feel are true for you. Put a circle around the boxes which reflect those you need to work on.

Token of Tolerance Inventory

- ☐ When my partner gets on my nerves, I can easily dismiss it.
- ☐ I am aware of my intolerance and immediately identify it and take reparative action.
- ☐ It is easy for me to accept my partner's opinions that contradict my own.
- ☐ I am comfortable when I perceive a weakness in my partner.
- ☐ I am patient and understanding when my partner disagrees with me.

Any box with a circle around it means you should be alert to this when working together, especially in conflict. Check the Token Tools at the end of this chapter for specific tips on improving tolerance.

Finding Empathy

"It is, what it is," Hallie scoffed, as she described her husband's response to anything that made her anxious. "It annoys me to death. Andrew always says that right when I am ready to blow my top, he sings those annoying words, 'It is … what it is …,'" she repeats, complete with mocking grimace and inflection. It is what it is.

She and I talked about that phrase, what it meant to her and what it might mean to her if she thought more about it. I told her about my favorite mindfulness guru and spiritual author, Eckhart Tolle, and how he had inspired me in my own life. (A more complete discussion of mindfulness will be found in the next chapter.) We discussed how hard it is to accept any present state; to wipe out all interferences and sit with a blank slate, as one is instructed to do if one aspires to Zen-like states of absolute tranquility. I told Hallie, that I, too, am baffled by this notion, but work hard to achieve it. I'm not sure I understand all that it encompasses, but I am a work in progress. What I do know is that the road to marital Zen-ness, where peace and love and stability intertwine, presents this same paradox—one that instructs you to work hard to do nothing. Just be.

For most people, the silly, ostensibly trivial things are usually harder to accept than the bigger, more complicated things. For example, one woman told me she has less tolerance for the popcorn smacking that resonates throughout the movie theater, than she does about the fact that her husband leaves for work every morning at 5:00 a.m. and has never enjoyed the opportunity for a weekday breakfast with her and their children. It's a universal phenomenon. It's the old toilet seat up or down argument and how to squeeze the toothpaste tube. It's the little things we have trouble dealing with. There are so many of them.

That's where Zen-ness comes in. By definition, marriage presupposes a certain obligation toward acceptance of our differences. This is easier said than done, for sure, but in general, there are two levels of interpersonal acceptance. The two levels of acceptance are apparent to most couples learning to live together in harmony; although they may not actually be articulated, most are familiar with them. Level one is learning how to live with snoring, picking, slurping, cracking, scratching, whining, farting, sloppiness, spitting, and yes, sometimes, breathing. Living together in peace requires a certain degree of surrender to the perpetual presence of noises, smells, idiosyncrasies, and just plain bad habits emanating from the love of your life. Not easy. Keep working on it.

Level two is learning how to accept your partner in spite of all, or most, of those imperfections, just as you hope he or she will accept you and your own shortcomings. Acceptance of yourself and each other is paramount to accepting the current state of "what is" in your relationship. Starting with where you are is mandatory in your work here. If you bypass this somewhat obvious step, you can inadvertently let unrealistic expectations sidetrack your position.

> What does *start with where you are*, really mean?
>
> It means not expecting things to be how they were before you had your baby.
>
> It means not expecting things to feel how they felt before one of you suffered from depression.
>
> It means less judgment, less disappointment.
>
> It means understanding that sometimes, it is what it is.
>
> And finally, it means you understand that truly accepting your current state will provide valuable cues and information that will eventually lead you to where you want to be.
>
> It's the difference between:
>
> *You left things a mess and I can't stand it!*
>
> and
>
> *I know you left things a mess because you were tired and had a hard day.*
>
> And that's a big difference.

Feeling accepted in a partnership increases the likelihood that change can take place. That's because people are more motivated to change if the appeal comes from a place of genuine admiration rather than contempt (Gottman, 1994). I'm sure you can attest to that from your own marriage. The less tolerance your partner expresses toward you at any particular time, the less motivated you will feel to change. Furthermore, the less patience your partner has for you at any particular time, the worse it probably feels.

Perhaps the most crucial component of true acceptance and validation of each other is the ability to empathize. Empathy is a complex concept, one that has been defined in many different ways throughout decades of research with marital relationships. For our purpose, empathy is the bridge to connectedness. It is what allows one partner to move away from self-centered thinking and move toward the other partner with sympathetic intentions. Simply put, it is the ability to identify with and understand the feelings, thoughts, and attitudes of your partner. Implicit in this construct is the ability to be aware, sensitive, perceptive, and able to communicate some level of compassionate understanding.

Understanding why your partner behaves a certain way or says certain things will lead to more productive interactions. In Chapter 9, the Token of Selflessness, we discussed how important it is to *first* acknowledge the emotional state of your partner, before asking for something or expressing something that you need. In the same way, it is now important for you to grab hold of the larger picture, that is, your relationship, while you navigate the temporary instability. Thinking about your partner first, and your relationship as a whole, will ground you when you are tempted to react impulsively. It may not be something that you feel like doing at a given moment, but it is important to hear, nonetheless. Your brain may still be in survival mode, which keeps you in self-preservation form. This may have provided some protection when things felt acute and desperate but now, it is no longer helpful. It does not leave room for someone else, and unless you intend to leave your marriage, nurturing the impulse to flee or retreat to your cave for the long haul, drawing away from your partner will get you nowhere.

How We Explain Each Other's Behavior

There is an interesting phenomenon that occurs in marriages as highlighted in Gottman's work. It's been shown that happier marriages tend to be more forgiving of each other's faults. Think about that statement. In happier marriages, the partners tend to be more forgiving of each other. At first glance, doesn't seem terribly profound. Say it again to yourself. It's so obvious. Of course, they are more forgiving, they are happier. Again, there is a reciprocal association. It is easier to be forgiving when you are in a stable and healthy relationship. If that is true, doesn't it also make sense that if you were more forgiving, it might make you happier? Perhaps.

In his research, Gottman found that in the happier marriages, when one partner does or says something negative, the other one is likely to perceive it as transitory and situational. That is, not reflecting the character of the partner. For example, negative emotions or words might be attributed to a bad mood or *He's had a rough day*. Positive behavior, on the other hand, is interpreted as intrinsic to the partner's character, such as, *He's such a caring person*. Couples who are happy are more likely to tolerate occasional negativity and ascribe it to a particular mood, moment, or external factor, rather than the person himself.

In contrast, unhappy marriages tend to view things in an opposite manner: Negative behaviors, instead of being seen as situational (bad mood) are interpreted as internal characteristics, *He's so inconsiderate*. Positive behaviors are seen as situational, such as, *Oh, he's just being nice because he came home early today*, and are not likely to last or generalize beyond that situation (Gottman, 1993).

Let's look at this a bit closer. Labeling each other's behavior with characteristics that are positive or negative is referred to as *attribution*. The notion of attribution in this context refers to the process by which partners explain the causes of, or meaning behind the behavior of others, such as, *He only brought me flowers because he was feeling guilty*. In distressed marriages, certain attributions for positive events will diminish the impact of those events (*He only came home early because he was out late last night*), and certain attributions for negative events will intensify the impact of those events (*She didn't make dinner because she's mad at me for what I said last night*). It's negativity on top of negativity. Unhappy couples are more likely than happy couples to blame their partner for marital stress and to see the partner's negative actions as intentional and selfish.

In happy marriages, as we saw above, the opposite pattern of attributions occurs. The impact of positive events is accentuated (*He made tea for me after dinner because he always thinks about what would feel good to me.*) The impact of any negative event is actually canceled out (*She was irritable because she has been working overtime all week*), clearly making things feel better.

In happy couples, the attributions can be viewed as excuses, so to speak, excuses in defense and behalf of the marriage. In unhappy couples, the attributions are maladaptive excuses that justify the disconnect, prolong the suffering, and are associated with later dissatisfaction (Bradbury & Fincham, 1990). Think about this carefully: When couples are satisfied with their marriages, they make relationship enhancing attributions, such that they make low-impact attributions for negative behaviors and allow positive events to have a great deal of influence. In contrast, when couples are less satisfied with their marriages, they make distressing maintaining attributions, meaning, they place more responsibility on the negative behavior or event (Holtzworth-Munroe & Jacobson, 1988). Simply put, the way you feel in your marriage has a direct impact on the way you credit or discredit various behaviors and events and even non-verbal cues.

If couples behave in a certain way because of how they think and feel, does it follow that we can teach ourselves to feel better in our relationships by changing the way we think and act? Cognitive behavioral therapists would certainly claim this is so. Pay attention to the way you are perceiving things in your marriage. Could you be misinterpreting? Misappraising? Over-reacting? It is possible for you to shift some of those appraisals in favor of your relationship? Would you be open to the possibility that your perceptions, at times, are not in sync with what is in front of you? Could there be an alternative way of interpreting things? Remember the CBT 101 skills you learned in Chapter 5? All of those tools can be used to soften the distress maintaining attributions that you make to explain your partner's behavior.

As we've said, you don't always have to believe in the long-term value of what you do at any given moment, you just have to act as if you do. The rest will follow. If you are hurt or angry, you can still act lovingly toward your partner. If you are scared or uncertain, you can still move forward in the direction of reconciliation. Paying attention to how you feel and of equal importance, paying attention to how your partner feels, creates the empathic groundwork from which strong connections are built.

Brain scripts

"I don't feel good today."

"What's wrong?"

"I dunno. I just don't feel good. My throat hurts"

"You were just sick last week."

"No I wasn't."

(Collective sigh.)

"So what do you want me to do?

"I have no idea. I just don't feel good. Can you feed the baby?"

"Sure."

"Are you mad because I don't feel good?"

"No I'm not mad."

"You sound mad."

"I'm NOT mad!"

"God, why is it so hard for you to take care of me when I'm sick?"

"Omg are we going there now? I SAID I WOULD FEED THE BABY!"

How many men and women claim that their partner doesn't understand what they are saying? In the above conversation, the husband is trying to fix things by helping her and she is feeling misunderstood and unloved. It's easy to see how miscommunications can easily disintegrate.

In the popular press, there are tons of self-help books on how men and women think differently. We touched on this with the caveman references in Chapter 10. In addition to our basic themes of affection (being nice to each other) and connection (feeling safe and cared for), let's return to the subject of gender differences. Without proper attention to those male versus female variables, we risk setting the stage for further misinterpretation.

There is a recognized stereotype that women have superior ability to feel the pain of others and experience compassion. Women frequently score higher than men on standardized empathy tests (Rueckert & Naybar, 2008). This is also the basis of a classic grievance among couples as noted in *The Male Brain*, described by neuropsychiatrist Louann Brizendine, "Men accuse women of being too emotional, and women accuse men of not being emotional enough" (2011). What's not clear is whether empathy and the ability to feel what the other is feeling is the result of nature or nurture.

Perhaps a quick lesson in neuroscience can shed some light. The recent discovery of *mirror neurons* in several areas of the brain has contributed to new understanding of empathy and emotional systems. Mirror neurons are named as such because they fire when someone performs an action and also when someone observes someone else perform that action. In other words, mirror neurons allow a person to experience what another person is experiencing without actually going through it.

Neuroscientist Marco Iacoboni says mirror neurons are the "only brain cells we know of that seem specialized to code the actions of other people and also our own actions" (Iacoboni, 2008). He goes on to explain that these brain cells help us understand others by presenting a sort of "inner imitation" of other people's behavior which then encourages us to copy the emotions that are linked with that behavior. For example, he states that we see someone smiling, our mirror neurons for smiling fire up, kicking off neural activity that actually evoke the feelings associated with a smile.

While sex differences in the brain are still up for debate, some experts maintain that there are two emotional systems working simultaneously: the mirror-neuron system (MNS), as described above and the temporoparietal junction system (TPJ), which appears to be involved in ability to reason about the contents of another person's mind (Saxe & Kanwisher, 2003). There are claims that men use the TPJ more, applying problem solving and analytical processes and women tend to use MNS more, relying on than emotional processes (Brizendine, 2011). If women are inclined to use the MSN (emotional empathy) system, *I feel what you feel*, men may be using the TPJ (cognitive empathy) system, such as, *I'm trying to fix your pain and make it go away*. This may account for the ever-present "you just don't understand!" coming from both sides of the dispute. Brizendine explains it like this: Basically, the MNS is activated in both men and women, but women appear to stay there longer, connecting to the emotions, while men move to the TPJ system, connecting with the cognitive processing.

Regardless of the neuroanatomical pathways, the key here is that we must do our best to understand that, there are both biological and environmental influences that account for differences in how we interpret and share emotions. Just as we learned in our caveman analogy from Chapter 10, marital satisfaction may hinge on a clear understanding of how these differences are expressed and accepted within your marriage. Expecting your partner to respond the way you would, or the way you would like him or her to, sets you up for disappointment at best and disaster at worst. Great comfort can be found in establishing mutual acceptance of each other's ways of thinking and eccentricities.

The Big Emotions

As we've seen with all previous Tokens, what applies to your partner and your marriage, also applies to you. A prerequisite for improving tolerance in your marriage is accepting yourself and what you've been through. This is difficult for anyone recovering from depression. The shame and stigma that unfortunately still exists, hits men especially hard.

Aaron and Suzy had been married 5 years when they had their first baby. After their son was born, Aaron was unprepared for his family history of depression to invade his private precious world. He was quick to identify it, but reluctant to let anyone in. Suzy was a loving wife who understood Aaron well, but was often frustrated by his tendency to shut down. Even when she felt close to him, he seemed most comfortable withdrawing from any conversation that felt even the slightest bit confrontational.

"Why didn't you tell me you had a doctor's appointment today?" Suzy asked as they drove home from dinner with her parents.

"It was no big deal."

"Well, I like to know. I like to hear how you're doing. What did he say? Are your meds right? Do you need to do anything different? Does he think things are going well?"

Aaron felt bombarded with questions and stared at the traffic in front of him.

"Aaron, how did it go? What did he say?"

"He said I'm fine."

Suzy has a choice here. She can either let go and let this conversation be, for now. Or she can push forward, and risk alienating Aaron or upsetting him. Or, she can try another tactic. Here we see a common illustration of how differently men and women deal with painful emotions. Both of them are anxious about the impact of Aaron's depression and, of course, his recovery and well-being. Suzy wants information and answers; Aaron just wants to be okay and be left alone for the time being.

Let's take a look at her options more closely:

She can:

1 Stop, try to drop the subject, and possibly feel angry that he is withholding and not forthcoming with information and emotions. She might feel shut out and hurt. She might pout and mirror his withdrawal by shutting down herself.
2 Pursue her line of questioning because this is important information, and if he is not complying with this treatment or if things aren't really going as well as he's saying, she should know about it. She can override his temptation to retreat and take the lead by insisting that he be specific about the appointment.

Or, she can:

1 Read his cues and recognize that this is how he is choosing to deal with his current discomfort. She may be aware that he is trying to cope with the shame he feels regarding his illness and prefers not to talk about it, at least not right now. She can try to respect that and sit beside him quietly, putting her hand on his leg or his arm, letting him know that she understands. She can hope to reopen the conversation later and she can say that to him.
2 She can make a relationship-enhancing attribution by telling herself *he must be upset about his appointment or about how he is feeling. We can talk about this later.*
3 She can articulate his discomfort as well as her own. She can help him identify that this is hard for him and she can let him know it's hard for her, too. She can model how talking about painful topics in a non-threatening, supportive way can be a safe experience. She can pave the way for him to join in, even if he is not ready to do so.

Withdrawal can feel like a comfortable option for some, particularly men, when things start to feel heated. In Gottman's approach to problem-solving strategies, his team concluded that the husband's actions—specifically, a tendency to withdraw from an argument—was most predictive of divorce (Gottman & Silver, 1999). A take home message for women is to learn how to first, identify this retreat into his cave. Second, gently enter it and share the space. Finally, find the best time, words, touch, and tone, to help him out.

Depression and recovery place a couple in an irrepressible emotional whirlwind. This is absolute and unavoidable. It can look something like this:

> *I'm trying to protect you, you're trying to protect me. I'm worried about you, you're worried about me. I'm angry, you're angry. I don't like this, you don't like this. I love you, you love me. We're both exhausted.*

If you consider that the goal of each interaction is to take care of *your partner's need*, you will increase the likelihood that your own needs will be met more sufficiently. Taking care of your partner's needs, in this context, means tolerating whatever emotional state may be predominant at the time. This doesn't mean you should surrender to negative emotions, of course not. It does mean you should be aware that your emotional response to any big emotion your partner is experiencing could potentiate it and make it worse.

The two big emotions that invade the marriage during this time of recovery from postpartum depression are shame and fear. These are the predominant components of the emotional residue we discussed earlier. Regardless of whether the depression hit the husband or the wife, the guilt and shame attached to the illness and the underlying fear and anxiety belong to both partners now. Believe it or not, one of the most effective ways to cut through some of the dialogue gridlock is to recognize these big emotions and name them for your partner.

> *I know this feels terrible. I imagine there are times you feel ashamed, but this is about you and me, not what other people think. It's about you feeling better and us getting stronger.*

Or,

> *I know you are scared. I can see how bad this feels for you. We are doing all the right things and we are on the right track and you won't always feel this way.*

Authors Love and Stosny (2007) explain how the unconscious fear-shame dynamic, as mentioned in Chapter 3, may well be the trigger for many or most marital disputes. They point out that the anxiety in one activates a shame-avoidant behavior, such as withdrawal or aggression, in the other, and vice versa. In a nutshell, they say that many issues of chronic disconnect are a result of misunderstanding how the other is experiencing anxiety or shame. They note, for example, that a woman's experience of discontent in the relationship makes her feel anxious, isolated, and afraid. She often responds to this by wanting to talk about it in order to reconnect. Her partner, on the other hand, may not want to talk about the relationship due to underlying feelings that he has failed in some way. They sum up this dynamic in this way: His shame is too great to allow him to understand her fear, and her fear keeps her from seeing his shame.

The unconscious fear-shame dynamic may also explain many problem areas for couples. For example, (a) Money: She is afraid they won't have enough money. He feels ashamed that he is an inadequate provider and responds by wanting more control or; (b) Sex: She may have anxiety about having sex, which inflames his dread of failure. You can see how each individual response could stimulate the area of vulnerability in the partner and lead to a cycle of misunderstandings. Here, again, we see the merit of helping each other, not just yourself, through this gridlock by identifying the issues, helping each other address the primary motivation for the discussion, and making elationship-enhancing attributions for your partner's behavior, rather than focus on the wrong thing.

Identifying the shame and the fear will help release your partner from profound and isolating emotions. This is true long after the depression subsides and well into treatment. People are inclined to carry the burden of big emotions along with them for extended periods of time. When this happens, remnants of shame and fear are likely to sneak into conversations when you least expect them! As this emotional residue infiltrates the air, communication will be compromised. Identify the big emotions. Accept that they are there. Tolerate them in your relationship for the time being. Learn how to navigate them with unconditional support.

Forgiveness

In Chapter 8, the Token of Compromise, we discussed the interference from negative mind-sets that potentially pull us away from our partner. Old emotions, unmet expectations, negative appraisals of past interactions are inclined to polarize a relationship. Learning to let go is essential and not as intimidating as it might seem at first.

Earlier in this chapter we saw how quickly the conversation collapsed from a sore throat to "You never take care of me!" Triggers from previous areas of pain and vulnerability are all over the place. Most often, couples are unaware that they are holding on to unconstructive feelings and resentments that continue to simmer well beyond the depression and recovery period.

Are you holding on to specific negative feelings and feel it is important for some reason that you continue to do so?

Do you realize by holding on you are making yourself feel worse?

Forgiveness is a complex construct without good definitions in the literature. It is a word that many people recoil from when they are in the throes of strong emotions. Most therapists know this to be true if they prematurely propose forgiveness as an ultimate objective and are met with immediate rejection.

Forgive him for totally abandoning me?
Forgive her for blaming me when I couldn't work?

Forgive him for yelling at me when I was sick?
Forgive her for treating me like a child when I was most vulnerable?

It is a well-known fact that people tend to hurt the ones they love. Actually, the assumption that humans are social animals who tend to be aggressive and hurt each other is addressed by Fincham and Beach (2001) in much of their extensive work on forgiveness. Couples in long-term relationships and marriages are constantly being challenged to take responsibility for whatever impulse there is to hurt each other with verbal or implicit attacks. Hopefully, most of the time, you try to communicate your disappointments with as much kindness as possible. Couples who are less sophisticated in their communication skills may be less able to do this and more apt to either display aggression or avoid the conflict all together.

Let's take a closer look at the concept of forgiveness and what it really means. Consider these points outlined by Fincham and Beach:

1 Forgiveness is intentional.
2 Forgiveness is unconditional.
3 Forgiveness is evident in your emotions, your thought process and your behavior.
4 Forgiveness is a process.
5 Forgiveness has an end-point.

In addition, forgiveness involves "conquering negative feelings and acting with good-will toward someone who has done us harm. It is this process, set in motion by a decision to forgive, that makes statements like 'I'm trying to forgive you' meaningful" (Fincham, 2004, p. 93). This notion of it being a process is important. While some things might *feel unforgivable* at any given moment, it is probably that it will not always feel that way. Moreover, if forgiveness is a process that means your intent to forgive is worth a great deal on its own and is likely to move you in the desired direction.

When you hang on to painful emotions, you teach your brain to believe all the subsequent impressions and interpretations related to it. Imagine that you were traumatized by that initial experience that made you feel so bad, which then imprinted that negative incident into your brain so that every time you think about it, it makes you feel terrible all over again.

For example,

Hallie told Andrew: "I will never forget that you screamed at me when I was two weeks postpartum because I didn't want your mother to come over. You told me to get over it and she had a right to see the baby! You knew I wasn't feeling good!"

Shelby told Matt: "Remember when I was crying every day and you never came and asked me what was wrong? You knew I was crying and you stayed in the other room. I know it's because you don't know what to do, but it feels like you don't care, even now."

Aaron told Suzy: "I used to hate it when you would badger me with questions to see how I was feeling. I just wanted to get out of my own head for a minute, but you would never let me."

It is as if the depression engraves these incidents into the recovery process and even as symptoms resolve old responses rest just beneath the surface. Forgiveness is the mechanism which enables your mind, body, and soul to release these memories and make room for more positive experiences and emotions.

The importance of forgiveness in marriage is supported by the finding that in couples married for twenty years or longer, partners rate the capacity to forgive as one of the most important factors contributing to marital durability, commitment, and satisfaction (Fennel, 1993). Although the thought of forgiving may feel daunting, remember that baby steps are a huge accomplishment in the right direction.

Observe how easily interactions disintegrate when you do not let each other off for intermittent misconduct:

"I'm trying to talk and you keep interrupting me."

You can respond with defensiveness, "Well, how can I talk if you won't stop blabbing! I can't get a word in edgewise."

Or,

You can respond with a sincere acknowledgement, "Sorry," and let the conversation continue.

Likewise:

"Why are your clothes all over the place?"

You can respond with defensiveness, "Because there is nowhere to put anything in this goddamn house, it's so small and I hate it and I cannot find anything I need!"

Or,

You can respond with a genuine personal responsibility and a smile, "Oops, I know, I'm a slob. Always have been."

How many times has your partner accused you of speaking out of turn when you didn't think you did? Or said you were being rude or hurtful when you didn't think you were? Or said you acted in a way that you didn't think you did? Remember not to get lost in the content and instead, pay attention to the process. What is happening? How is your partner feeling? How can you best intervene to de-escalate the situation rather than make it worse? Can you say you are sorry, even if you are not sure you did anything wrong?

Saying you're sorry does not mean you actually did what your partner thinks you did. In the example above, you might not have been interrupting during the conversation but your partner was anxious to speak and wanted more attention than you were giving so when you said anything at all, it felt intrusive. Saying you're sorry sometimes means you are sorry that your partner is feeling that way. In other words, you may not be sorry for what you said or did, but you may certainly be sorry that it hurt your partner's feelings since that is not at all what you intended.

We saw earlier in this chapter that when people believe that they are being criticized, they are less likely to change. When your concerns are expressed with love and support instead of contempt or belittling, you are more likely to be effective in communicating your needs and desires. Learning to tolerate the small and the big things in marriage is much like learning to live with a bum knee, or any chronic pain. If you understand that there will always be parts of the relationship that don't feel good, you will get better at picking your battles and developing strategies to cope with the things you don't like.

Why Forgive When You Can't Forget?

Is there something your partner did or said during the recent depression and recovery period that you are having a hard time forgiving?

Think about the pain that comes with holding on to whatever it is that you cannot forgive right now. Think about the negative energy it inflames and the toll it takes on your peace of mind. The act of forgiveness actually serves to transform that negative energy into positive feelings and has been shown to improve the way people feel about themselves and about their relationships (Kachadourian, Fincham, & Davila, 2005). Simply put, you'll feel better if you can address any negative attitude you have toward your partner about past transgressions especially any that relate to feeling misunderstood or mistreated while depression overshadowed your relationship.

Mulling it over and over in your mind is likely to further entrench the existing negativity.

Rumination, when you go over something in your mind repeatedly, can contribute to the maintenance of depression. This response style actually makes you to focus how bad you feel. In fact, it has been shown that rumination intensifies distress and increases negative thinking (Moberly & Watkins, 2008). It is believed that ruminating about what your partner did or said that you find blameworthy is likely to create a chronic state of ambivalence in your relationship. We have discussed the potential for damage to the relationship if ambivalence is left unattended. Regarding forgiveness, it appears that ambivalent individuals who ruminate about the misbehavior of a partner are least likely to ultimately forgive (Kachadourian et al., 2005). It's almost as if the ambivalence and rumination get caught in a vicious cycle, one reinforcing the other.

In other words, as pointed out earlier, attitude matters. Both you and your partner need to think about how you both feel about things that were said or not said, done or not done, throughout the depressed state. You need to believe in the possibility that you will both feel better if you learn how to release yourselves from this pain. It has been said that an attitude of benevolence toward the offending partner is what enables us to forgive. This is not achieved by simply avoiding the issue or overcoming the hurt. Rather, it involves approaching your partner and acknowledging the behavior. In this way, forgiveness is a liberating and honorable choice, motivated by self-respect and a desire to free oneself (Holmgren, 1993).

Fred Luskin, another pioneer in the work on forgiveness, teaches us that the practice of forgiveness can actually reduce anger, hurt, depression, and stress. It can also lead to feelings of hope, compassion, love, and greater self-confidence. This can only take place, however, after sufficient grief work has taken place. In order to grieve, people must be clear about their feelings and the action they feel has offended them (Luskin, 2002). Keep in mind that forgiveness does not necessarily imply reconciliation, justice, or condoning the wrongdoing. It means that you change the story, from one of feeling like a victim to feeling like the hero by deciding to take the steps necessary to feel back in control of your life.

Do not sit alone with your bad feelings. Do not allow your partner to sit alone with bad feelings. Even if, or especially when, you find you cannot let go of pain, avoidance behaviors will quickly derail your efforts here. In the interest of constructive and affectionate problem solving, it will not be helpful if you insist you are justified in feeling this way and that your anger or resentment or unwillingness to forgive is likely to erode of all good will between the two of you. This is, perhaps, that hardest part. It feels tempting to stay in the grief when you feel you have been wronged. The challenge, as Luskin points out, is to find the strength to find the peace you seek. You will find that letting go and trying to forgive plays an important role in both your physical health and psychological well-being. In study after study, results show that those who are forgiving tend to have lower stress levels and better relationships (Fincham, 2003). There is also evidence that forgiveness is associated with fewer health problems in general and a lower incidence of depression, heart disease, stroke, and high blood pressure (Lawler et al., 2005). Why? Because refusing to forgive is toxic for your body and increases your susceptibility to stress and disease.

Remember that actions on behalf of forgiveness engage behaviors that move *toward* the wrong-doer, rather than avoidance. In other words, in order to begin to forgive, you need to fundamentally *care* (about your partner, what he or she did, what the transgression was, how it feels now, and how you hope to feel once you move past this) and you need to deal directly with whatever the wrong-doing was. There is great power that can be derived from this process of pain and ultimate forgiveness. Forgiveness does not mean what the other person did or said is okay. It does not minimize how much pain was inflicted or how much hurt you have suffered. It means you have made a decision not to let that pain make you feel bad anymore by truly letting go of it. It means you are no longer going to make yourself feel sick or bitter or sad over what was done or said. Although it does not excuse what was done, you are now in a better position to move forward from the pain. There is great personal freedom in taking ownership of how we respond to how others treat us or make us feel.

Forgiveness is only possible within the context of tolerance. Lessons in tolerance will make you a more loving person. Though this has enormous social, cultural, and religious implications, its relevance here is most striking. Without tolerance for the little displeasures as well as some unavoidable indiscretions, relationships remain stuck. Learning to coexist without comment, without attitude, and without judgment at any given moment is a challenge, indeed. However, like all of the Tokens, it is something that can develop with practice and determination.

Tokens Tools of TOLERANCE

1 **Disregard bad habits.** *Omg, he is so annoying. I can't stand to be in the same room with him sometimes.* Yes, well, that happens. In all marriages. The truth is we all have maddening habits or foolish inclinations, or routines that get on each other's nerves. To be honest, most of these things go fairly unnoticed until a bad mood, sleepless night, or some other vulnerability settles in. Then, all bets are off and the slightest pick of the finger, or clearing of the throat, or more infuriating irritations feel like the final straw. Once perspective is recalibrated and things become more focused, you will realize that these annoyances mean little in the larger picture. Remember that just because something *feels* bad, doesn't mean it *is* bad.

Try this:
Write a list of your partner's five most annoying habits. This should be easy, right? Go ahead, write them down, in plain view, all the things that drive you nuts on a fairly regular basis. Next, pick one of the five things. Only one. Pick the one that you will no longer let annoy you. For two days. Forty-eight hours. Let it go. Tell yourself whatever you have to, to make this easier for you. For instance, *So what if he bites his nails? It helps him relax. I don't have to watch. I can leave the room. It's okay if he bites his nails. I might prefer that he doesn't, but I don't have to let it drive me crazy. This is his problem, not mine.*

2 **Accept mediocrity.** Everything is not going to be the way you want it. Whether we are talking about the laundry or your marriage, for now, it's okay that things are just what they are. You can work toward high aspirations, but in the meantime, lower your expectations just enough to settle into the current state. When you both can resist looking back to where you've been and forward to where you want to be, you will be able to focus on each other.

Without a doubt, we live in a culture dominated by goals of perfection and supreme excellence in most things that we do. It's exhausting just to think about the demands we place on ourselves! In your marriage, it will feel better if you release yourself from those impossible standards and cozy up to the way things are right now.

Try this:
Often we feel burdened by our own internal pressures of how we think thing should be. *Should* is a nasty word when you are working on feeling better. Make a list of three "should" statements that reflect pressures you currently feel.
For example:
- I *should* have lost all my baby weight by now.
- My partner *should* remember to do the chores without being asked.
- I *should* get everything done in the house before I go to bed.

Next, make a list of corrective statements, or ones that would feel more restorative using the CBT 101 tools that you learned in Chapter 5.
- It's okay that I haven't lost all my baby weight. I've been busy and I've been tired and I'm working hard to make things feel right in my family. I will focus on staying healthy and strong.
- It's all right for me to remind my partner to do a specific chore or, I can choose to take care of it by just doing it myself. I'm sure it all evens out in the end.
- It's not as important that I get everything done as it is to get a good night's rest. Maybe I need to reprioritize my list to make sure I get to bed at a decent hour.

Now, you make your list.

3 **Be patient in the presence of big emotions.** In this chapter we looked at shame and fear as two of the most prominent emotions that can saturate the foundation of recovery from depression. There are many other emotions that might be central to your personal experience. Try not to let the intensity of the emotions take precedence over your intention to stay focused on what needs to be said or done. Use caution and compassion when attempting to diffuse these emotions.

Try this:
Sometimes our inability to stay present and patient is compromised when emotions run high. Try to have an open mind. Remember that strong emotions are not bad for your relationship. Fighting is not bad for your relationship. What *is* bad for your relationship is withdrawal, avoidance,

criticizing and blaming. Having an open mind means you are trying to increase your tolerance for the random appearance of strong emotions. Increase your resilience by:

- Clear your mind. Write down things you are worried about and put it away. This enables you to de-clutter your head and stay focused on what you need to do at the moment.
- If you hear or feel something that makes you uncomfortable, take a deep breath and name that feeling to your partner. Ask yourself if something is scaring you and try to reflect on why this is so upsetting. Try to identify the meaning associated with your strong emotional response.
- To improve your ability to stay present when emotions are high, you need to trust in your relationship. If you do not feel like this is something you can do, please seek help from a professional who can help you reconnect on this fundamental level.

4. **Pause.** Impulsivity is not always your friend. Unless you are stealing your partner from work to meet at a favorite park with a picnic lunch during the middle of a work day, being impetuous in your responses to a tense situation can rapidly escalate the emotional climate. Remember you are learning how to accept the presence of strong emotions. Try not to take it personally. Stop. Breathe. Wait. Proceed carefully.

Try this:
- Devise a plan of action and have a back-up. Make a list of people you can call or things you can do if your comfort level plummets. I am not talking about a volatile or violent situation. I am talking about you feeling uneasy because your partner is experiencing an emotion that is hard for you to bear because it hurts you both so much. Ideally, the two of you should stay plug in and stay there. If this is not possible, let your partner know how you are feeling and take a break.
- Keep an ongoing list of things that you like to do; things that make you feel good; things that are creative or inspiring, things that help you feel more relaxed. When you are in a relaxed state, your capacity for tolerance increases. Everyone knows how hard it is to put up with sensory overload, such as, noises, bright lights, loud music, whining, when feeling agitated.

5. **Be forgiving if you cannot yet forgive.** In our discussion of forgiveness, we touched on how complicated it can feel when painful emotions impede the course you two are taking. While the concept of forgiveness can feel overwhelming in the face of powerful resistance, do not forget that you can still make the choice to act in a forgiving manner. Being sympathetic

to each other's discomfort or difficulty without judgment will help you solve the problems that are solvable. Do your best to release yourself and your partner from the strain of constant scrutiny.

Try this:
- Chances are, you and your spouse are both planning on living a lifetime together, which means you will be forgiving each other pretty much on a regular basis.
- Make a pledge to yourself—say it aloud or write in down because both of these efforts will help ingrain it in your mind—to try to forgive your partner, even before he or she does something that hurts you. Remember that at the core of forgiveness is your willingness and readiness to liberate *yourself*. Assume an attitude of compassion and forgiveness, even when there is nothing particular to forgive.
- Make a list of the things you would like to be more forgiving of, regarding your partner. Have your partner do the same. Find a good time to discuss your lists and explore what you think is getting in the way of both of you following through with this list.
- Now make a list of anything that you would like to be forgiven for, even small things will help you both feel better.

13

TOKEN OF LOYALTY

*I'd marry you all over again
if I knew you weren't going to annoy the living shit out of me.*

—Someecards.com

We live in a busy world. People and relationships are often pulled in a hundred directions, daily calendars are hectic, and patience is thin. For many, priorities at work and at home often intertwine in ways that are counterproductive, despite one's best efforts to make everything fall into place neatly. Everyone feels over-scheduled at times, and often there doesn't feel like there is enough time in the day to do what needs to be done. Our to-do lists roll over into tomorrow, increasing the burden. Some believe they are running too fast, spinning too hard, tweeting too much, texting too many, and simply, exhausting themselves, leaving little time for themselves or their marriage.

Sound like you?

Marriage, of course, is the utmost platform for the expression of loyalty, the final Token. Loyalty has many meanings, within many contexts, but it is most often linked with commitment to a relationship. When young couples dream of a "happily ever after" life together, their fantasy rarely includes visions of sleep deprivation, mood disturbances, and intermittent arguments that can feel so bad, it can make them wonder why they ever married this person in the first place. This is precisely when the Token of Loyalty comes into play. Loyalty is the duty you feel to remain connected despite moments or hours or days when it feels tempting to disengage.

The day-to-day activities that may feel routine at the time, are the shared experiences and memories that build on each other and strengthen the marital connection. The sense of loyalty is what ultimately binds you together; it's what keeps you there even when it's hard, it's what makes it possible to prioritize when things get overwhelming, it's why it feels so bad when your heart breaks from misunderstandings, and why it feels so right, when you are both in sync.

This sense of responsibility to the marriage underscores every other Token. Although presented as the final Token, as the ultimate objective for your work here, the virtue of loyalty is what has given you the desire to do this work in the first place. This continuous loop puts the Token of Loyalty in position to act as champion on behalf of all the other Tokens. It is the blanket that can hold all the other Tokens in place.

Read each statement and check the ones you feel are true for you. Put a circle around the boxes which reflect those you need to work on.

Token of Loyalty Inventory

- ☐ I know, I hope, I intend, and I believe that my partner and I will remain together and happy.
- ☐ Any areas of distrust in our relationship feel surmountable.
- ☐ The integrity of our marriage is solid and I make my partner a priority.
- ☐ I try hard to be fair and make my spouse feel cared for.
- ☐ I feel comfortable talking about what our relationship means to me with my partner.

Any box with a circle around it means you should be alert to this when working together, especially in conflict. Check the Token Tools at the end of this chapter for specific tips on strengthening loyalty.

The Circle of Affection

When sitting with couples, I often draw a diagram so they can visualize this concept of being overwhelmed, which is both obvious and neglected by the couple. On a piece of paper, I draw two circles in the middle, labeling each with their names. Using the entire page, I draw circles in the space surrounding their two spots, labeling each with people, events, obligations, pressures on the couple, etc., anything and everything that impacts their lives, trying to make it as personal to their own experience as possible. Next, I draw a circle around the "couple."

It ends up looking something like Figure 13.1.

I say: *Look at all of these pressures coming at you from all sides. For the most part, they are constant and they are persistent. We all have them, they are part of life. For a moment, let's move all of these circles over to the side. Let's pretend they aren't there. Let's just look at this blue circle, the one with the two of you inside.* I emphasize the circle by repeatedly tracing the outline while they observe.

I wait.

How does it feel in there? I ask.

The responses are interesting:

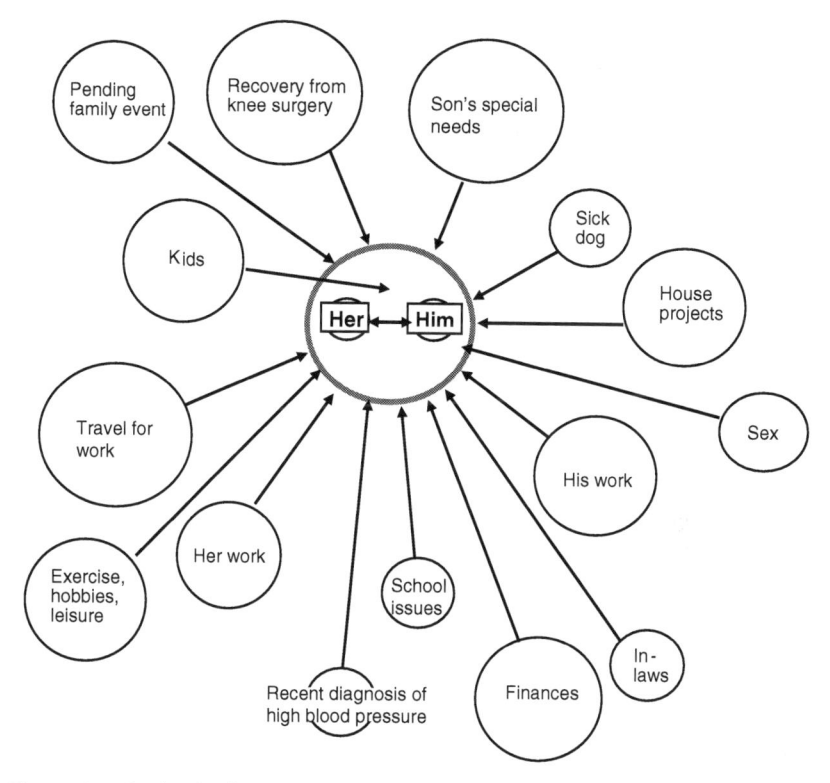

Figure 13.1 Circle of Affection

    Total silence. Some facial expression with raised eyebrows and lip biting.
I presume they are trying to understand the question being asked.
Or,
    Awkward giggling, glancing back and forth to each other, waiting for the other one to respond.
I presume they understand the question but are tentative about how they actually feel or how thy think the other will feel about how they feel if they say it aloud.
Or,
    Request for clarification. "What do you mean, how does it feel?"
I presume they understand the question, but haven't spent much time/energy focusing on the marriage as a separate entity from all the pressures from the outside. They can barely fathom the existence of themselves alone and therefore cannot formulate a response. They have rarely considered themselves as a circle in and of itself, as opposed to how they relate to the other external circles.
    They respond with reference to external circles. "We would be fine if such-and-such wasn't happening."

Or, "She has been upset, because...."
They do not understand the question.
Or,
They oversimplify. "We're fine."
I presume they understand the question but are unable or unwilling to elaborate.
Or,
They respond with authentic reference to emotions they are currently experiencing. "We're okay. But I miss him. There's no time just for us, anymore."
They understand the question.

The circle of affection in this illustration is the space that the two of you occupy with zero distractions, either from the outside or the inside. It is a sacred symbolic space that you can return to when you feel overwhelmed or long to reconnect. It is a space that can partially sustain itself with the presence of pure intentions and the absence of external circles. In order for this state to maintain, both partners must put the Token of Loyalty into practice.

Dedication to Each Other and the Marriage

When you think about the word *loyalty*, it probably conjures up a host of synonyms that we all grew up striving for in our long-term relationships. Words like devotion, faithfulness, reliability, dedication, fidelity, commitment, and trustworthiness; all components of a healthy relationship, to be sure. Expanding on this definition is the unspoken pledge you make to each other to take care of the relationship and cherish each other.

According to the authors of the book, *Why Loyalty Matters,* couples who value loyalty to their spouse, family, and friends are more satisfied with their lives than those who do not value loyalty (Keiningham & Aksoy, 2009). It seems that many couples, in pursuit of happiness, neglect the relationship itself, hoping that by acquiring things or experiencing events or looking good, they will find what they are looking for. Keiningham and Aksoy state, "The most important factor that separates happy people from unhappy people is our relationships with others" (p. 21), which, of course, is the foundation of this book. Loyalty translates into happiness. People are happier at home and at work when they feel a commitment to the relationship.

If loyalty is one of the hallmarks of a healthy relationship, this last Token represents a final test, of sorts, of the bond between two partners during difficult times. When more marriages are likely to end in divorce than not, the capacity to emerge from the challenge of depression with something greater, something stronger is a goal to work toward if it is not something you feel at the moment.

With introspection there can be great insight and rediscovery that may lead to you a sweet spot in your marriage. For example, my husband and I have a yearly ritual, since we were engaged on Valentine's Day, to write a poem, or prose, or letter, or some written tribute to our marriage and how we feel about each other. It isn't easy to do, especially when the good stuff is not rising to the surface, but it's an exercise of loyalty and one that has proven to be valuable to us over the years. Create your own tradition. At the risk of sounding cliché, I truly do believe that taking responsibility by checking in on the ongoing emotional state of one's marriage is precisely what helps it endure.

Remember Gottman's (2007) concept of turning toward each other from Chapter 2? He says that we have a choice, we can turn toward or we can turn away from our partner. Even when we are tired, or sad, or angry, or scared. For example, imagine you are talking on the phone to an old friend from college and having fun reminiscing about past adventures. In walks your partner, visibly tired and upset. You put your friend on hold and ask if your partner is okay. The response is, "No, not really." At that moment you have a choice. You can ignore or postpone any attention to your spouse's mood and return to your friend (turning away). Or, you can wind things up with your friend until another time and see what's up with your partner (turning inward).

Gottman says this is how couples build trust; by choosing to be there for each other when the need arises. If you resist turning inward and choose to turn outward, you might find that you begin to acknowledge that alternatives to this relationship exist. Once you allow yourself to think things like—*I'm not in the mood for this again; who needs this bullshit; why do I stay in this relationship; I can do better than this; if I were with someone else I wouldn't have to feel this way*—you initiate a course of non-committing behaviors and thoughts.

In order to stay focused on and loyal to your relationship, turning inward needs to be the default response. If it doesn't feel that way to you now, practice by making a mental list of the benefits of your relationship and see if they outweigh the costs. If you feel as though you are losing more than you are gaining, you are moving in the opposite direction. If the benefits prevail, then continue to turn toward your partner.

Do it now. Think about the things that brought you two together in the first place. Do a rapid re-assessment of what attracted you to your partner. Think about how that feels. Find a way to express it to your partner. Speak it, write it, text it, Skype it, make it rhyme, make it a game, make it funny, make it serious, make it real. Make a date, make a phone call, reach out. Do it with your eyes closed, your eyes open, your arms around each other, or across state lines. You can be eating dinner, or naked in bed. You can sing it, whisper it, or shout it from the roof top. The only criteria are that you are alone and that you mean what you say.

An Attitude of Gratitude

In a groundbreaking study, researchers were able to determine the effect of gratitude on mental health over time, and found that those assigned to journal about the things they were grateful for, showed an improvement in mood, coping behaviors, and physical health symptoms compared to those who wrote about daily hassles or more routine life events. The researchers instructed participants to engage in self-guided exercises involving "counting their blessings" either on a weekly basis for 10 weeks or on a daily basis for 2 or 3 weeks. Those in the gratitude group reported higher positive affect and physical well-being, such as higher levels of alertness, enthusiasm, determination, and energy, than those in the control group. In addition, those in the gratitude group experienced less depression and stress, were more likely to help others, exercised more regularly, and made greater progress toward achieving personal goals (Emmons & McCullough, 2003).

This study generated tremendous interest in the effect of gratitude on mental health. Specifically, gratitude seems to inspire people to reframe otherwise negative experiences as potentially positive experiences. This reframing leads to fewer depressive symptoms. Presumably, the expression of gratitude is not likely to coexist with negative emotions, and therefore may reduce feelings of envy, bitterness, anger, or greed (McCullough, Emmons, & Tsang, 2002). Certainly, depressive symptoms can indeed exist side-by-side with positive emotions, but the enormity of the depressive symptoms is likely to be weakened by the presence of more positive emotions (Lambert, Fincham, Gwinn, & Ajayi, 2011).

It follows, then that incorporating gratitude into your life and relationship has huge benefits; from feeling better emotionally and physically, to potentially protecting you from depressive symptoms. Cultivating gratitude means you take the time and make the effort to appreciate the things in your life for which you are thankful. The big things. The small things. The relationships, the events, and opportunities that should not be taken for granted. It is easy to overlook the good things in your life. Try not to.

Being grateful for the joy that is present in your life is good for you. And good for your marriage.

"Tend and Befriend"

While doing research for this book, I came across a study that thoroughly intrigued me. Shelley Taylor of UCLA proposed an alternative theory to the well-known "fight-or-flight" response to stress. The initial groundwork for understanding the physiology of mind–body interactions was pioneered back in the 1930s and characterized as fight-or-flight, referring to the survival-based and physiological response to threat. Basically, when faced with danger, many species either lash out, or run away.

I was surprised to discover that the overwhelming research pertaining to the fight-or-flight response has been conducted on males, particularly, male rats. The justification for this bias toward male subjects was due to the cyclical variation in neuroendocrine responses in women's reproductive cycles, which might confound the results. The fight-or-flight response itself might also be directly impacted by female cycling, thus, evidence regarding a fight-or-flight response in females has been inconsistent (Taylor et al., 2000). Taylor proposes something completely different from the fight-or-flight response. She asks, "But what if the equivocal nature of the female data is not due solely to neuroendocrine variation, but also to the fact that the female stress response is not exclusively, nor even predominantly, fight-or-flight?" (Taylor et al., 2000, p. 412).

Taylor claims that human female responses to stress have evolved to maximize the survival of self and offspring through caretaking responses and affiliating with social groups for support. She calls this pattern, "tend and befriend" and states that in times of stress, women don't necessarily go into fight-or-flight mode. Rather, their instinctive response is to take care of their young (tend) seek the comfort of others, particularly other women (befriend).

If we generalize this theory and incorporate it into our belief that women tend to take on greater responsibility than men for repairing the marital connection, it has interesting implications. What this means is that there may be a biological basis for a woman's response to hunker down and deal with marital stress, while a man's instinct is to fight or flee (withdraw).

Evolution aside, if we apply the tend and befriend pattern of behavior to the marriage itself, it makes sense that the woman's response to a perceived stress or disconnect is to initially tend to the marriage and turn to the marital relationship itself for relief, as well as to others outside the marriage for additional support. Affiliation feels better to most women than does isolation. Tending to the marriage and befriending your partner is a wonderful way to frame the work you are doing here. After all, a strong friendship is at the heart of every good marriage and loyalty to that friendship is the bond that holds it all together.

Mindfully Married

Even in good, strong marriages, most partners tend to be locked into their own fixed points of view. Sometimes, without knowing it, you might resort to emotional and habitual patterns and presume you are behaving in the best interest of your relationship. Nonetheless, your relationship will thrive when you step out of your routine (which may or may not be working for you) and open your heart to the possibility that the way you have been doing things may not have always served you best.

Mindfulness is a buzz word that gets a great deal of attention these days. This is a good thing—the general principles of mindfulness seem to be associated with substantial feelings of well-being. For our purposes, being mindful within your marriage refers to your conscious awareness of how things impact both of you, thereby increasing your feelings of control and connection. When mindful, emotional reactivity is likely to decrease and problem-solving capabilities are enhanced.

In *Dropping the Baby and Other Scary Thoughts* (Kleiman & Wenzel, 2010), we discussed the question of whether or not people can change the way they think and feel. We believe they can. Here are some techniques and exercises to help you do so.

- **Controlled breathing.** It's hard to breathe comfortably when distress levels are high. This can set off a cycle of anxiety, rapid breathing, more anxiety, panic-driven thoughts or responses. Learning to breathe in a controlled manner can help you feel more in control of a situation. Controlled breathing comes from your abdomen, not your chest, and is referred to as "belly breathing" (Kabat-Zinn, 1990). Put one hand on your chest and the other on your belly. Inhale as you take a deep breath from your abdomen. As you inhale you should feel your belly expand. The hand on your chest should not move. After a brief pause, slowly exhale, keeping your focus on your breathing. Your belly should go back down as you exhale. Your complete attention should remain on your each breath. It is suggested that you make the time to do this for 15 minutes each day, whether or not you feel like it. In time, your breathing can actually be used as a tool to relieve anxiety.
- **Mindfulness meditation.** Meditation has been practiced for centuries and offers great relief for anxious states. Kabat-Zinn defines mindfulness as the "awareness that emerges through paying attention on purpose, in the present moment, and nonjudgmentally to the unfolding of experience moment by moment" (2003, p. 145). In other words, mindfulness requires that you remain in the present moment, no judging, no regrets about the past or worries about the future, with focused attention.

    Sit comfortably with your eyes closed, with your back upright. Do your best to relax the muscles of your body and take note of your bodily sensations and the sounds around you. Try to notice them without judgment. Let your mind settle into the rhythm of breathing as noted above. Stay focused on your breathing. When your mind wanders, gently redirect your attention to your breathing. Just notice it, but do not think about it. The goal is to try to be aware of the sensations your body is experiencing while you quiet the thinking part of the experience. Stay with this process for at least 10 minutes. If this feels too long or impossible, try not to be discouraged. Mindfulness is a skill that takes time to develop, but some of the techniques can become second nature to you in time. After some practice, you will notice that you can use it during times of stress to help you slow down and breathe for efficiently. Research shows that mindfulness meditation can actually create structural changes in the brain which can help you experience less depression and anxiety and more joy (Hölzelab et al., 2011).

The art of being mindful is more than practicing mindfulness techniques. It is also a state of mind. Taking things for granted is, in a way, the opposite of being mindful. When we take things for granted, we forget to notice their value. Mindfulness refers to the practice of paying attention with intent and without judgment. It is simply a way to describe the art of noticing things we normally don't notice. It is a way of deciding or choosing what will be the focus our attention, rather than letting our random, distracting thoughts take over.

If we borrow from the general concepts of mindfulness training and apply it to the Token of loyalty, the emphasis is on the following three principles.

1. **Be present in your marriage**
   If you're not careful, you might reject this directive. People say they are too busy, too preoccupied, too distracted to be mindful. How ridiculous does that sound? The suggestion to increase our ability to pay attention to the little things and appreciate the *now* rather than ruminate about the past or fret about the future is a provocative one. The impulse to remain true to our preoccupied musings is a strong one, and it is hard work to stay focused on the present moment. Take a minute. Take a breath.

"Everyone needs a thing," one of my clients taught me "Mine is the alarm on my cell phone. I have it set to remind me to breathe," he chuckles as he hears how difficult something so easy can be. Another client told me the she attached a clear sticker on the upper corner of her car windshield with the word "gratitude," reminding her every time her eye glanced in that direction, to stop and be grateful.

If you are familiar with my previous books, you know that the bracelet I give to postpartum women is a "thing" to help guide busy brains back toward the heart of their healing. People use alerts on their cell phones, rubber bands on their wrists, and, of course, there are Apps for just this purpose, literally, to remind you to be present. Whatever approach works best for you, learn to pay attention. Not to the noise in your head. Not to the thoughts that spin and snowball out of control. Not to the countless events, feelings or circumstances that may call into question your loyalty to the marriage. Stop the world around you and take notice of each other. Be mindful of your marriage. Stay there with each other, if only for a moment. Baby steps will take you in the right direction. Savor the moment.

2. **Trust the process**
   The work you have done here is virtually renewing your vows. By taking this on, you have made the commitment to turn your attention back to your marriage after probably months of distraction, between the baby

and the depression. There is nothing mysterious here. Things will get better because you are doing this. Don't peer too far ahead. Don't wonder if old pain will return to haunt you. Stay loyal to each other and the belief that good things will continue to unfold. One of the most important precepts of mindfulness teachings is learning how to simply, take notice. To resist the temptation to judge, or worry, or think. Just notice. Experience. Be. Trust the course of your work here and believe it will make a difference. Quieting your thinking brain is hard to do without continual efforts, but the practice is worth it if you stick with it. There are a number of good books to help guide you through this. One of my favorites is *Full Catastrophe Living* (Kabat-Zinn, 1990).

3 **Balance**
To repeat a concept we introduced in the first chapter, balance is key. Below are just a few examples of how this manifests as a component of loyalty and keeping the bigger picture in mind.
- Learning to accept what is rather than wish for what you can't have.
- Accepting your partner's flaws instead of feeling irritated and resentful.
- A sacrifice should not feel like a loss, it should feel like an investment.
- Learn to let the little things slide, as long as you can do that honestly and without resentment.

If you work on finding moments in which you can be present, notice the feeling, pay attention to the marriage, enjoy the clarity, and balance the good with the bad, you will find that believing in your marriage will help channel the positive forces between the two of you. When you replace your uncertainty with loving energy and acts of compassion, things can begin to fall into place. There's a plaque we have posted in our waiting room. It reads: *She believed she could ... And she did.* Believing in yourself and in your marriage carries great power. Own that power and use it wisely. Believing that things will feel better is the first step toward achieving your desired outcome.

Token Tools for LOYALTY

1 **Find the *you and me*.** We've seen how difficult it can be to unearth the two of you from the fallout of childbirth and depression. You and me. Just us.

Try this:
- Draw a circle of affection for you and your partner. Fill out the circles with all external pressures. Then, draw a circle around the two of you, as described earlier in this chapter.

- Ask your partner how it feels, just the two of you, alone together.
- Talk about some of the things that might be getting in the way. Is there anything that you can both do a better job of ignoring, or managing, or channeling in another direction?
- What do the two of you need to do now, to bring your focus back on the two of you? Make a plan and follow through with it.

2. **Spend time together.** It sounds simple and cliché but in the midst of so many distractions and obligations, couples spend less time together by default. You need to build this in, time together becomes the bridge between all the other priorities and your relationship.

Try this:
- Put your phone away. Away. Not on the kitchen counter. Not in your pocket. Away. You cannot expect to find time together if you remain more connected to your electronic devices than you are to each other. Disconnect from work and all contact with others. There can be no "us" with social media in the background.

3. **Practice mindfulness in your marriage.** Although we have discussed mindfulness in terms of a solitary experience, you can also enjoy the benefits in tandem with your partner. Have fun with it.

Try this:
- Sit outside. Listen to the sounds you hear. Try to see how many different sounds you pick up. The birds. The cars. The airplanes. The wind. The leaves falling. Remember to breathe. Slowly. In and out. In and out. Together.
- Find a time to sit alone with your partner. Practice being together without speaking. Sit together, look at each other. No talking. This is hard, and you might find yourselves giggling before long. That's okay. It's a playful and anxious reaction to the pressure of obligatory closeness. It makes everybody uneasy. Still, if you can force your way through it, sharing the space in a mindful way can promote and level of intimacy that might otherwise not be experienced.
- Have you ever just sat back and observed the flow of your marital state? Do you like the way it feels? Do you think paying attention to the nuances of your relationship will help you both feel more connected? Sit with this for a minute (or two). Think about your marriage in ways you have not thought of it before. Pay attention to the things you have not paid attention to before. Think about what you partner may want from you. See if you can make that happen.

4. **Be intentional.** Make your marriage a top priority. Some things will be out of your control, to be sure. Yet, your pledge to take care of each other and the marriage has the potential to trump everything else. Recall the earlier chapters of this book when we emphasized mutual respect. If your sole objective is to care about your partner, everything else will fall into place. It does not mean you will always agree or always feel good. It does mean that your heart is in the right place and that energy leads to better outcomes.

   An intentional marriage is one in which both of you are aware and deliberate about creating and maintaining a sense of connection over the years. Intentional couples think about their relationship on a regular basis. Intention goes beyond commitment. It needs to be acted upon.

   Try this:
   - Create a ritual. Pick a day. Pick a time. Something that you both can rely on and look forward to. Do not let excuses or distractions get in the way of making this happen. Where will you meet? What will you do? Why are you doing this?
   - Examples of affectionate rituals and traditions that work for some couples:
   - Saying "I love you" often and meaning it.
     - Meeting every Friday night without children for a glass of wine and hors d'oeuvres to end the week.
     - Buying a single rose for your partner and putting it somewhere where he or she can find it and doing this every year for a milestone day.
     - Making a cup of tea for your partner when he or she settles in for the night after the kids are in bed.
     - Making a pizza together and watching a favorite TV show in front of a fire on a weekend when kids are sleeping.
     - Having a weekly date night.

5. **Make it work.** When I was anxious about getting pregnant for the first time, my mother asked me if I wanted to be pregnant. I said, unequivocally, yes! But I was nervous. *Was this the right time? Should I wait? Was I ready?* She responded, "You'll be nervous whether you get pregnant tomorrow, or next year. So just get pregnant. You will learn to manage it and you'll be fine." She was right. We can make ourselves crazy with fretfulness when, sometimes, we just have to act *as if* it's exactly the way we want it to be. This is actually what you are doing by reading this book. You want your marriage to feel more connected, so you are going through the motions and learning tools to augment that connection. Choose to make it work. Trust your marriage.

Try this:
- Close your eyes and let your partner walk you through your house, including the steps. This is an old trust-building exercise that is harder to do than you might think.
- Exchange each other's passwords. If this causes uneasiness in either of you, have a discussion about this.
- Many people mistakenly presume that in good marriages, you can worry less about things that you say and do because, well, because it's just good. In good marriages, you must still monitor your words and your behavior.
- Sit down and have a conversation about trust and loyalty between the two of you. What does this mean to you? Are you both on the same page? Are there ways in which one of you is disappointed? Consider how your expectations of loyalty may be impacting your relationship if you are not in sync. See how you might modify some of those expectations.

14

BUMPS IN THE ROAD

That which does not kill us makes us stronger

—Friedrich Neizsche

Over and over we hear that marriage is good for us. Married couples tend to live longer, be healthier both physically and mentally, and experience less depression than unmarried people. In this book, we have introduced each Token of Affection as an approach toward a stronger and revitalized connection.

We have predominantly focused on marriages that are primed for affection and attention. Our goal has been to embrace the challenge of postpartum depression and help you reclaim the connection the two of you shared before the aftermath took its toll. Recognizing that not all marriages are in a position to focus on the positive and frankly, not all partners are in the mood to be affectionate or forgiving, it is important for us to take a look at relationships that continue to struggle.

Hurt and pain is an inevitable part of every marriage. The pain associated with love is substantial and can leave a mark that is forever embedded in the heart of any relationship. Still, we know that marital satisfaction is associated with good mental health and well-being. This is just one of many reasons why taking care of your marriage is essential.

We cannot ignore the reality that, in some instances, injuries to the marriage can make it feel broken beyond repair. The common theme that arises in both literature and in clinical offices is a pervasive sense of devaluation (Leary, Springer, Negel, Ansell, & Evans, 1998). Ranging from insensitive teasing to betrayal through infidelity, the injured party often attributes the transgression to a lack of caring for the relationship. *How can you treat me this way if you value our relationship?* Hurts can be so profound and so deep that reconciliation feels unattainable. That doesn't mean it *is* unattainable, it means it may feel that way.

In Chapter 4 we reviewed some behaviors that can disrupt your effort to reconnect. Now that you reached this point of your work, consider these three relationship dynamics that may be insidious enough to periodically cut short your progress as a couple.

Couples or partners who do not want to change. Sometimes, the status quo is good enough. There might be a number of reasons for this. Some couples feel stuck with their current interactive patterns, dysfunctional or not. Or, they might be naive regarding their level of dysfunction and believe that this is just the way it has to be. Or, they might not be willing to do the work. Long-term change requires a commitment to the process, as we've seen, and this commitment implies trial and error and the possibility of rejection or intermittent failure. This may be a risk that some people are not willing to take.

Sometimes I see this play out when couples constantly defend each other's carelessness in the relationship. Or, when one or the other makes excuses for bad behavior. Couples who engage in constant battle with each other may seek a secondary gain from these heated exchanges, such as vying for control or seeking stimulation from the clash of words. Systems that have been in place within a marriage over time, whether functional or dysfunctional, feel familiar and therefore, may be resistant to change.

Neglect. As we've seen, total disregard can kill any connection. If your marriage is not your top priority when things feel bad, it means no one will advocate for the marriage, and it's hard to get back on track. Neglecting the marriage may feel safer than neglecting each other, but in the long run, the relationship suffers from lack of attention and nourishment.

Loss of spirit. Every so often, I see a couple who comes into my office with a level of mutual hopelessness that is palpable and oppressive. The heaviness permeates the room. In general, this despair that feels ominous and irrevocable to them may be a signal to me that they have significant healing to do before they can embark on reconnection work. It does not necessarily point to irreconcilable differences, but it does necessitate careful scrutiny of the couples' experience, the extent of their emotion residue and withdrawal and motivation for change.

Caution: Detour Ahead?

In sickness and in health. For better or for worse. These are the best of times; they are the worst of times. The clichés are endless. The meanings are the same: The blessing of a loving partnership can carry the burden of deep pain. Let's take a look at specific questions and complex situations that arise as couples navigate this tender territory and determine whether Token-work is appropriate. All of the following scenarios are tremendously complicated. For our purpose, we will briefly address how each may impact the work you are doing here. Keep in mind that any constant high level of distress or worrisome behavior needs immediate attention from both of you and most likely, requires professional help.

Here is a sampling of some of the questions we often hear when we talk about doing work as a couple with our clients. We will take a closer look at each of these below:

1. What if I'm too angry?
2. My partner thinks the idea of using Tokens is silly and won't help. Can I use the Tokens by myself?
3. Our marriage felt bad long before we had a baby. What does that mean?
4. Will the Tokens work if my partner is just a jerk?
5. What if my partner cheated on me? Am I wasting my time doing this work?
6. I'm ashamed to admit it but I'm just not sure if there has been abuse in our marriage and I am not sure how to proceed.
7. I am worried that my partner and I might be drinking too much. Can this get in the way of moving forward together?
8. I continue to struggle with the loss of my baby and cannot seem to focus on my marriage.
9. How do I know if my marriage is beyond hope?
10. What if my partner hurt me so badly I am unable to forgive?
11. How do we know if we need couple's therapy?

1 What If I'm too Angry?

You might be. Or might just feel like you are. The difference is one of severity. If you really are too angry, then it would be best for you to embark on some individual therapy in order to better understand the nature of your anger and how to proceed. In the absence of this understanding your anger can easily morph into hostility and contempt, both of which are incongruent with this work.

If, on the other hand, you just *feel* too angry, that's different. Slight distinction, but important nonetheless. It is the difference between the existence of a true state of being (unbridled rage) and your perception (*I feel like I could burst!*). One is out of control. One is under control.

Anger is not incompatible with this work. Anger, as we've seen, can be a fierce marker of strong emotions, not all of which are negative. Anger can result from any number of intimate experiences that do not necessarily signal trouble. Talk about it, explore it, cry about it, fight about it. Do not avoid doing the work because you are angry. Confront your anger and make the decision to move beyond it, either by addressing it and letting it go, or seeking professional support. Intermittent feelings of anger, even intense anger, are normal and not necessarily problematic. On the other hand, unremitting anger, even low levels, if constant, can be destructive and a hindrance to this work. In fact, any strong negative emotion that feels chronic has the potential to interfere with this work. Be sure you pay attention to negative emotions that could interrupt this process.

2 *My Partner Thinks the Idea of Using Tokens Is Silly and Won't Help. Can I Use the Tokens by Myself?*

Of course you can. And you should.

Sometimes, either partner might not in the mood to work on the marriage.

Sometimes, men think intimacy is a waste of time, or, something you do in order to have sex, or, something women are better at than men. On the other hand, sometimes it's the woman who feels that working on the marriage is futile and she's not optimistic about where that might lead.

I am a firm believer that relationships can get better and stronger when only one partner takes the first hard step toward improving something in the marriage. Even troubled marriages can benefit when only one spouse seeks help or actively engages in self-help strategies, such as the Tokens. On average, that spouse is the wife. Women are more likely to engage in the process of therapy than men. And when they do, especially if it is relational by design, women in therapy will improve their skills for problem-solving in their marriages. It can be a secondary gain for being treated for postpartum depression! Whether you are in therapy by yourself or working with the Tokens by yourself, as long as it's couples-based work, with the goal of reconnection, you can both make progress. You will learn practical skills that you can put into practice in your marriage which will then benefit both of you.

3 *Our Marriage Felt Bad Long Before We Had a Baby. What Does that Mean?*

To begin with, it means that having a baby put extraordinary pressure on your already strained marriage, which is not a good way to create strong foundation. It means you might have to work harder than couples that did not feel this level of stress before having their baby. And finally, it means you might additionally want or need to reassess the fundamental connection criteria: Are the two of you good friends? Do you care about each other's happiness and well-being?

Unhappy relationships are not doomed to remain unhappy. The added stress of a baby, combined with postpartum depression and the aftermath, makes finding a new state of equilibrium challenging. First and foremost, you need to have a discussion about this and determine whether you are both on the same page. Self-help books are a good start but they will only scratch the surface of a marriage that was broken prior to the enormous stress of recent months. If you haven't had couple's therapy, now would be a good time. Let the birth of your baby and the recovery from depression be the impetus to move forward in a stronger and healthier direction. I operate under the assumption that most marriages can recover from loss love. It is not easy to do. With the right support and commitment to the process, your marriage can feel better.

Remember that only the two of you can really decide whether the Tokens are enough or whether you could benefit from professional help. Only you can determine if enough is enough. Do not forget that marital conflict is inevitable, no matter how happy and healthy your marriage is. And, as we have seen, it can be good for a marriage if careful skill is applied when addressing the point of controversy. Do not avoid confrontation. Just figure out how to bring your love into your fight. Remember that sometimes the best way (even if paradoxical) to get something to change is to accept it. Conflicts will happen. How you approach it, how personally to take it, how resentful you feel, can potentially make things worse. As corny as it sounds, love is the best antidote to conflict. Your fights will be better, that is, more productive, if you bring a Token or two into each one.

4 Will the Tokens Work If My Partner Is Just a Jerk?

First, let's talk about husbands. When I wrote *The Postpartum Husband* (2000), it was intended to be useful for the compassionate, loving husband who didn't have a clue as to how to respond when his formerly in control, happy, high functioning wife suddenly felt incapacitated and overwhelmed by crushing emotions. It was not written for the husband who didn't care or wasn't interested in helping or making things better.

This is an important distinction.

Is your husband acting like a jerk? Or is he a jerk? If he is really a jerk, that is, if he really doesn't care, is self-absorbed, narcissistic, or otherwise not invested in the relationship over a period of time, that would almost certainly disqualify him from Token-work.

Most of the time, that is not what is happening. Most of the time, husbands can frustrate their partner because they really do not understand something. We discussed this when we looked at the differences between how men and women think and experience emotions. Frustrations and resentments that emerge from this kind of miscommunication may be maddening but they are not destined for disaster. Once you've established that *your husband is not a jerk*, but may be acting like one at times, you can conclude that moving forward with this work is a good thing. You husband needs information and understanding. And you, most likely, need to do a better job of understanding what makes him tick and why he is continually disappointing you. Is it all him? Or is part of it you?

What if your wife is acting like a jerk? What does that look like? Within the context of postpartum depression, some women respond to their husband's depression with skepticism or impatience. Something like, *Oh great, now I have to take care of YOU, too!* Often, this kind of hasty and insensitive response is due lack of information and some good psychoeducation is helpful. If women are not trained to look for it, they may miss the depressive symptoms their partner is dealing with and thereby respond inappropriately and unsupportively. For men who feel their wives are not being helpful, ask yourselves the same questions we posed above: Is it all her? Or is part of it you? Have you successfully conveyed to her how you are feeling and what you need?

5 What If My Partner Cheated on Me? Am I Wasting My Time Doing this Work?

The question of whether infidelity is the cause or the consequence of marital distress is up for debate and certainly varies from relationship to relationship. Still, the devastating impact is indisputable; in fact, the literature suggests it is the primary cause of divorce (Amato & Previti, 2003). While it may currently feel unforgiveable to you, consider this: While many people believe forgiveness in this context to be a sign of weakness (*he betrayed you and you are staying in your marriage?!*), and somehow excusing the misbehavior or enabling it to happen again, not all people see it this way.

The majority of the literature on forgiveness focuses on the transformative nature of the forgiveness process and views it as an act of strength, rather than weakness, as it requires the injured party to acknowledge and face the mistreatment and to work toward transcending the injury and eventually moving beyond it. Forgiving does not appear to increase the likelihood of repeated hurt of this nature in the future (Braithwaite, Fincham, & Lambert, 2009). If tackled successfully, it is seen as a positive antidote to the distress.

So, while it may feel extraordinarily contradictory, the important consideration is where the two of you are in terms of commitment and loyalty to the marriage. If your partner cheated and wants out of the marriage, there may be little room for discussion. If, on the other hand, there is remorse and an expressed desire to turn back toward your relationship and dig in, it is recommended that the two of you find a good therapist to help you explore your options. The bottom line is this: The feelings of betrayal, abandonment, devastation, humiliation, loneliness are excruciating. They are not, however, necessarily incompatible with the hard work and ultimate goal of reconnection. It is possible.

6 I'm Ashamed to Admit It but I'm Just Not Sure If There Has Been Abuse in Our Marriage and I Am Not Sure How to Proceed.

Let's start with the obvious. If your partner makes you feel bad, on any level, that is not okay. That being said, some inexcusable behavior may rear its ugly head from time to time and though it is troubling, it may not automatically be a deal breaker, such as angry outbursts, rude interactions, offensive name-calling, and other inappropriate conduct that will surely bring progress to a standstill. Although these behaviors need to be addressed and stopped, they can be worked with when the two of you are putting energy toward renewing your connection.

If you are not sure whether there is abuse in your relationship, consider this: Verbal or emotional abuse may be present if there is a *chronic pattern* of ignoring, screaming, humiliating, threatening, name-calling, degrading, bullying, or mocking you. All of these are hurtful tactics that, if persistent, are contrary to the connection building work you are doing here.

Any form of physical aggression or violence should never occur. Ever. Period. If it does, you must separate yourself from the situation/relationship and seek help immediately. Physical violence can take many forms, such as hitting, pushing, slapping, punching, kicking, burning, restraining, biting, shoving, or throwing objects. Threatening to do any things is also aggressive and unacceptable. Keep in mind that physical or sexual abuse within a relationship is not always as apparent as you might think. For example, it might be that your partner doesn't listen to you when you say you don't feel like being touched. Or your partner might continue to touch you in ways that feel bad to you and does not respect your wishes. If you think something is wrong, trust your instincts. Any form of physical, sexual, emotional, or verbal abuse is dangerous to a marriage. Tokens of Affection will not help. You must both seek professional help before any work on your own to repair the connection is attempted.

Of particular concern in the context of the perinatal period is the issue of violence against women during pregnancy and the postpartum period. Although pregnancy appears to be a time of increased risk for violence, there is no current national estimate of the prevalence of violence against pregnant women. Consequences of pregnancy-related violence include postponed prenatal care, low birth weight of the babies, premature labor, fetal trauma, unhealthy maternal behaviors, and health issues for the mother (Jasinski, 2004).

Take a look at these sobering statistics:

- Domestic violence has been identified as a prime cause of miscarriage or stillbirth, and of maternal deaths during childbirth (Mezey & Bewley, 1997).
- One study found a significant relationship between pregnancy, domestic violence, and suicide: pregnant women who attempt suicide are very likely to have been abused (Stark & Flitcraft, 1996).
- Between 4 and 9 women in every 100 are abused during their pregnancies and/or after the birth (Taft, 2002).

Please do what you need to do to keep you and your baby safe. That takes priority over trying to work on the relationship if hostility or contempt is present.

If you are not sure whether or not there is abuse going on, ask yourself:

- Does my partner repeatedly belittle me and make me feel bad about myself?
- Do I feel controlled by my partner?
- Do I hesitate to bring things up because I am afraid he might react excessively?
- Has my partner caused physical harm or pain to my body in any way?
- Does my partner threaten me, the baby, and our other children?
- Does my partner constantly blame me for things that go wrong?
- Is my partner becoming more and more aggressive?
- Have I ever felt unsafe with my partner?
- Does my partner apologize and promise never to hurt me again, but still does?

If you answered "Yes" to any of these questions, you may be in a risky and unhealthy relationship. If you need help, call the national domestic violence hotline: (800) 799-SAFE (7233).

7 I Am Worried that My Partner and I Might Be Drinking too Much. Can this Get in the Way of Moving Forward Together?

Interestingly, recent research shows that married women consume more alcohol than long-term divorced or recently widowed women. They suggest it is in part due to the fact that they live with men who had higher levels of alcohol use (Reczek, Pudrovska, Carr, Umberson, 2012). The researchers said this new information contradicts earlier notions about marriage and alcohol and they did not expect to find that married women drank more than those who are divorced or never married. They did note that, overall, men drink more than women, and women's increased drinking after marriage might be an effort to match their husband's tendencies.

The abuse of any substance doesn't mix well with marriage. Yet, there seems to be more and more young couples worrying about one or the other or both partners enjoying just a bit too much of a good thing. I saw a couple who both enjoyed a glass of wine now and again, but he also liked to smoke marijuana after work to "wind down." He didn't see anything wrong with this, but his wife didn't like it, so he found himself smoking outside before coming in the house, or smoking in the basement when his wife was putting the kids to bed. When she would confront him, he would argue that her drinking was no better than him getting stoned. That argument didn't go anywhere fast!

One of my rules of thumb is that things are only a problem if they are a problem. Got that? What that means is, if you can drink two drinks a night and it doesn't cause a problem for you or your partner, then, perhaps that's fine. If your drinking bothers your partner or causes other problems in your life, like your weekends are ruined because you are feeling sick, or hung over, or unable to participate with your family, then it's a problem. That doesn't mean you have a drinking problem, but you might have a problem in your marriage if your partner and you don't see eye to eye about this.

Back to the original question, what is worrying you about the current drinking patterns? Typically, if someone is wondering if they are drinking too much, they probably are. That doesn't mean they have a drinking problem. If, however, they are thinking this, then something about their current pattern of behavior needs to be adjusted so things can feel more in control.

Consider some of these danger signs:

- Do you fight about drinking or drug use?
- Have you have had to make excuses for yourself or your partner because somehow drinking or drug use got in the way?
- Does either of you regularly state that drinking or drug use makes dealing with the marriage or the fighting, easier?
- Does drinking or drug use make it easier for two of you feel good together, which is the only time you enjoy each other's company?
- Do either of you experience a noticeable change in behavior when you drink too much, such as becoming more aggressive, belligerent, or argumentative?
- Is there any hiding or sneaky behavior regarding alcohol or drug use?
- Do you find that being drunk or high is the only time the two of you can express how you really feel?
- Have you both isolated yourself from friends and family to somehow mask the drinking or drug use?
- Has social drinking led to a compulsive need for alcohol to ease tension or deal with day to day stress?
- Do either of you find yourselves drinking or using drugs more because the other one wants you too?

Remember that the abuse of any substance can damage a relationship. Make sure the two of you are expressing your concerns and addressing the problem if there is one. Not always, but often, an accusation of substance abuse is met with denial or dismissal. If you are worried about your partner, be careful how you introduce this issue, and, like always, do it with compassion and affection. Keep all the Tokens in mind, when times are hard. Remember you are collaborating as a team, find a safe place to talk, express yourself with love. If you are wondering about your own drinking or drug use, I would urge you to discuss this with your partner and take the steps you need to take to feel more in control of the choices you make.

8 I Continue to Struggle with the Loss of My Baby and Cannot seem to Focus on My Marriage.

There is no loss as profound as the loss of a child. The toll it takes on a marriage is nothing less than life shattering. As dreams are quashed and life as you know it is brought to a screeching halt, nothing will make sense for a long while. When this happens, issues within marriages are often put on hold while both partners cling to each other and resist each other simultaneously.

If you and your partner are struggling with the unspeakable loss of your baby, strengthening the marital connection will have its benefits but healing comes first. If you feel you are too numb, in too much pain, too emotionally detached, or just going through the motions, put all of this work aside until your personal resources are replenished.

There are a number of reasons why connections become threatened after a loss. Primarily it is due to (a) communication breakdown, (b) differences in how you both grieve, (c) blame and guilt that pervade the home, and (d) one or both partners turn to substance use or other potentially damaging outlets for relief from the pain.

As if the loss of the baby isn't cruel enough, many bereaved parents fear that their marriage may not survive this devastating loss. Despite a widespread belief that divorce is an inevitable result of the insurmountable stress on the marriage following the death of a child, a 2006 survey conducted by the Compassionate Friends Organization debunked this myth. They found that the divorce rate was 16%, far below the national divorce rate of 50%, and 4% reported that the divorce was due to problems that existed prior to the loss of the child (Loder, 2006). It seems that rather than acting as a catalyst to divide the couple, a child's death can actually bring couples together (Hardt & Caroll, 2006).

The Tokens, if used judiciously, can promote long-term healing for a grieving couple. The space carved out by this loss leaves a hole in the soul of your marriage; one that takes more time than imaginable to heal. The work involved with reconnecting after the loss of a child is not only, not contraindicated, it is essential, but it might have to wait until both partners have taken care of themselves and feel ready to address the relationship.

9 How Do I Know If My Marriage Is Beyond Hope?

Nothing is beyond hope. It might feel that way, but unless there has been some behavior that cannot be ignored, such as abuse, relationships have the capacity to be more flexible than it might feel at the moment. Feelings of despair or hopelessness consume all fibers of our being. It's hard to see past it and believe that it won't always feel like this. The one criterion that must be present in order to even entertain the possibility of a positive progression is that both of you want to work on the marriage. In the absence of a mutual desire for reconnection, one of you may continue to spin your wheels in the opposite direction which takes you nowhere.

If you or your partner are totally overwhelmed and feel desperate for a way back together or a way out of the marriage, it is time to sit down and have a conversation about your future, if you haven't already done that. You also need to carefully consider whether you are staying in the marriage for the wrong reasons, such as for the kids, or not to hurt your spouse. These reasons, though admirable to an extent, may actually make things worse for your children and your spouse in the long run.

Try therapy on a trial basis. Make a short-term commitment to each other to find a good therapist and see how an objective professional can help. Give it 2 to 4 months of weekly sessions to determine if it can help at all. If one of you has totally checked out of the marriage, therapy will not help. You can fake it for a while, but you'll be wasting your time.

10 *What If My Partner Hurt Me so Badly I Am Unable to Forgive?*

As we discussed in Chapter 12, forgiveness can be a long, long process and one that can feel impossible to achieve when first setting out. So again, there is a difference between it feeling like you are unable to forgive and actually being unable to forgive. Each circumstance is different; each couple is different. In order to determine that forgiveness is possible or not, it requires a soulful and introspective journey that only you can take. It calls for absolute transparency with regard to the issues and subsequent emotions on your part and on the part of the offending partner. You may also want to call in reinforcements from supportive communities, such as your church or synagogue, or a professional therapist. Be careful not to misconstrue some of the well-meaning counsel from loving friends and family members who can, in their attempt to protect you, confound the situation. You need consider all of the variables with clarity and fairness.

Even if your pain feels insurmountable, this does not mean you will be unable to forgive. Give yourself time to suffer through and surround yourself with as much support as you can. Never presume a relationship is hopeless unless you have worked extremely hard to prove otherwise. Remember also that forgiveness is less about the other person and more about you. Even though it may feel as though your partner is undeserving of your forgiveness, we now understand that forgiveness is really a gift you give yourself; the act of forgiving someone offers great benefits to your physical, psychological, emotional, and spiritual self. Finally, bear in mind that any wrongdoing which feels impossible to forgive is, more likely than not, the one you should try hardest to forgive. This is simply because it may be difficult to fully move past the pain, until you do.

11 *How Do We Know If We Need Couple's Therapy?*

Consider these words that may have been spoken in moments in time that felt insurmountable.

I can't believe you did that!
I can't believe I'm married to you!
If you don't like it, then just leave!
I cannot stand the way this feels right now!
You are never there for me!
You just don't understand me!
Why would you act like that?

Any of these sound familiar? All marriages go through rough patches. All marriages have moments, hours, days, or weeks that feel, well, irreconcilable. In the heat of the moment, it can feel catastrophic and then, later, it can be forgotten or resolved. Sometimes it's amazing how quickly couples can move from laughter to rage in the blink of an eye. That's what love can do to you every now and then.

Yet, most of the time, statements like those above reflect transient, emotionally charged exchanges that, with time, skill and healing, resolve. When these situations fail to resolve, however, or if negative feelings become chronic instead of transitory, then professional help is certainly a more viable option than ending the marriage.

Here are some situations where therapy may be helpful:

- When the negative interactions outweigh the positive ones.
- When either or both of you are thinking about separating or divorcing.
- When either or both of you are drifting away from the partnership instead of working on issues together.
- When you find that you fight about the same things over and over again, and these fights are not productive or if they continuously lead to harsh, negative emotions.
- When being with your partner no longer feels fun, meaningful, comfortable, or pleasing in any way.
- When you feel stuck and everything you try feels useless.
- If touching or being touched feels unappealing, intrusive, abrasive, tedious, or repulsive on a regular basis.
- When either of you feel withdrawn or apathetic about the relationship.
- When either one of you think you need to go or suggests therapy.

Here are some goals of couple's therapy:

- To decrease withdrawal and avoidance issues;
- To modify any dysfunctional behavior;

- To improve communication and problem-solving strategies;
- To reframe how you view the relationship, making sure there is a strong "us" in the equation.
- To accentuate and strengthen the positive qualities;
- To learn how to appropriately express painful emotions;
- To reinforce all of the Tokens and restore a meaningful connection.

People decide to enter therapy for many reasons. Consider the couples we have discussed thus far in the book: Hallie and Andrew came in for therapy because Hallie felt she needed more support and Andrew agreed to come with the misguided intent to prove her wrong. Shelby and Matt sought therapy when her distress made him feel helpless and they both agreed they needed to address the disconnect. Carrie decided to come to therapy alone, since Jon thought their private lives were no one else's concern. As she learned new skills and gained confidence, she was able to convince Jon that their marriage would benefit from their mutual effort. Aaron started therapy when his symptoms of depression interfered with his ability to function well at work. He initiated the process and deemed it vital to his desire to return to work. Suzy was extremely supportive and joined his sessions to learn how to cope with his inclination to retreat from the marriage.

If you are thinking about therapy, don't wait too long. According to Gottman (Gottman & Silver, 1999), couples typically wait 6 years from the time they first encounter relationship trouble to make the decision to talk to a professional about it! By that time, the work is harder because the negativity may be more entrenched. It makes sense to seek the help with your level of distress is mild to moderate, rather than waiting until it feels out of control.

Finally, remember this: If you think therapy will help and your partner isn't interested in joining you, go alone. You can (and should!) ask him or her to join you when you are both ready.

The above scenarios merely scratch the surface of the various circumstances that can hinder or postpone Token work. Do your best to respect where the two of you are at any given point in time, then make a determination whether sharing more of yourselves with each other feels right to you at this time.

15

WHAT'S NEXT?

It is not a lack of love, but a lack of friendship that makes unhappy marriages.

—Friedrich Nietzsche

The majority of this book has focused on moving beyond postpartum depression, beyond the injuries inflicted onto the marriage by the often mysterious and always painful course of the illness. We have taken you past the destructive force and into a space of renewed hope and resilience for your relationship. That being said, let's go full circle for a moment and remember that all marriages go through tough times after a baby is born, even when neither partner is depressed. The reason we reemphasize this is to reassure you that some degree of marital distress after having a baby is widespread and experienced by most couples as a normal consequence of this life transition. However, vulnerability in any of the Token domains can potentially fracture the base of a relationship, which can either be ignored, left to rock the foundation indefinitely, or it can be restored.

The good news is that skillful realignment of the marital relationship after the birth of the baby can help create new and secure bonds. With the right tools and Tokens, couples are able to reconnect in ways that bring new meaning to their marriage and their family. Here's the best news: A couple's belief and sense of confidence in the future of the relationship has been linked with not only better relationship functioning, but also with a lower incidence of future episodes of depression (Whitton et al., 2007). Therefore, when factoring the risk of subsequent depressions into this mix of babies, depression, and your marriage, it becomes imperative that the two of you focus on reclaiming your marriage. Your perception of how things are going is a vital part of this process.

Integrity of the Tokens

The Tokens of Affection, by their very nature, demand a certain belief in yourself and in your marriage. The use of these Tokens is the ultimate act loyalty. After all, if you didn't believe in your marriage and seek to reinforce your connection, you would never have engaged in this process initially.

Each token—Esteem, Collaboration, Compromise, Selflessness, Sanctuary, Expression, Tolerance, and Loyalty—all have the capacity to self-generate.

This means:

- When you have regard for yourself and your relationship (Esteem), your partner will respect you more.
- If you work with your partner (Collaboration), your partner will ally with you when you need it.
- When you practice give and take (Compromise), your partner will be more likely to cooperate.
- When you take care of others (Selflessness), you will be taken care of.
- When you create a safe spot to *be present* with your partner (Sanctuary), your partner will join you in spirit.
- When you express yourself with consideration and skill (Expression), you increase the likelihood that your partner will return the effort.
- When you are more accepting (Tolerance), your partner will be more understanding.
- If you trust the efforts your partner has put into your marriage (Loyalty), you will feel encouraged and grateful.

In other words, when you pay it forward, on behalf of your marriage, you will get more in return. This is a law of reciprocity in healthy relationships. Each time you invest with a Token Tool, you increase the likelihood that your partner will either learn or benefit from that effort.

As we conclude this journey of introspection and affection, let's take a final look how your perception can affect your behavior, and how you are now in position to monitor your progress, create new pathways, cultivate resilience, and experience joy in your relationship again.

What You Believe Is True May Not Be True

Have you ever found yourself in a situation where someone responds in a way that surprises you? Consider a simple example of two people at work with their boss:

Person #1: Did you see the way he looked at me? He must be so angry. Geez.

Person #2: Really? He didn't look angry to me. He looked confused. Like he didn't understand what you meant.

Person #1: I think he's still mad because I turned that assignment in late yesterday. He probably hates me now.

Person #2: Nah. I think you weren't clear just now, and he was trying to understand. Plus, I heard he was leaving early today because he isn't feeling well.

We have seen how easily a person's perceptions can mislead them straight into the funhouse of distorted mirrors where nothing is what it seems, or they can smooth the path ahead by softening the edges. You have more choice in this matter than you might think. We saw this in Chapter 5 when we introduced CBT 101, and we saw it again when we discussed attributions in Chapter 11. Your mindset is crucial to your eventual progress or lack thereof. You have learned that if you misinterpret, misattribute, or misconstrue a thought of your own, or of someone else, your perception will be distorted and your response may be inappropriate or unhelpful. Our understanding of something can feel as if it is real, but it is largely based on how we perceive it. In fact, depressed patients who perceived their spouses as highly critical of them were significantly more likely to relapse during follow-up than were those who perceived that they were less criticized (Kwon, Yuri, Lee, & Bifulco, 2006). The key word here is *perceived*. There is not a measure of how critical the spouses were, only that they were perceived as critical.

It appears that people who do not perceive that they are being criticized (even when living with an objectively determined critical partner) may be protected somewhat by their ability to redirect the criticism off of them. Conversely, people who perceive they are being criticized, even when living with a critical partner, by objective standards, may be at risk for depression relapse (Hooley & Teasdale, 1989).

This does not mean that you should yield to criticism. That would contradict every single thing the book stands for! It means you should be careful not to jump to conclusions which could misinform you or lead you to take things personally when disagreements get heated between the two of you. There is much research to support the importance of improving marital interactions in preventing relapse in depression. Protecting yourself or your partner from depression should be part of your mutual long-term recovery plan. Both of you need to continue to be mindful of this and advocate for yourselves and each other.

Hall Monitor

Someone needs to keep an eye on things in a relationship. It would be nice if good relationships just stayed good and healthy for the long haul, but we know that this is not the case. Strong, stable relationships, no matter how happy or healthy, require ongoing attention and constant tweaking of skills.

Remember when you were in elementary or middle school and someone was designated as hall monitor to maintain order? Think of the rules, be clear, be firm, be nice, don't break your own rules, don't be obnoxious, don't miss anything and, above all, be fair! Let's face it, being a hall monitor was a dirty job, but somebody had to do it! Well, somebody has to do it in your marriage too. When you feel you are headed for trouble, in a big way, such as how the relationship feels in general, or in a small way, such as feeling uneasy about a recent negative interaction, one of you needs to step back into the role of marriage monitor.

It doesn't have to be the same person each time, but it can be. You can also alternate, depending on the circumstances. It doesn't matter who steps up, or how many times, because, remember, you are not keeping score! What matters is that one of you must take the initiative to pull back out of the fray and acknowledge the current state. This can diffuse it and keep it from escalating. Escalation is your greatest enemy. It will obscure every bit of clarity you thought you had and lead to an irreversible momentum. Back out gracefully. You will not be abandoning the relationship itself, only the objectionable moment that is poised to lead the two of you off course.

Despite stereotypes about women taking on the role of relationship caretaker, research also shows that men regard their marital union as a vital part of their well-being, if not survival. Divorced men do not live as long as married men. They are prone to alcoholism, suicide, physical and mental illnesses, and car accidents. Men may not talk about it as much, but they are deeply motivated to sustain the life of their marriage.

Both of you are in position to be the one, at any given moment, to embrace the paradox: break out of the tense moment in support of the greater good. Do not make the mistake in believing that the longer you perseverate, or argue in circular fashion, the greater the likelihood that you will get your point across. Actually, the opposite is more likely to occur. Every time you retreat from a potential standoff, you are preserving power and decelerating the negative energy.

Resilience

In my book, *Therapy and the Postpartum Woman* (2009), there is a section on resilience, defined as the capacity to recover from stress, adversity, or misfortune. A person's vulnerability to stress and capacity for resilience is complex and can be understood as both contributing to depressive illness as well as providing protection from it. One of our goals here is to reduce the damage of relational immobilization and isolation. We have discussed that ongoing stress can threaten disconnection, specifically in this context, the stress of a new baby and postpartum depression.

In the early 1990s, psychologist Judith Jordan introduced the notion of relational resilience. Challenging the common notion that resilience represents some type of intrinsic hardiness endowed to a lucky few or heroic people, Jordan (1991) highlights resilience as a human capacity that can be learned, developed, and reinforced through relationships. In fact, in therapy, many couples learn to use moments of conflict to demonstrate that points of disagreements can be opportunities to enhance the genuineness of the relationship and strengthen confidence in connection. The research does show that individuals with higher self-esteem and a sense of self-worth tend to share characteristics of greater resiliency. Simply put, take care of yourself, take care of your relationship, and protect yourselves going forward. After all, doesn't the individual locus of control truly lead to mutual empowerment? Can we (should we?) separate the two when we are talking about connection?

It is well known that stress generates more stress. It follows, then, that one of your goals should be to foster resilience. Based on theories of optimism versus pessimism, research has shown that there are characteristics that appear to be associated with better coping and therefore, better outcomes (Scheier, Carver, & Bridges, 1994). Several years ago, The Postpartum Stress Center adapted some of these characteristics to our model for the treatment of postpartum depression. The qualities listed below are believed to be associated with the manner and success with which people cope with stress. Therefore, the more you can relate to any or all of these qualities in your own life, the more likely your response to stress will lead to successful, adaptive functioning.

Take a look at the list below and check the ones you feel you could use some continued work with.

Characteristics of Positive Adaptation

Copyright © 1999 by The Postpartum Stress Center. Adapted from work of Carver, C., Scheier, M., Weintraub, J., 1989.

- ☐ **Positive reinterpretation and personal growth.** The ability to learn and grow from, and transform a negative experience into one a positive one.
- ☐ **Active coping.** The ability to take action that makes a difference and improves management of symptoms or problems.
- ☐ **Planning.** The development of strategies that are future oriented and focused on specific behaviors that will maximize coping.
- ☐ **Seeking social support.** The ability to resist isolation and reach out to connections outside the marital relationship.
- ☐ **Humor.** The ability to smooth out differences and boost moods by inserting gentle and loving playfulness and laughter.
- ☐ **Ability to accept and trust current state.** One's capacity for self-awareness regarding the present, without regretting the past or worrying about the future.
- ☐ **Rearranging priorities.** Having the flexibility to modify expectations, as well as the practical day-to-day demands, in order to keep things in perspective.
- ☐ **Insight.** Self-awareness, in particular, how it relates to the pros and cons of the relationship and problem-solving.

- **Capacity for or interest in intimacy.** The motivation for closeness and familiarity that provides the very air you both breathe.
- **Self-expression.** The ability to say what you need to say, feel what you need to feel, do what you need to do on behalf of your marriage.
- **Spiritual search.** Finding ways, words, times, to think about, seek out, and connect with that which takes you to a private and personal space between you and the power of your connection with the universe.

By identifying areas in which you are strong, as well as areas in which you are vulnerable, you can fortify your ability to respond to challenges in your marriage with better personal resources. Those qualities you are good at—keep working with them. Those you are weaker in—see if you can improve on anything of them; challenge yourself to incorporate these characteristics into your relationship. As you continue to lean toward your partner in this way, you will establish and reinforce features that have been linked with positive adaptation. That means your relationship will feel better because it will *be* better.

Neuroplasticity

Okay, this is a big word for the end of the book, right? It's an important one. It refers to a process that will help you move forward through this work long after you have finished reading. Neuroplasticity refers to the brain's ability to reorganize neural pathways or create new ones. The point is this: It is never too late to learn, to grow, to change. Let's see how this works.

What you have done up to this point is learn specific connection-enhancing techniques. Some have been short-term feel good interventions, others have been more enduring strategies. Let's face it, romantic dinners, scheduled date nights, and intermittent hugs are nice for a relationship, but rarely ensure long-term satisfaction. Next, you must practice, practice, practice. Especially, if you are exercising muscles you rarely use, it's even more necessary for you to practice. Applying these skills may come naturally for some people. If you are not one of those people, you must first talk to your brain.

Yes, you should tell your brain that you are learning new skills and need help. Your brain is quite comfortable with the current pathways. In order for you to develop new ones, you need to alert your brain, for instance, you can start with affirmations. *I am developing new skills. I am surrounding myself with loving thoughts about my partner. I am embracing our relationship.* Remember that your brain is hard-wired to respond to messages it gets. It doesn't know if you are faking it or not. As you continue to practice by repeating affirmations and taking actions to authenticate your words, new neural pathways begin to be formed in order to accommodate the new information. That's an oversimplification of a function that is way too complicated for most of us to really understand. Scientists who study the brain tell us one of the best ways to keep our brains sharp is to learn something new or try an old activity differently. It seems that our brains create neural passages to sustain that new knowledge or skill. Exercises to stimulate this plasticity include things like (a) switching things up, such as using your non-dominant hand for certain tasks, brushing your teeth, for example, or (b) restricting your senses, such as by showering with the lights off, or (c) changing routines, such as by experimenting by taking a new driving route to work.

Every time you repetitively focus on or practice a new skill, or try something you are not used to doing on behalf of your marriage, you may be creating a new pathway that becomes easier as you continue to incorporate it into your routine. Today's imaging techniques have enabled researchers to precisely map functioning of different parts of the brain. Wherever we focus our attention is where new neural connections will be made!

Neuroscientist and psychology professor Richard Davidson teaches us that our emotions and thoughts are predictable and rooted within the structure of our brains. He calls his work "affective neuroscience" (Davidson & Begley, 2012), which he describes as the study of the brain mechanisms that are the basis of our emotions.

A shout out to cognitive behavioral therapists everywhere, Davidson's work is based on the notion that thoughts can change your brain. He refers to an experiment done at Harvard (Pascual-Leone, 1996) in which subjects were taught to perform with one hand, a five-finger exercise on a piano keyboard connected by a computer musical interface. The subjects were instructed to perform the sequence of finger movements smoothly, without pausing and without skipping keys, while paying particular attention to the beat of the metronome. Subjects were studied for five consecutive days, and each day they had a 2-hour practice session, then tested. When tested, they used neuroimaging to determine how much of the motor cortex had been involved in the learning process. To no one's surprise, the intense practice had expanded the relevant region in the brain.

Of particular interest, however, was what happened with the second half of the volunteers. This group was instructed to *think* about practicing the exercise on the piano. In other words, they played the music in their heads, imagining how they would move their fingers, but did not actually touch the keys. What the imaging revealed was that the region of motor cortex that controls the piano-playing fingers also expanded in the brains of the subjects who only imagined playing the music—precisely as it did in those who actually played it. The discovery was evidence that mental exercise has the power to alter the physical composition of the brain.

Therefore, your job now is to practice, practice, practice! Whether you actually say the words you are learning to say, or do the things you are learning to do, it will count toward your connection-building efforts if you think about this work, imagine yourself reconnecting the way you hope to, and believe in the promise of your heartfelt vows you once made to each other.

WHAT'S NEXT?

12 Keystones to Token Work

1. Apply yourself to your marriage.
2. Small changes can make a huge difference.
3. Small acts of disrespect can annihilate many acts of love.
4. Small sacrifices can create limitless gratitude.
5. Take your good intentions and wrap them around each point of controversy.
6. Be accountable.
7. Take risks.
8. Don't expect changes too quickly.
9. You have the right to remain separate and the right to impose togetherness.
10. Be patient with one another.
11. Prepare for setbacks.
12. Lean in. Reinforce small movements in the right direction.

Take a good look at this list of 12 truths. They are just another way of saying what we have already said in other ways throughout your work here. They are reminders that the affection the two of you exchange during good times and during difficult times will be an investment in the enduring well-being of your marriage. If you share the common goal of a warm and loving relationship, some of this work will pay off without you even taking notice. Still, getting out from under the sticky web of depression is harder than just feeling better. Some couples describe it as the wreckage after the storm. Others, say it is an opportunity to rediscover each other. Remember, you have a choice as to how you will respond to most things. It may not always feel that way, but you do.

Read each of the above truths aloud to yourself, one at a time, and ask yourself a question related to your contribution to this process.

1. Am I applying myself? Am I taking too much for granted?
2. What small changes have I seen or participated in? In what ways are things slightly different (better?) than before we have a baby and before we suffered through depression?
3. Have I inadvertently disrespected my partner? Do I sufficiently understand the profound damage that can have on our connection? Can I do my best to not disrespect my partner? Ever?
4. Am I making small sacrifices on behalf of my partner? Even when I don't feel like it? Limitless gratitude. Sounds nice, doesn't it? Once you decide this is where you'd like to be, you will find the way and use the tools to secure that spot. It's one of those things that self-generates. Once you see how good it feels, it will become more natural for you to reinforce it than resist it. When you reach that sweet spot, you will know because sacrifices no longer feel like sacrifices. They feel like gifts.

5. When we disagree, do I regress to a frustrated state of defeat, or do I rise to the occasion and cling to our shared goal of renewed connection?
6. Am I taking responsibility for the choices I make and the consequences of my actions? Am I just waiting for my partner to fix things or change his or her behavior or do I believe in the power I have to make difference?
7. Can I slip out of my comfort zone long enough to see if that leads to positive and restorative changes? Do I even know what that means? Do I understand how I may be getting in my own way?
8. Am I willing to let this take its natural course which may run parallel to the work we are doing? Do I understand that our commitment to work on reviving our connection is not mutually exclusive from the truth that time really does help heal wounds and some of this will just feel better because we are persevering together?
9. Am I continuing to take care of myself alone and what I need to do to feel complete and at peace with myself? At the same time, do I feel entitled to fight for my marriage and for the parts of the relationship that my partner requires a bit of extra encouragement? Can I tell the difference between those times when we should take care of ourselves versus when we should take care of each other?
10. Am I giving my partner the opportunity to make mistakes? Do I understand that it is likely that my partner does not interpret things the way I do and this can lead to gridlock unless one of us is able to keep the larger picture in mind. Always.
11. Do I keep in mind that obstacles will continue to test us? Babies will challenge us. Depressive thinking will taunt us. Your efforts will intermittently feel exasperating. Perhaps, futile. Keep moving in the direction of connection.
12. Am I seeing the "us" in our relationship or do I continue to push back? Am I able to zero in on the two of us despite the distractions of everyday life? Am I able to extract the two of us from the equation of me + you = us (+ baby + depression) = new us? Can I remember every step toward each other is a stride toward the connection we crave?

Token Check-In

Finally, we recommend that you pay regular and continuous attention to each Token: Esteem, Collaboration, Compromise, Selflessness, Sanctuary, Expression, Tolerance, and Loyalty. By now, you can better understand that although they are distinct entities, they all have common characteristics and will continually overlap. Your proficiency in one area will bring about greater confidence when applying a subsequent Token with which you feel less comfortable.

Perhaps most important at this stage is the recognition that the Tokens are forever. This is not a recovery plan in response to the devastation of depression. It is a plan for a lifetime together. It's a commitment to a lifestyle and dedication to your partnership. By strengthening these areas of communication, affection, and connection, you will be securing your ability to navigate and withstand future challenges. Reclaiming your marriage is just the beginning. Recognizing that the two of you now have the strength to take care of yourselves and each other in ways that are mutually rewarding and growth-enhancing is quite an achievement. Good marriages require this loving attention. When good marriages are besieged by unforeseen suffering which tests your relationship and resolve, this loving attention is even more crucial.

Check in with each other. Check in with your *self*.

Be kind. Be attentive. Be available.

Find the conviction to speak when something needs to be said and the courage to stop speaking when you need to listen.

I assure you that if you take care of yourself and your marriage in these ways, the rest will take care of itself. Expect good things to happen.

REFERENCES

Acitelli, L. (1988). When spouses talk to each other about their relationship. *Journal of Social and Personal Relationships, 5,* 185–199.

Acitelli, L. (1993). You, me, and us: Perspectives on relationship awareness. In S. Duck (Ed.), *Understanding relationship processes 1: Individuals and relationships* (pp. 144–174). London, England: Sage.

Acitelli, L. (2002). Relationship awareness: Crossing the bridge between cognition and communication. *Communication Theory, 12*(1), 92–112.

Acitelli, L. (2008). Do relationship reflections help or hurt relationship satisfaction. In J. Forgas & J. Fitness (Eds.), *Social relationships: Cognitive, affective and motivational processes.* New York, NY: Psychology Press.

Agnew, C., & Etchenberry, P. (2006). Cognitive interdependence: Considering self-in relationship. In K. Vohs & J. Finkel (Eds.), *Self and relationships: Connecting intrapersonal and interpersonal processes.* New York, NY: Guilford Press.

Amato, P., & Previti, D. (2003). People's reasons for divorcing: Gender, social class, the life course,and adjustment. *Journal of Family Issues, 24*(5), 602–626.

American Psychiatric Association. (2000). *Diagnostic and statistical manual of mental disorder* (4th ed., text rev.). Washington, DC: Author.

Andrews, F., Abbey, A., & Halman, L. (1992). Is fertility-problem stress different? The dynamics of stress in fertile and infertile couples. *Fertility and Sterility, 57,* 1247–1253.

Areias, M., Kumar, R., Barros, H., & Figueiredo, E. (1996). Correlates of postnatal depression in mothers and fathers. *The British Journal of Psychiatry, 169*(1), 36–41.

Barnes, D. (2006). Postpartum depression: It's impact on couples and marital satisfaction. *Journal of Systemic Therapies, 25*(3), 25–42.

Beach, S., Fincham, F., & Katz, J. (1998). Marital therapy in the treatment of depression: Toward a third generation of outcome research. *Clinical Psychology Review, 18*(6), 635–661.

Beach, S., Sandeen, E., & O'Leary, K. (1990). *Depression in marriage: A model for etiology and treatment.* New York, NY: Guildford Press.

Becker, R. (n.d.) Defending the caveman. Retrieved November 5, 2012, from http://www.defendingthecaveman.com

Benazon, N., & Coyne, J. (2000). Living with a depressed spouse. *Journal of Family Psychology, 14*(1), 71–79.

REFERENCES

Berk, L., Tan, S., Fry, W., Napier, B., Lee, J., Hubbard, R., & Lewis, J. (1989). Neuroendocrine and stress hormone changes during mirthful laughter. *American Journal of the Medical Sciences, 298*, 390–396.

Berk, R. (2001). The active ingredients in humor: Psycho-physiological benefits and risks for older adults. *Educational Gerontology, 27*, 323–339.

Bernal, G., & Baker, J. (1979). Toward a metacommunicational framework of couple interaction. *Family Process, 18*, 293–302.

Biglan, A., Hops, H., Sherman, L., Friedman, L., Arthur, J., & Osteen, V. (1985). Problem-solving interactions of depressed women and their husbands. *Behavior Therapy, 16*, 431–451.

Bowlby, J. (1969). *Attachment and loss: Volume 1. Attachment.* New York, NY: Basic Books.

Bradbury, T., & Fincham, F. (1990). Attributions in marriage: Review and critique. *Psychological Bulletin, 107*, 3–33.

Braithwaite, S., Fincham, F., & Lambert, N. (2009). Hurt and psychological health in close relationships. In A. Vangelisti (Ed.), *Feeling hurt in close relationships* (pp. 376–399). Cambridge, England: Cambridge University Press.

Brizendine, L. (2011). *The male brain.* New York, NY: Three Rivers Press.

Broderick, J. (1981). A method of derivation of areas of assessment in marital relationships. *The American Journal of Family Therapy, 9*, 25–34.

Brown, B. (2012). *Daring greatly: How the courage to be vulnerable transforms the way we live, love, parent and lead.* New York, NY: Gotham Books.

Buehlman, K., Gottman, J., & Katz L. (1992). How a couple views their past predicts their future: Predicting divorce from an oral history interview. *Journal of Family Psychology, 5*, 295–318.

Butler, B. (2005). Laughter: The best medicine? *Oregon Library Association Quarterly, 11*(1), 11–13.

Butzer, B., & Kuiper, N. (2008). Humor use in romantic relationships: The effects of relationship satisfaction and pleasant versus conflict situations. *The Journal of Psychology, 142*(3), 245–260.

Byrne, A., & Hansberry, J. (2007). Collaboration: Leveraging resources and expertise. *New Directions for Youth Development, 114*, 75–84.

Carstense, L., Gottman, J., & Levenson, R. (1995). Emotional behavior in long-term marriage. *Psychology and Aging, 10*(1), 140–149.

Carver, C., Scheier, M., & Weintraub, J. (1989). Assessing coping strategies: A theoretically based approach. *Journal of Personality and Social Psychology, 56*(2), 267–283.

Choi, H., & Marks, N. (2008). Marital conflict, depressive symptoms, and functional impairment. *Journal of Marriage and Family, 70*(2), 377–390.

Cohen, C., & Bradbury, T. (1997). Negative life events, marital interaction, and the longitudinal course of newlywed marriage. *Journal of Personality and Social Psychology, 73*, 114–128.

Cowan, P., & Cowan, C. (1988). Changes in marriage during the transition to parenthood: Must we blame the baby? In G. Michaels & W. Goldberg (Eds.), *The transition to parenthood: Current theory and research* (pp. 114–154). New York, NY: Cambridge University Press.

Cowan, C., & Cowan, P. (1992). *When parents become partners: The big life change for couples.* New York, NY: Basic Books.

REFERENCES

Covey, S. (1990). *Seven habits of highly effective people.* New York, NY: Simon & Schuster.

Cox, M., Paley, B., Burchinal, M., & Payne, C. (1999). Marital perceptions and interactions across the transition to parenthood. *Journal of Marriage and the Family, 6,* 611–625.

Davidson, R., & Begley, S. (2012). *The emotional life of your brain: How its unique patterns affect the way you think, feel, and live — and how you can change them.* New York, NY: Plume Publishing.

Dennis, C., & Ross, L. (2006). Women's perceptions of partner support and conflict in the development of postpartum depressive symptoms. *Journal of Advanced Nursing, 56,* 588–599.

Ditkoff, M., Moore, T., Allen, C., & Pollard, D. (2005). The ideal collaborative team. Retrieved October 13, 2012, from http://www.ideachampions.com/downloads/collaborationresults.pdf

Emmons, R., & McCullough, M. (2003). Counting blessings versus burdens: Experimental studies of gratitude and subjective well-being. *Journal of Personality and Social Psychology, 84,* 377–389.

Fennel, D. (1993). Characteristics of long-term marriages. *Journal of Mental Health Counseling, 15,* 446–460.

Fincham, F. (2003). Marital conflict: Correlates, structure and context. *Current Directions in Psychological Science, 12,* 23–27.

Fincham, F. (2004). Communication in marriage. In A. Vangelisti (Ed.), *Handbook of family communication* (pp. 83–104). Hillsdale, NJ: Erlbaum.

Fincham, F., & Beach, S. (2001). Forgiving in close relationships. *Advances in Psychology Research, 7,* 163–198.

Fincham, F., Beach, S., & Davila, J. (2004). Forgiveness and conflict resolution in marriage. *Journal of Family Psychology, 18,* 72–81.

Fincham, F., Beach, S., Harold, G., & Osborne, L. (1997). Marital satisfaction and depression: Different causal relationships for men and women? *Psychological Science, 8,* 351–357.

Fry, W. (1992). The physiological effects of humor, mirth, and laughter. *Journal of the American Medical Association, 267,* 1857–1858.

Fry, W. (1994). The biology of humor. *Humor: International Journal of Humor Research, 7,* 111–126.

Gaynes, B., Gavin, N., Meltzer-Brody, S., Lohr, K., Swinson, T., Gartlehner, G., ... Miller, W., (2005). Perinatal depression: Prevalence, screening accuracy, and screening outcomes. *Evidence Report: Technology Assessment, 119,* 1–8.

Gill, D., Christensen, A., & Fincham, F. (1999). Predicting marital satisfaction from behavior: Do all roads really lead to Rome? *Personal Relationships, 6,* 369–387.

Gold, K., Sen, A., & Hayward, R. (2010). Marriage and cohabitation outcomes after pregnancy loss. *Pediatrics, 125*(5), 1203–1207.

Gordon, A., Impett, E., Kogan, A., Oveis, C., & Keltner, D. (2012). To have and to hold: Gratitude promotes relationship maintenance in intimate bonds. *Journal of Personality and Social Psychology, 103,* 257–274.

Gotlib, I., & Beach, S. (1995). A marital/family discord model of depression: Implications for therapeutic intervention. In N. Jacobson & A. Gurman (Eds.), *Clinical handbook of couple therapy* (pp. 411–436). New York, NY: Guilford Press.

REFERENCES

Gottman, J. (1979). *Marital interaction: Experimental investigations.* New York, NY: Academic.

Gottman, J. (1993). *What predicts divorce? The relationship between marital processes and marital outcomes.* New York, NY: Psychology Press.

Gottman, J. (1994). *Why marriages succeed or fail: And how you can make yours last.* New York, NY: Fireside.

Gottman, J. (2007). *And baby makes three.* New York, NY: Crown Publishing.

Gottman, J., Coan, J., Carrere, S., & Swanson, C. (1998). Predicting marital happiness and stability from newlywed interactions. *Journal of Marriage and the Family, 60,* 5–22.

Gottman, J., & Krokoff, L. (1989). Marital interaction and satisfaction: A longitudinal view. *Journal of Consulting and Clinical Psychology, 57*(1), 47–52.

Gottman, J., & Levenson, R. (1992). Marital processes predictive of later dissolution: behavior, physiology and health. *Journal of Personality and Social Psychology, 63,* 221–233.

Gottman, J., Markman, H., & Notarius, C. (1977). The topography of marital conflict: A sequenced analysis of verbal and nonverbal behaviors. *Journal of Marriage and the Family, 39,* 461–477.

Gottman, J., & Silver, N. (1999). *The seven principles for making marriage work.* London, Engand: Orion Publishing.

Guerrero, L., & Andersen, P. (1994). Patterns of matching and initiation: Touch behavior and touch avoidance across romantic relationship stages. *Journal of Nonverbal Behavior, 18*(2), 137–153.

Hall, J. (1984). *Nonverbal sex differences: Communication accuracy and expressive style.* Baltimore, MD: The Johns Hopkins University Press.

Hall, J., & Veccia, E. (1990). More "touching" observations: New insights on men, women, and interpersonal touch. *Journal of Personality and Social Psychology, 59*(6), 1155–1162.

Hardt, M., & Caroll, D. (2006). When a child dies. Retrieved April 23, 2013, from http://www.compassionatefriends.org/pdf/When_a_Child_Dies-2006_Final.pdf

Hobfoll, S., Ritter, C., Lavin, J., Hulszier, M., & Cameron, R. (1995). Depression prevalence and incidence among inner-city pregnant and postpartum women. *Journal of Consulting and Clinical Psychology, 63,* 445–453.

Holmgren, M. (1993). Forgiveness and the intrinsic value of persons. *American Philosophical Quarterly, 30*(4), 341–352.

Holtzworth-Munroe, A., & Jacobson, N. S. (1988). Toward a methodology for coding spontaneous causal attributions: Preliminary results with married couples. *Journal of Social and Clinical Psychology, 7,* 101–112.

Hölzelab, B., Carmodyc, J., Vangela, M., Congletona, C., Yerramsettia, S., Gardab, T., & Lazara, S. (2011). *Psychiatry Research: Neuroimaging, 191*(1), 36–43.

Hooley, J., & Teasdale, D. (1989). Predictors of relapse in unipolar depressives: Expressed emotion, marital distress, and perceived criticism. *Journal of Abnormal Psychology, 98,* 229–235.

Iacoboni, M. (2008). The mirror neuron revolution: Explaining what makes humans social. *Scientific American.* Retrieved February 6, 2013, from http://www.scientificamerican.com/article.cfm?id=the-mirror-neuron-revolut

Jack, D. (1991). *Silencing the self: Women and depression.* Cambridge, MA: Harvard University Press.

REFERENCES

Jacobson, N., & Margolin, G. (1979). *Marital therapy: Strategies based on social learning and behavior exchange principles.* New York, NY: Brunner/Mazel.

Jasinski, J. (2004). Pregnancy and domestic violence: A review of the literature. *Trauma, Violence, & Abuse, 5*(47), 47–64.

Johnson, S. (2008). *Hold me tight: Seven conversations for a lifetime of love.* New York, NY: Little, Brown and Company.

Jordan, J. (1991). Empathy and self boundaries. In J. Jordan, A. Kaplan, J. Miller, I. Stiver, & J. Surrey (Eds.), *Women's growth in connection: Writings from the Stone Center* (pp. 34–37). New York, NY: Guilford Press.

Kabat-Zinn, J. (1990). *Full catastrophe living: Using the wisdom of your body and mind to face stress, pain, and illness.* New York, NY: Bantam.

Kabat-Zinn, J. (2003). Mindfulness-based interventions in context: Past, present, and future. *Clinical Psychology: Science and Practice, 10*(2), 144–156.

Kachadourian, L., Fincham, F., & Davila, J. (2005). Attitudinal ambivalence, rumination and forgiveness of partner transgressions in marriage. *Personality and Social Psychology Bulletin, 31,* 334, 342.

Keiningham, T., & Aksoy, L. (2009). *Why loyalty matters: The groundbreaking approach to rediscovering happiness, meaning and lasting fulfillment in your life and work.* Dallas, TX: BenBella Books.

Keita, G. (2007). Psychosocial and cultural contributions to depression in women: Considerations for women midlife and beyond. *Journal of Managed Care Pharmacy, 13*(9), S12–S15.

Kleiman, K. (2000). *The postpartum husband: Practical solutions for living with postpartum depression.* Bloomington, IN: xlibris.

Kleiman, K. (2009). *Therapy and the postpartum woman: Notes on healing postpartum depression for clinicians and the women who seek their help.* New York, NY: Routledge.

Kleiman, K., & Raskin, V. (1994). *This isn't what I expected: Overcoming postpartum depression.* New York, NY: Bantam.

Kleiman, K., & Wenzel, A. (2010). *Dropping the baby and other scary thoughts: Breaking the cycle of unwanted thoughts in motherhood.* New York, NY: Routledge.

Kwon, J., Yuri, L., Lee, M., & Bifulco, A. (2006). Perceived criticism, marital interaction, and relapse in unipolar depression — findings from a Korean sample. *Clinical Psychology and Psychotherapy, 13,* 306–312.

Lambert, N., Fincham, F., Gwinn, A., & Ajayi, C. (2011). Positive relationship science: A new frontier for positive psychology? In K. Sheldon, T. Kashdan, & M. Steger (Eds.), *Designing the future of positive psychology: Taking stock and moving forward* (pp. 265–279). Oxford, England: Cambridge University Press.

Lawler, K., Younger, J., Piferi, R., Jobe, R., Edmondson, K., & Jones, W. (2005). The unique effects of forgiveness on health: an exploration of pathways. *Journal of Behavioral Medicine, 28*(2), 157–167.

Laws, K. (2010). First concrete evidence that women are better multitaskers than men. University of Hertfordshire. Retrieved November 11, 2012, from http://www.alphagalileo.org/ViewItem.aspx?ItemId=81458&CultureCode=en

Leary, M., Springer, C., Negel, L., Ansell, E., & Evans, K. (1998). The causes, phenomenology, and consequences of hurt feelings. *Journal of Personality and Social Psychology, 74,* 1225–1237.

REFERENCES

LeMasters, E. E. (1957). Parenthood as a crises. *Marriage and Family Living, 19,* 352–355.

Levant, R., & Pollack, W. (Eds.). (1995). *A new psychology of men.* New York, NY: Basic Books.

Loder, P. (2006). When a child dies. Retrieved April 23, 2013, from http://www.compassionatefriends.org/pdf/When_a_Child_Dies-2006_Final.pdf

Love, P., & Stosny, S. (2007). *How to improve your marriage without talking about it.* New York, NY: Broadway Books.

Lovestone, S., & Kumar, R. (1993). Postnatal psychiatric illness: The impact on partners. *The British Journal of Psychiatry, 163,* 210–216.

Lukas, C., & Andrews, R. (2006) Four keys to collaboration success. Fieldstone Alliance. Retrieved April 1, 2013, from http://www.fieldstonealliance.org/client/articles/Article-4_Key_Collab_Success.cfm

Lun, J., Kesebir, S., & Oishi, S. (2008). On feeling understood and feeling well: The role of interdependence. *Journal of Research on Personality, 42,* 1623–1628.

Luskin, F. (2002). *Forgive for good.* New York, NY: Harper Collins.

Man cave (n.d.) In *Wikipedia.* Retrieved November 6, 2012, from http://en.wikipedia.org/wiki/Man_cave#cite_note-ohio-8

Manning, M. (1994). *Undercurrents: A life beneath the surface.* New York, NY: Harper Collins.

Martin, R. (2007). *The psychology of humor: An integrative approach.* Burlington, MA: Elsevier.

Marks, M., Wieck, A., Checkly, S., & Kumar, C. (1996). How does marriage protect women with histories of affective disorder from postpartum relapse? *The British Journal of Medical Psychology, 69,* 329–342.

Mattessich, P., & Monsey, B. (1992). *Collaboration: What makes it work.* St. Paul, MN: Amherst H. Wilder Foundation.

McCullough, M., Emmons, R., & Tsang, J. (2002). The grateful disposition: A conceptual and empirical topography. *Journal of Personality and Social Psychology, 82,* 112–127.

Mezey, G., & Bewley, S. (1997). Domestic violence in pregnancy. *British Journal of Obstetrics & Gynecology, 104,* 528–531.

Miller, M. (1996). *Intimate terrorism: The crisis of love in an age of disillusion.* New York, NY: W. W. Norton & Company.

Moberly, N., & Watkins, E. (2008). Ruminative self-focus and negative affect. *Journal of Abnormal Psychology, 117*(2), 314–323.

Murray, S., Holmes, J., MacDonald, G., & Ellsworth, P. (1998). Through the looking glass darkly? When self-doubts turn into relationship insecurities. *Journal of Personality and Social Psychology, 75,* 1459–1480.

Neff, K. (2003). The development and validation of a scale to measure self-compassion. *Self and Identity, 2,* 223–250.

Neff, K. (2011). *Self-Compassion: Stop beating yourself up and leave insecurity behind.* New York, NY: William Morrow.

Neff, K., Kirkpatrick, K., & Rude, S. (2007). Self-compassion and adaptive psychological functioning. *Journal of Research in Personality, 41,* 139–154.

Neff, K., Rude, S., & Kirkpatrick, K. (2007). An examination of self-compassion in relation to positive psychological functioning and personality traits. *Journal of Research in Personality, 41,* 908–916.

Nolen-Hocksema, S. (1987). Sex differences in unipolar depression: Evidence and theory. *Psychological Bulletin, 101*, 259–282.

Noller, P. (1980). Misunderstanding in marital communication: A study of couples' nonverbal communication. *Journal of Personality and Social Psychology, 39*(6), 1135–1148.

Notarius, C., Benson, P., Sloane, D., Vanzetti, N., & Hornyak, L. (1989). Exploring the interface between perception and behavior: An analysis of marital behavior in distressed and nondistressed couples. *Behavioral Assessment, 11*, 39–64.

Offer, S., & Schneider, B. (2010). Multitasking among working families: A strategy for dealing with the time squeeze. In K. Christensen & B. Schneider (Eds.), *Workplace flexibility: Realigning 20th century jobs to 21st century workers* (pp. 43–56). Ithaca, NY: Cornell University Press.

O'Hara, M. (1986). Social support, life events, and depression during pregnancy and the puerperium. *Archives of General Psychiatry, 43*, 569–573.

O'Hara, M., & Swain, A. (1996). Rates and risk of postpartum depression — A meta-analysis. *International Review of Psychiatry, 8*(1), 37–54.

Orloff, J. (2011). The power of generosity and anonymous giving. Retrieved January 21, 2013, from http://www.huffingtonpost.com/judith-orloff-md/generous_b_1151535.html

Pace, M., & Sandberg, J. (2012). Emotions and family therapy: Exploring female and male clinicians' attitudes about the use of emotion in therapy. *Journal of Systemic Therapies, 31*(1), 1–21.

Patel, V., Rodrigues, M., & DeSouza, N. (2002) Gender, poverty & postnatal depression: A cohort study from Goa, India. *American Journal of Psychiatry, 159*, 43–47.

Paris, R., & Dubus, N. (2005). Staying connected while nurturing an infant: A challenge of new motherhood. *Family Relations, 54*, 72–83.

Pascual-Leone A. (1996). Reorganization of cortical motor outputs in the acquisition of new motor skills. In J. Kinura & H. Shibasaki, (Eds.), *Recent advances in clinical neurophysiology* (pp. 304–308). Amsterdam, The Netherlands: Elsevier Science.

Paulson, J., & Bazemore S. (2010). Prenatal and postpartum depression in fathers and its association with maternal depression: A meta-analysis. *Journal of American Medical Association, 303*(19), 1961–1969.

Paykel, E., Emms, E., Fletcher, J., & Rassaby, E. (1980). Life events and social support in puerperal depression. *British Journal of Psychiatry, 136*, 339–346.

Petruzzello, S., Landers, D., Hatfield, B., Kubitz, K., & Salazar, W. (1991). A meta-analysis on the anxiety-reducing effects of acute and chronic exercise. *Sports Medicine, 11*, 143–182.

Pike, G., & Sillars, A. (1985). Reciprocity of marital communication. *Journal of Social and Personal Relationships, 2*, 303–324.

Real, T. (1997). *I don't want to talk about it: Overcoming the secret legacy of male depression*. New York, NY: Fireside.

Real, T. (2008). *The new rules of marriage*. New York, NY: Ballantine Books.

Reczek, C., Pudrovska, T., Carr, D., & Umberson, D. (2012). *Alcohol, marital status, and marital transitions: Quantitative and qualitative evidence*. Denver, CO: American Sociological Association.

Rogers, C., & Farson, R. (1987). Active listening. In R. Newman, M. Danziger, & M. Cohen, (Eds.), *Communication in business today*. Retrieved from http://www.go-get.org/pdf/Rogers_Farson.pdf

REFERENCES

Rueckert, L., & Naybar, N. (2008). Gender differences in empathy: The role of the right hemisphere. *Brain and Cognition, 67*(2), 162–167.

Ryan, R., & Deci, E. (2008). A self-determination theory approach to psychotherapy: The motivational basis for effective change. *Canadian Psychology, 49*, 186–193.

Salmela-Aro, K., Aunola, K., Saisto, T., Halmesmäki, E., & Nurmi, J. (2006). Couples share similar changes in depressive symptoms and marital satisfaction anticipating the birth of a child. *Journal of Social and Personal Relationships, 23*(5), 781–803.

Saxe, R., & Kanwisher, N. (2003). People thinking about thinking people: The role of the temporo-parietal junction in "theory of mind." *NeuroImage, 19*(4), 1835–1842.

Sayer, A., & Goldberg, A. (2006). Lesbian couples' relationship quality across the transition to parenthood. *Journal of Marriage and Family, 68*(1), 87–100.

Scheier, M., Carver, C., & Bridges, M. (1994). Distinguishing optimism from neuroticism (and trait anxiety, self-mastery, and self-esteem): A reevaluation of the Life Orientation Test. *Journal of Personality and Social Psychology, 67*, 1063–1078.

Schnarch, D. (1997). *Passionate marriage*. New York, NY: W.W. Norton & Company.

Shapiro, A., Gottman, J., & Carrère, S. (2000). The baby and the marriage: Identifying factors that buffer against decline in marital satisfaction after the first baby arrives. *Journal of Family Psychology, 14*, 59–70.

Sheffield, A. (2003). *Depression fallout: The impact of depression on couples and what you can do to preserve the bond*. New York, NY: Harper Collins.

Simon, R., & Barrett, A., (2010). Nonmarital romantic relationships and mental health in early adulthood: Does the association differ for women and men? Journal of Health and Social Behavior, 51, 168–182.

Smalley, S. (n.d.). Stuart Smalley. Retrieved January 18, 2013, from http://en.wikipedia.org/wiki/Stuart_Smalley

Stamp, G. (1994). The appropriation of the parental role through communication during the transition to parenthood. *Communication Monographs, 61*, 89–112.

Stanley, S., Markman, H., & Whitton, S. (2002). Communication, conflict, and commitment: Insights on the foundations of relationship success from a national survey. *Family Process, 41*, 659–675.

Stark, E., & Flitcraft, A. (1996). *Women at risk: Domestic violence and women's health*. London, England: Sage.

Surrey, J. (1984). *The self-in-relation: A theory of women's development* [Work in Progress, No. 13]. Wellesley, MA: Stone Center Working Paper Series.

Swendsen J., & Mazure, C. (2000). Life stress as a risk factor for postpartum depression: Current research and methodological issues. *Clinical Psychology Science and Practice, 7*, 17–31.

Taft, A. (2002). Violence against women in pregnancy and after childbirth: Current knowledge and issues in healthcare responses. *Australian Domestic and Family Violence Clearinghouse Issues* [Paper 6]. Retrieved April 15, 2013, from http://www.austdvclearinghouse.unsw.edu.au/PDF%20files/Issuespaper6.pdf

Taylor, S., Klein, L., Lewis, B., Grunewald, T., Gurung, R., & Updegraff, J. (2000). Biobehavioral responses to stress in females: Tend and befriend, not fight or flight. *Psychological Review, 107*(3), 411–429.

Thompson, J., Whiffen, V., & Aube, J., (2001). Does self-silencing link perceptions of care from parents and partners with depressive symptoms? *Journal of Social and Personal Relationships, 18*, 503–516.

Tolle, E. (2004). *The power of now*. Vancouver, B.C., Canada: New World Library.

Tomlinson, P. (1996). Marital relationship change in the transition to parenthood: A reexamination as interpreted through transition theory. *Journal of Family Nursing, 2*, 286–305.

Walters, M., Carter, B., Papp, P., & Silverstein, O. (1988). *The invisible web: Gender patterns in family relationships.* New York, NY: Guilford Press.

Wegner, D., & Giuliano, T. (1982). The forms of social awareness. In W. Ickes (Ed.), *Personality, roles, and social behavior* (pp. 165–198). New York, NY: Springer-Verlag.

Whiffen, V. (1988). Vulnerability to postpartum depression: A prospective multivariate study. *Journal of Abnormal Psychology, 97*, 467–474.

Whiffen, V. & Gotlib, I. (1993). Comparison of postpartum and nonpostpartum depression: Clinical presentation, psychiatric history, and psychosocial functioning. *Journal of Consulting and Clinical Psychology, 61*, 485–494.

Whitton, S., Olmos-Gallo, P., Stanley, S., Prado, L., Kline, G., St. Peters, M., & Markman, H. (2007). Depressive symptoms in early marriage: Predictions from relationship confidence and negative marital interaction. *Journal of Family Psychology, 21*, 297–306.

Wisner, K., & Stowe Z. (1997). Psychobiology of postpartum mood disorders. *Seminars in Reproductive Endocrinology, 15*, 77–89.

Wisner, K., Parry, B., & Piontek, C. (2002). Postpartum depression. *New England Journal of Medicine, 347*, 194–199.

Wisner, K., Sit, D., McShea, M., Rizzo, D., Zoretich, R., Hughes, C., ... Hanusa, B. (2013). Onset timing, thoughts of self-harm, and diagnosis in postpartum women with screen-positive depression findings. *Journal of the American Medical Association Psychiatry, 13*, 1–9.

Zelkowittz, P., & Milet, T. (1997). Stress and support as related to postpartum paternal mental health and perceptions of the infant. *Infant Mental Health Journal, 18*(4), 424–435.

INDEX

Page locators in *italics* indicate figures and tables.

abuse: abusive language, 71; described, 63; mental or physical abuse, 193–95; and risks to the connection, 55; substance abuse, 195–96
acceptance vs. contempt, 158–59
accepting influence and collaboration, 93–94, 100
accepting mediocrity, 171–72
active listening, 69–70, 139, 142–43, 147, 154
adaptation, positive adaptation, 205–6
addiction, 63–64
affection. *See* Tokens of affection
affirmations: dedication to each other and the marriage, 179; quieting your critical voice, 90; and self-compassion, 86; and self-esteem, 79
alcohol abuse, 195–96
ambivalence, numbness and ambivalence, 36–37
anger: being too angry, 190–91; getting past recent anger, 89; and letting go of negativity, 87–88
anxiety, 26–27
approach track to connectedness, 39–40, *39*
assumptions and compromise, 111–12
attachment theory, 48
attitude: and collaboration, 94–95, 96; and forgiveness, 169–71; of gratitude, 180

attribution, explaining each other's behaviors, 160–61
authority, accepting influence and collaboration, 93–94, 100, 103–6
awareness, selfless support model, 121–23

baby blues, 27
bad habits, disregarding bad habits, 171
balance and mindful marriage, 184
balanced response and cognitive behavioral therapy (CBT), 75–76
barriers to compromise, 106–8
barriers to expression, 152–53
behavior: behavioral obstacles to using the Tokens, 62–64; childish behavior and selfless support model, 123–24; effective communication and behaviors to avoid, 70–71; explaining each other's behavior, 159–63
being nice to each other, 141–44, 154–55
being present in your marriage, 183
being right, 103–4, 109–10
biased cognition and cognitive behavioral therapy (CBT), 73–74
bickering, 103–4, 107–8
black and white thinking, 106
brain scripts, explaining each other's behaviors, 161–62

calming down and compromise, 108–9
C.A.R.E. (common purpose, attitude, respect, and expectations), 95–97
caring for each other: common purpose and collaboration, 95–96; role

reversals and the connection, 50–52; selfless support model, 119–24; tolerance and big emotions, 163–66

challenges to marriage and relationships: being too angry, 190–91; and deciding if therapy would be helpful, 199–200; devaluation, 188; feeling bad prior to having a baby, 191–92; inability to forgive, 198; infidelity, 193; loss of a child, 197; loss of spirit, 189; mental or physical abuse, 193–95; neglect, 189; not wanting to change, 189; substance abuse, 195–96; thinking the Tokens are silly, 191; thinking your partner is a jerk, 192–93; wondering if the marriage is beyond hope, 197–98

change: not wanting to change, 189; openness to change, 100–101

checking in with partner, 89–90

children: fighting in front of children, 71; loss of a child, 197

circle of affection, 176–78, *177*

co-dependence, 83

cognitive behavioral therapy (CBT): black and white thinking as barrier to compromise, 106; described, 28, 72–77; and neuroplasticity, 206–7

cognitive interdependence, 83

collaboration: about, 20, 92; and accepting influence, 93–94; and attitude, 94–95, 96; and C.A.R.E., 95–97; and current married state, 21–23, *22*; as dance of togetherness, 97–98; self-generative capacity, 202; separate but together, 98–99; token inventory, 92; token tools, 99–101

comfort, Tokens of affection and building the connection, 61–62

commitment to relationship: and connectedness, 14–16; Tokens of affection and building the connection, 61, 64

common goals. *See* shared vision and goals

common language, 153–54

common purpose, attitude, respect, and expectations (C.A.R.E.), 95–97

communication: active listening, 69–70, 139, 142–43, 147, 154; behaviors to avoid, 70–71; collapse of communication and postpartum depression, 10, 35–36; Dos and Don'ts, 71–72; effective communication techniques overview, 65–67; how to begin a discussion, 67–68; hunting and man cave metaphor, 129–30; and marital satisfaction, 139–41; numbness and ambivalence, 36–37; and relationship expectations, 16–19; Tokens of affection communication code, 67; using "I" statements, 68–69. *See also* connection strategies; expression

community of respect, 79–80, 88

compassion, self-compassion, 84–86

compassionate negotiation, 59–60

competitive edge, 100

compromise: about, 20, 102; barriers to, 106–8; and current married state, 21–23, *22*; process over content, 103–4; self-generative capacity, 202; token inventory, 102–3; token tools, 108–12; as win-win situation, 104–6

confrontation: fear of confrontation as barrier to compromise, 107; marital satisfaction and communication, 139–40

the connection: approach track to connectedness, 39–40, *39*; barriers and risks to, 54–56; connectedness and current married state, 14–16; and disengagement of couples, 38–39; and feelings of fear and shame, 42–45; importance of, 47–48; and misperceptions, 49–50; and ongoing issues, 52–54; and partner support, 53–54; reconnecting and expression, 144–47; and role reversals, 50–52; and strong marriages, 41–42; symptoms of weakening connection, 45–47; and Tokens of affection, 60–62; Tokens of affection as reconnection tool, 6, 64

connection strategies: active listening, 69–70; behaviors to avoid, 70–71;

INDEX

connection strategies (*continued*): communication Dos and Don'ts, 71–72; effective communication techniques overview, 65–67; how to begin a discussion, 67–68; using "I" statements, 68–69

contempt, 71

contentment and building the connection, 61–62

controlled breathing, 182

couple identity, relationship awareness, 82

critical evaluation and cognitive behavioral therapy (CBT), 75

curiosity: attitude and collaboration, 96; and expression, 147, 154–55

current married state: assessment of, 4, 12–13, 21–23, *22*; communication and relationship expectations, 16–19; and connectedness, 14–16; effects of depression on, 8–12; and family rules, 13–14; and onset of postpartum depression, 7–8; relationship awareness, 11–12; and Tokens of affection, 19–23, *22*

defensiveness: selflessness inventory, 114; and using "I" statements, 68–69

depression. *See* postpartum depression

Depression Fallout (Sheffield), 8

devaluation, 188

Diagnostic Statistical Manual of Mental Disorders (American Psychiatric Association), 26

differentiation and collaboration, 98–99

discussions: gender and starting difficult discussions, 115; how to begin a discussion, 67–68; sanctuary and difficult discussions, 128

disregarding bad habits, 171

divorce, mentioning divorce and effective communication, 71

domestic violence, 194–95

Dropping the Baby and Other Scary Thoughts (Kleiman and Wenzel), 5, 150, 182

drug abuse, 195–96

ego: checking your ego at the door, 99; and giving to get, 115–16; sensitivity vs. self-involvement, 114

emotional abundance, 78–79

emotional control, 114

Emotional Freedom (Orloff), 126

emotional needs, awareness and selfless support model, 121–23

Emotionally Focused Therapy (EFT), 48

emotions: calming down and process of compromise, 108–9; emotional repression, 128; feeling bad prior to having a baby, 191–92; lasting emotions and postpartum depression, 30–35, *34*; and over giving, 116–18; tolerance and big emotions, 163–66, 172–73. *See also* negativity

empathy and tolerance, 157–59

enthusiasm, attitude and collaboration, 96

esteem: about, 20, 79; and community of respect, 79–80, 88; and current married state, 21–23, *22*; letting go and letting in, 86–89; and low self-esteem, 79–81; relationship awareness, 81–82; relationship integrity, 82–84; self-compassion, 84–86; self-generative capacity, 202; token inventory, 79–80; token tools, 89–91

expectations: barriers and risks to the connection, 54; and collaboration, 96–97; recalibrating expectations, 100

explicit relationship awareness, 11–12, 81–82

expression: about, 21, 138; and active listening, 139, 142–43, 147, 154; barriers to, 152–53; being nice to each other, 141–44, 154–55; and curiosity, 147, 154–55; and current married state, 21–23, *22*; gender and humor, 148–49; health and humor, 149–52, 155; how you say things, 145–46; and reconnecting, 144–47; satisfaction and communication, 139–41; self-generative capacity, 202; token inventory, 138–39; token tools, 153–55; what you do, 146–47; what you say, 145

INDEX

fair fighting rules, 107, 135
family history and legacies, 55
family rules and current married state, 13–14
fear: fear of confrontation as barrier to compromise, 107; fear-shame dynamic, 42, 165–66; feelings of fear and the connection, 42–45
feeling bad prior to having a baby, 191–92
fighting: fair fighting rules, 107, 135; in front of children, 71
finding the you and me, 184–85
5:1 ratio of positive and negative interactions, 33
forgiveness: inability to forgive, 198; and infidelity, 193; and tolerance, 166–71, 173–74
forthrightness and therapist's role, 1–2
Four Keys to Collaboration Success (Lukas and Andrews), 97
friendship and marriage, 135

gender: accepting influence and collaboration, 93–94; and big emotions, 163–64; and compromise, 105; and explaining each other's behavior, 162–63; and fear-shame dynamic, 42–45; female stress response, 180–81; gathering and man cave metaphor, 130–32; and humor, 148–49; hunting and man cave metaphor, 129–30; and nonverbal communication, 146; and postpartum depression, 6, 25–26, 28–29, 42; and relationship awareness, 82, 127, 128–32; and starting difficult discussions, 115
generosity: selfless support model, 119–24; selflessness token tools, 124
genetic barriers and risks to the connection, 55
giving back to partner, 91
giving first, 124
giving, over giving, 116–18, 125–26
giving to get, 114–18
giving up competitive edge, 100
goals. *See* shared vision and goals
gratitude, attitude of gratitude, 180

guilt: guilt-free time for sanctuary space, 136; and postpartum depression, 10–11, 28, 32

harsh startup and how to begin a discussion, 67
health and humor, 149–52, 155
healthy thinking and cognitive behavioral therapy (CBT), 74–76
Hold me Tight (Johnson), 48
hugging and relaxation, 83–84
humor: and gender, 148–49; and health, 149–52, 155
hunting and man cave metaphor, 129–30

"I" statements, 68–69
identity, couple identity and relationship awareness, 82
implicit relationship awareness, 11–12, 81–82
inability to forgive, 198
infertility, 55–56
infidelity, 63, 193
influence, accepting influence, 93–94
integrity, esteem and relationship integrity, 82–84
intensity of interchange, 97–98
intentional marriage, 186
interdependence and relationship integrity, 83–84
interpersonal psychotherapy (IPT), 28
Intimate Terrorism (Miller), 78
inventory, 138–39
inventory. *See* Token inventory
isolation: dance of togetherness and collaboration, 97–98; and low self-esteem, 79; and postpartum adjustment, 47

keeping score, 104–5, 111
kindness, 124

laughing, humor and health, 149–52, 155
letting go and letting in, 86–89
listening: active listening and expression, 69–70, 139, 142–43, 147, 154; respect and collaboration, 96
loss of a child, 197

loss of spirit, 189
loyalty: about, 20, 175–76; circle of affection, 176–78, *177*; and current married state, 21–23, *22*; dedication to each other and the marriage, 178–80; mindful marriage, 181–84, 185; self-generative capacity, 201–2; "tend and befriend" stress response, 180–81; token inventory, 176; token tools, 184–87
lying, 63

magic ratio of positive and negative interactions, 33
The Male Brain (Brizendine), 162
man cave metaphor, 128–32
manipulation, 63
marriage: and acceptance of differences, 158; and compassionate negotiation, 59–60; dedication to each other and the marriage, 178–80; and emotional abundance, 78–79; and explaining each other's behavior, 159–63; and friendship, 135; and importance of connection, 47–48; marital satisfaction, 9–12, 29–30, 139–41, 168; mindful marriage, 181–84, 185; as partnership of good efforts, 57–59; romanticized notions of, 78; strong marriages and the connection, 41–42. *See also* challenges to marriage and relationships; the connection; current married state
meditation, 182–83
mental abuse, 193–95
mindfulness: mindful marriage, 181–84, 185; and tolerance, 157–58
mirror-neuron system (MNS), 162–63
misperceptions: and the connection, 49–50; email and texting, 144
multitasking, 130–32

name-calling, 71
negativity: attributions and explaining each other's behaviors, 160–61; being too angry, 190–91; and compromise, 103, 105, 110–11; and forgiveness, 169–71; harsh startup and how to begin a discussion, 67; healthy thinking and cognitive behavioral therapy (CBT), 74–77; letting go and letting in, 86–89; vs. being nice to each other, 141–44
neglect, 189
negotiation, compassionate negotiation, 59–60
neuroplasticity, 206–7
neuroscience, 162–63
new cave metaphor, sanctuary, 132–34

ongoing issues: barriers and risks to the connection, 54; and the connection, 52–54
open-mindedness, attitude and collaboration, 96
openness to change, 100–101
over giving, 116–18, 125–26
overreacting, barriers to compromise, 107

paradoxical thought patterns, 2–3
partner support and the connection, 53–54
Passionate Marriage (Schnarch), 83–84
patience and tolerance, 172–73
perceptions: and depression, 41; misperceptions and the connection, 49–50; and using the Tokens, 202–3
personal sanctuary space, 136–37
physical abuse, 193–95
physiological effects of humor, 149–52
positive adaptation, 205–6
postpartum depression: approach track to connectedness, 39–40, *39*; benefits of therapy, 10; and case history experiences, 3–4; communication with partners, 10, 35–36; described, 25–26; and disengagement of couples, 38–39; and feelings of guilt, 10–11, 28, 32; forthrightness and therapist's role, 1–2; and gender, 6, 25–26, 28–29, 42; and lasting emotions, 30–35, *34*; and loss of esteem, 79; and marital satisfaction, 9–12, 29–30; marital satisfaction and communication, 140–41; numbness and ambivalence, 36–37; onset of, 7–8, 24, 27–28; and

INDEX

paradoxical thought patterns, 2–3; "silencing the self" and depression risk, 52; symptoms, 26–27; treatment, 28. *See also* communication

The Postpartum Husband (Kleiman), 192

Postpartum Stress Center, 9, 134

power: accepting influence and collaboration, 93–94; and compromise, 102, 105, 109–10

practice and effective communication, 66

predispositions, barriers and risks to the connection, 55

presumptions and compromise, 111–12

private time, 128, 129, 136

problem solving skills: and being nice to each other, 142–43; marital satisfaction and communication, 140–41; tolerance and big emotions, 163–66

process over content, 103–4

psychological effects of humor, 149–52

reconciliation: and compromise, 102, 109–10; letting go and letting in, 87–89

reconnecting, 144–47

relationship awareness: described, 11–12; designation of relationship monitor, 203–4; esteem, 81–82; relational resilience, 204–5

relationship esteem, 80

relationship integrity, 82–84

relaxation, hugging and relaxation, 83–84

resilience, relational resilience, 204–5

respect: and collaboration, 96; esteem and community of respect, 79–80

rituals, sanctuary as new cave metaphor, 133

role reversals and the connection, 50–52

rumination, 169–70

sacrifice and compromise, 105–6

sanctuary: about, 20–21; and current married state, 21–23, *22*; and man cave metaphor, 128–32; and new cave metaphor, 132–34; self-generative capacity, 202; token inventory, 128; token tools, 135–37

secrets, 63

self-compassion, 84–86

self-criticism, 90

self-esteem, 80–81

self-integrity, 84

self-sabotage, 117

selfless support model, 119–24

selflessness: about, 20; and current married state, 21–23, *22*; giving to get, 114–18; over giving, 116–18, 125–26; self-generative capacity, 202; selfless support model, 119–24; sensitivity vs. self-involvement, 113–14; token inventory, 114; token tools, 124–26

sense of self, lasting emotions and postpartum depression, 30–35, *34*

sensitivity vs. self-involvement, 113–14

separate but together, 98–99

Seven Habits of Highly Effective People (Covey), 107

shame: fear-shame dynamic, 42, 165–66; feelings of shame and the connection, 42–45

shared vision and goals: and compromise, 105, 108; using "we" and "us" pronouns, 90. *See also* collaboration

shared vs. personal sanctuary space, 136–37

"silencing the self" and depression risk, 52

silent treatment, 71

socialization, accepting influence and collaboration, 93–94

solutions, working toward solutions, 99

spending time together, 185

stonewalling, 63

strength-based reliance, 83–84

substance abuse, 195–96

suffering and self-compassion, 86

support, selfless support model, 119–24

supportive psychotherapy, 28

surrender and compromise, 102, 108

suspiciousness, 63

symptoms: anxiety, 26–27; and paradoxical thoughts, 2–3; postpartum depression, 26, 31–32; role reversals and caring for each other, 51–52; symptom surplus and marital connection, 56

INDEX

teasing, 71
temporoparietal junction system (TPJ), 162–63
"tend and befriend" stress response, 180–81
thank you, saying thank you, 143, 153
Therapy and the Postpartum Woman (Kleiman), 43, 128, 204
therapy, deciding if therapy would be helpful, 199–200
This isn't What I Expected (Kleiman and Raskin), 50–51
togetherness: dance of togetherness and collaboration, 97–98; separate but together, 98–99
Token inventory: collaboration, 92; compromise, 102–3; esteem, 79–80; expression, 138–39; loyalty, 176; sanctuary, 128; selflessness, 114; tolerance, 157
Token tools: collaboration, 99–101; compromise, 108–12; esteem, 89–91; expression, 153–55; loyalty, 184–87; sanctuary, 135–37; selflessness, 124–26; tolerance, 171–74
Tokens of affection: behavioral obstacles to using, 62–64; and building the connection, 60–62; communication code, 67; and compassionate negotiation, 59–60; and current married state, 21–23, *22*; described, 4–5, 19–21; designation of relationship monitor, 203–4; and giving to get, 116; and importance of individuality and self-determination, 22; integrity of, 201–2; and marriage as partnership of good efforts, 57–59; and neuroplasticity, 206–7; perceptions and misperceptions, 202–3; and positive adaptation, 205–6; regular check-ins with, 209–10; and relational resilience, 204–5; as tool for reconnecting, 6, 64; 12 keystones to, 208–9. *See also* collaboration; compromise; esteem; expression; loyalty; sanctuary; selflessness; tolerance
tolerance: about, 20, 156–57; and big emotions, 163–66, 172–73; and current married state, 21–23, *22*; explaining each other's behavior, 159–63; and finding empathy, 157–59; and forgiveness, 166–71, 173–74; self-generative capacity, 202; token inventory, 157; token tools, 171–74
Tolle, Eckhart, 157
tone of voice and effective communication, 70–71
tools. *See* Token tools
trusting the process and mindful marriage, 183–84
12 keystones to Token work, 208–9

unconditional selflessness, 126
uncoupling, 63
Undercurrents (Manning), 43

vulnerability: as catalyst, 3; fear of confrontation as barrier to compromise, 107; and fear-shame dynamic, 42; forthrightness and therapist's role, 1–2

"we" and "us" pronouns, 90
Wenzel, Amy, 5
what you do, 146–47
what you say, 145
Why Loyalty Matters (Keiningham and Aksoy), 178
withdrawal: and fear-shame dynamic, 42, 165–66; gender and stress response, 181
working toward solutions, 99

yelling and effective communication, 70–71
yielding to win, 93–94

Made in the USA
Middletown, DE
18 September 2019